Open Country, Iowa

SUNY Series in the Anthropology of Work

June Nash, Editor

OPEN
COUNTRY
IOWA

Rural Women, Tradition and Change

DEBORAH FINK

State University of New York Press

Published by
State University of New York Press, Albany

©1986 State University of New York

All rights reserved

Printed in the United States of America

For information, address State University of New York
Press, State University Plaza, Albany, N.Y., 12246

Library of Congress Cataloging-in-Publication Data

Fink, Deborah, 1944-
    Open country, Iowa.

    (SUNY series in the anthropology of work)
    Includes index.
    1. Rural women—Iowa—Case studies.   2. Women—
Iowa—Case studies.   3. Rural women—United States—
Case studies.   I. Title.   II. Series.
HQ1438.I7F56   1986   305.4′09777   86-967
ISBN 0-88706-317-9
ISBN 0-88706-318-7 (pbk.)

To Open Country women

Contents

Acknowledgments

My primary debt of gratitude is to the women of Open Country, Iowa, who participated in the research. Many Open Country women and men welcomed me into the community, gave their time and energy for interviews, offered emotional and social support during the times I navigated roughly through particular situations, and listened to my preliminary conclusions, volunteering their opinions and analyses in return.

Several scholars at Iowa State University furthered the research: Leonard Eggelton of the poultry extension service allowed access to poultry record flock data and reports. William Owings, also a poultry extension specialist, spent time explaining the economics of current Iowa egg production. Margaret Liston, a retired Iowa State University home economist, explained the survey work she did in the 1930s. Carl and Lucille Malone, who were county extension agents in the 1940s and later became extension faculty, discussed their work with rural Iowans and what they learned from this work. Robert Rohwer, a former Iowa State College rural sociologist and a farmer in northwest Iowa, shared his work and his insights. Louie Hansen, the Iowa State University Extension Research Development Specialist located in Spencer, talked to me about Iowa's central points and about his needs assessments for the Open Country area.

Students and colleagues at Iowa State University and the University of Iowa, along with a number of coparticipants at professional meetings, journal referees, and editors gave helpful insights as I wrote. Judith Block, my production editor at SUNY Press, gave astute and tactful advice. Rebecca Henderson, Kathy Hickok, and Dorothy Schwieder were among those who devoted precious time to reading drafts and offering comments. Their advice and encouragement were invaluable.

A few people were closely attuned to the project from the onset. My sister Kate Hansen, a Nebraska farm woman, offered astute reflections on her life on the farm and was able to ask honest questions at all points. Working on this project together allowed us to assimilate and to put into perspective some of our shared experiences in rural Nebraska in the 1950s. Horace and Mary Autenrieth provided intellectual, moral, and material support, which cannot be adequately enumerated here, but which will never be forgotten. George Fink and Philip Fink shared their mother with Open Country and kept her rooted in reality. They have been a source of enthusiasm, joy, and hope. A.M. Fink, a Great Enabler for twenty years, has listened to my ideas as they formed, spent time with me in Open Country, shared his boyhood experiences in rural South Dakota, and read and reread drafts and papers. Too unfailingly supportive to be a good critic, he has given timely and sensitive encouragement that has kept me on track.

CHAPTER 1

Introduction

In 1885, when Elsa's mother, Mary, was eleven, she moved to Iowa with her parents and her uncle and aunt.[1] They were leaving a farm in the eastern United States to begin farming in a northwestern Iowa community. Several other relatives and co-religionists moved there about the same time. Their lives in Iowa centered around their farms and the church they built toether. Mary married a farmer from the church circle in 1898; three years later, Elsa, the oldest of five daughters, was born.

Like her mother, Elsa spent her days in the midst of a society of kinsfolk on her farm and in the religious and social activities of the church. She attended both a small parochial school and a rural public school. Before completing her high school education, she changed to a normal education course and received her teaching certificate in 1919. After teaching in rural grade schools for two years, she too married a local farmer, Martin.

As a farm woman, Elsa kept a flock of poultry and helped to milk cows, in addition to raising two sons and two daughters. Elsa, her mother, and other kinswomen helped each other with housework and caring for babies; a sister became her most intimate friend; and Elsa and Martin shared major farm tasks with his brother and brother's wife. They went to church on Sundays and ate Sunday dinners with kinsfolk. Once a week Elsa gathered with other church women to sew and visit.

The four children learned farm work, helping out in the fields, the barn, and the home. With cousins as companions to share the trials of growing up in rural Iowa, they began their educations in rural schools and belonged to 4-H clubs in which they had poultry, beef, dairy, and sewing projects. Although seemingly destined to take up farming and produce yet another generation of Iowa farmers, they were not to remain in rural Iowa; World War II interrupted the continuity. Both sons were drafted, and the daughters followed the wartime exodus out of rural Iowa. They went to college and got jobs and, eventually, husbands outside of the rural community. Although one of the daughters farmed for a short time with her husband, none returned to live near Elsa and Martin.

In pondering the changes in her life between her marriage in 1921 and my interview with her in 1982, Elsa said, "The war changed everything." Her children, along with many of the other young people of the church, had moved away. During World War II, Elsa got her first refrigerator, and both she and her husband began to realize more and more material comforts in their farm life. In 1955 they gave up their poultry and dairy enterprises so they could spend their winters in the southwest and in the scattered homes of their children. Since that time, they have travelled extensively—even as far as Europe.

While Elsa's material means were far greater than what she had imagined in the first years of her marriage, her everyday social world became fragmented as her kinswomen died or moved away. By 1982 the 120 acres that she and Martin owned were rented to Elsa's sister's grandson. Elsa's grandnephew's wife, urban-born, did not meld into the kind of close familial network that Elsa had known from her pre-World War II years on the farm. Where women of the previous generation had situated themselves within a cushion of mothers, sisters, daughters, nieces, cousins, and granddaughters, Elsa found herself with no close female kin in the community.

In the years since the first white settlement in Iowa in the 1830s, strong-minded women have agitated for women's political rights and entered what were previously male preserves in business and professions. Only a few rural women entered this stream; the majority have not been self-conscious agents of change. But, however nonpolitical, none of the women have escaped the effects of the profound changes of this century. This book is about Elsa and the other women of a rural Iowa community which I call Open Country, the majority of whom were more absorbed in the immediacy of raising children, making a living, and meeting daily crises than in changing the world. Yet largely without conscious planning, the world of these women—their family farms, their ethnic/religious groups and their small towns—were transformed during World War

II and its aftermath. The women were a part of the rural social nexus, and their story is also a story of the rural community.

A basic premise of this book is that the material reality of women in a small, rural community is significant. These women struggled to make a living and to create links with each other in order to have some control over their world. Kinship and the way that family membership has defined and expressed the meaning of being a rural woman is at the core of any understanding of the possibilities and limitations of Open Country women's experiences. The kinship system has not been autonomous, however. Community culture and national politics and economics have also interacted as women have worked toward a sustainable society in which people can grow, share lives with loved ones, and do what gives meaning to their lives.

Women's work in reproduction and production has involved three distinct kinds of relations to the household and to the market: First, women have worked within the household or farm to produce the food, clothing, and personal services that have, to varying degrees, sustained the rural population. Second, still working within the household economic operation, they have produced goods (such as butter and eggs) that they have exchanged for other goods outside the household. Third, they have worked outside the household economic operation to earn money to support the household. Over time, the relative significance of these kinds of work has shifted. Where much of women's time was occupied by production within the home or family business in the early twentieth century, recently women have more frequently worked outside the household.

This trend toward women's increased employment outside the home can be interpreted in different ways. One way focuses on the improvements in women's lives as they have earned more money. With larger units of production, less labor has been tied up by inefficient production units, and women have, consequently, enjoyed increased leisure time. Women who work outside the home for pay may have happier, more fulfilling lives (Friedan 1963). A further consideration of this trend toward women working outside the home foresees the effects of many women coming together in the workforce: through interaction with each other in the work setting women might become increasingly conscious of who they are as women workers and thus more likely to press for such things as better pay, job security, and maternity leave.

On the other hand, researchers who have examined rural development in diverse settings have asserted that women have shouldered extra burdens with development and that women, have not realized the primary benefits of development (Anand 1983; Moen, Boulding, Lillydahl and Palm 1981). Some have suggested that, with increased education and training, women will become full participants in the mainstream of economic development (Bescher-Donnelly and Smith 1981; Boserup 1970). Others, arguing that women have assumed low-paying, dead-end jobs in the secondary labor market, have implied that the marginalization of women may be an essential and fundamental effect of capitalist development (Benería and Sen 1981; Young 1980). Consistent with this latter analysis, this book points to some of the contradictions in viewing rural industrialization in terms of continuing progress toward general, shared prosperity. Since U.S. rural development has been used in many ways as a model for development programs around the world, this assessment of the benefits and losses experienced by women contributes to an evolving understanding of the human factors in technological and economic change.

The transformation of Iowa's rural society is usually explained in terms of the mechanization of farm production; specialization in corn, soybeans, and hogs; and concentration of land and capital in fewer, larger, and more costly farming operations. In the case of Elsa and Martin, they began farming by milking fourteen cows; keeping a few horses, pigs, beef cattle, and chickens; and planting varied croppings of corn, hay, and oats. In 1982 their grandnephew raised only corn and soybeans. Where Elsa and her husband had used horses, milk pails, and a great deal of hand labor, their nephew used chemical sprays and fertilizers and a combine, which cut and threshed the crops in one step. This expensive machinery could have paid for itself only by being used on more than the 200 acres Elsa and her husband farmed at the peak of their working lives.

Of equal significance to Elsa, however, was the demographic change in the rural community. While people have steadily moved from rural to urban areas throughout the century, the massive political and economic realignments of the World War II period greatly accelerated the movement. This exodus effected qualitative changes in rural social life and fragmented the tightly knit kinship groupings that had been the basis for Elsa's life before the war. Increased mobility had also deposited in Open Country strangers like Elsa's grandnephew's wife, who had different ideas about religion, social expectations, and aesthetic standards. The functions of the family and the workings of the family farm have shifted with the demographic change as well as with political and economic changes.

Rural life in the 1980s is substantially more economically varied than it was before 1940. Among those who have stayed in Open Country, fewer are farming and more are commuting to factory jobs in nearby cities. Government programs of welfare, food stamps, hot lunches, medicare, medicaid and farm aid have replaced some of the functions of the church and family. In addition, these programs have provided employment for women in the form of professional and other service jobs. Like women everywhere, rural women are appearing in labor force statistics in increased numbers. Unlike many urban women, however, rural women's labor force participation emerges from a particular rural history of work in family business operations. Ignoring this history can be likened to looking at a dive and seeing only the splash.

Open Country

The community called Open Country is located in a northwest Iowa county. Open Country is rural, not in having an exclusively agrarian economy, but in having no population aggregates greater than 2,500. The rural part of the entire county, the basis for the statistics used in this study, includes seven small towns and at least six other named wide spots on the roads. The county contains part of one small city (population 5,000), but this city is not discussed in detail herein. My fieldwork in Open Country focused on the south central part of the county and included two small towns, Center and Farmtown, each with a population of approximately 1,000.

Farmsteads, empty farmhouses, and nonfarm dwellings line the roadsides in the country. Iowa's natural tree cover, heaviest in the southeastern area of the state, becomes sparse in the northwest where the elevation is higher and rivers are fewer. Most of the existing trees in Open Country have been planted as windbreaks around farmhouses or in towns. Almost all of the farmland is planted in corn or soybean crops each year; only the erosion-prone land around creeks is usually left in pasture. The view from the country is of wide open spaces with trees enclosing farmsteads. Towns have paved streets lined with trees, houses, businesses, and the many private cars that are the only means of transportation in Open Country.

Open Country's fertile, rolling land is composed of glacial till and loess. The richness of the soil, together with an average rainfall of 25 inches per year, dependably produces abundant crops without irrigation. With hybrid seeds, herbicides, pesticides, and fertilizers, the corn yields have tripled since World War II. Iowa leads the nation in the production of corn and hogs, is second in the production of soybeans, and is third in the production of beef (ICLRS 1983:14,46). Open Country, with corn, soybean, hog, and beef production, is an integral part of the Iowa farm economy.

Center and Farmtown, like other rural towns, were founded to meet the educational, marketing and supply, medical, and recreational needs of the farmers, and they have remained dependent on farm trade. Before 1940 farm produce constituted the only local production sold outside of Open Country to bring money into the community. In the early days of settlement, towns were spaced so that farmers could reach them by driving no more than five miles. With the coming of cars and better roads, businesses in the smallest towns died out, leaving empty stores, schools, and houses to be razed by farmers seeking more acres on which to plant. Center and Farmtown, both large enough to survive into the 1980s, are now primarily farm service centers, with grain elevators, farm implement dealerships, feed stores, and service stations dominating the business districts. Both have kindergarten-through-grade-twelve public school systems. Center was established as the county seat in the geographic center of the county and survives because of the business brought to town by the courthouse. Farmtown, ten miles to the southwest, developed as a railroad town and has continued as a small retail center despite the closing of rail service in 1980.

While some social distance has always existed between farm and town people, any set social boundaries between town and country or between country neighborhoods are arbitrary, with one social or ethnic cluster blending into the next. Neighbors, whether in town or on the farm, have usually worked and socialized together, and kinship ties have crosscut all political boundaries.

The oldest people in Open Country are the children of pioneer settlers. By the 1870s, a few ranchers and homesteaders had settled in Open Country, but the major settlement and planning of towns occurred in the 1880s after the railroad was built. Newcomers like Elsa's ancestors settled in ethnic/religious communities, usually centered around a church or meetinghouse. While these communities attracted some European immigrants, most of the settlers moved from earlier residences in the eastern United States or Canada. Irish Catholics came as railroad workers, acquired land, and became farmers. A group of Germans moved into Open Country from Illinois and settled around a Lutheran church. The Norwegians settled into a compact area, but were bifurcated into a Lutheran group and a Quaker group. The English and Scots were dispersed, many of them living in towns. Most of their descendants have migrated from Open Country, but the original nuclei of the Presbyterian, Methodist, and Congregational churches were English, as were some of the early Quakers. The Irish have largely left the farms, some of them victims of hard times and some pulled away by opportunities outside of farming. In recent years, Hollanders from other Iowa Dutch settlements moved onto farms vacated by Irish.

Of the ethnic groups, the Hollanders, with their conservative Dutch Reformed church, are most self-consciously protective of their ethnic boundaries. Other churches and the Quaker Meeting remain as reminders of past ethnic diversities, but this is now more a matter of style than substance. Several of the churches merged, as intermarriage, population mobility, and loss of native language blurred the most obvious distinctions. Today the overall ethnic character is mixed northern European, mostly Protestant, with a minority of German and Irish Catholics. The work ethic is strong, as is the belief in independence and free enterprise. Republicans dominate party politics and unfailingly fill all local offices. In being Caucasian and politically conservative, Open Country is similar to many other rural midwestern communities.

Feminism and Rural Women

This study is about rural social process, the ongoing building and shaping of patterns of human interaction in Open Country. It is explicitly feminist in that it is based on the assumption that women have been major participants and have stories to tell that will clarify the events that have shaped rural life and made it distinctive. Feminist analytical perspective, focusing on women's activities, is not dominant either in urban America or in Open Country. Common consensus associates rural areas with farming and farming with men; concomitantly, most rural studies have been about male farmers. Rural people have concurred in attributing greater importance to men than to women. Open Country joined with the rest of rural Iowa to defeat the state Equal Rights Amendment of 1980, an episode which indicates that most Open Country people share a broad, pervasive antipathy toward explicitly feminist issues. Being acknowledged as rightfully assuming authority over women in the community as well as in the home, men have held most of the prestigious and powerful public offices and women have viewed themselves as background supporters of the major (read, male) citizens of the community.

Acknowledging that most people conceptualize society in male terms, however, is not the same as saying that men alone have constructed the institutions of Open Country society. Feminist scholars have determined that women have their own sets of beliefs and patterns of action, that these are not completely derivative from men's beliefs and actions, and that they are integral to understanding society as a whole. Gender, the social (as opposed to biological) fact of being female or male, is a primary basis of social organization in all societies.

Further, significant variation is found among women in a given society. In the United States, gender depends on variables of race and class: being a woman has a different meaning for a poor, black woman than for a wealthy, white woman. Gender is not a static, homogeneous fact; it is continually being redefined. Historically, the daily reality of an Open Country farm woman's life shaped what she did and the way she related to men, and consequently the concrete meaning of being a woman. As daily life changed, women internalized new images of womanhood, images that have not necessarily been the same for all women of Open Country. Today, for example, because of increasing limitations imposed by rural poverty, a poor woman will structure her life on different premises and will see different life choices than a rich woman, and this will be subject to continuing change as the economic structure develops further. In addition, there are individuals who, because of unique experiences or innate propensities, conceptualize themselves as women in idiosyncratic ways: there have always been dissenters.

Rather than uniformity, there is typically a mosaic of different traits within a society, and a minority trait may be significant in providing the germ of change in the overall consensus. For example, only a small minority of Open Country women worked outside the family business operation in the early years of this century; today, a more substantial minority does. The changing pattern of variation helps to illuminate the concrete possibilities women face. Statistics are potentially useful in ferreting out diversity. Yet many who have studied society from women's perspective have discovered that existing statistical records have been inadequate to describe the incidence and nature of women's experiences. Using statistical records regarding the work of Open Country women is particularly difficult.

One example of statistical inadequacy is illustrated in the situation of Martha, a farm woman who came to Open Country with her husband in 1949. In 1982 Martha's work on the farm included bookkeeping, running errands, helping to count and check cattle, helping to artifically inseminate cows, hauling grain from the fields during harvest, weeding soybeans, buying cattle, and cooking for hired men. Martha was statistically listed as not working. While Martha's husband was accurately listed as a farmer, statisticians assigned Martha no title that described the work she did. At one time, almost every farm had a woman who did work similar to Martha's without receiving a wage or salary. A few of these women were recorded in the census as unpaid family farm workers, but the majority were listed as economically inactive, a gross distortion of the reality of their daily lives.

Karen, a farm woman in her twenties, typifies another problem with a static statistical summary. In 1982 Karen had been married five years and had two small children. She and her husband were taking over her parents' farm and starting an extensive hog enterprise. In addition to work in the house and on the farm, she did sewing and tailoring for income (at the interview, she had just completed dresses for a wedding party), baked and decorated cakes for weddings and other celebrations (also for income), sold pigskins, kept a paying boarder in her home; and was a part-time bartender in Center. As a bartender, Karen was listed statistically as a part-time, unskilled worker, but nothing in the statistical record illuminated the complexity of her work. While Karen was exceptional in the variety and extent of her work, many women juggled multiple part-time, temporary jobs to meet family and personal needs. Yet the census characterizations of the workforce seem to be most representative of those who do permanent, full-time work of one kind. In other words, the workforce statistics in our society are most adequate in delineating the work of middle-class men.

Glenda Riley (1981:56), describing the lives of ninteenth century Iowa frontierswomen, pointed to the irony of their being considered "not gainfully employed." Rachel Rosenfeld (1984:1), who co-authored a 1980 national survey of farm women, reported that the women in her survey sample were also likely to report that they did not work unless they held paying jobs in businesses such as offices, stores, or factories. Women themselves, as recipients and carriers of male-centered culture, tend to downplay the significance of their work. This book goes beyond this denial by focussing on what women have actually done and the context in which they have operated.

Once beyond the narrow definition of *work* in terms of what women do outside the home for pay, we immediately run into the difficulty of defining what work is and what it is not, an issue that penetrates to the heart of the controversy over women's place in society. The difficulty is not solely analytical; it is a basic societal contradiction. Women and men everywhere express contradictory views of women's work both in their statements and their behavior. Rather than attempting to construct a suitable definition of *work*, I use the word without precise definition in this book, and tighten the analysis by describing the economic and social significance of the activities which I will work. Clearly, the way society utilizes women's work on the one hand and the way it evaluates that work on the other hand creates paradoxes.

Looking at women's work in this way has methodological implications. Therefore, rather than relying solely on written records, the women themselves have been interviewed and, whenever feasible, their stories are presented in their own words. Although published statistics were used, they have been used in context; that is, they have been interpreted, not merely offered at face value.

Field Research in Open Country

Studying social patterns in rural Iowa posed definite challenges for me as an anthropologist seeking to become part of the women's community. Since a rural area is, by definition, sparsely peopled, the subjects of study were few and far between. Rather than having a single arena of action, I drove from one setting to another. In addition, unlike many cultures where public and private spheres merge in daily activities, Iowans, indeed all Americans, make a clear distinction between public and private. Much of their work and their most significant social interaction goes on in private and thus is not open to public observation. Data collection hinged on being introduced to people and receiving invitations, which I frequently solicited.

Generally rural Iowans are friendly and generous. Many readily welcomed me into their homes. Yet this hospitality did not necessarily mean that we were able to get to know each other. Rural people's special appreciation of privacy stems from the fact that at one level everyone is acquainted. Residents of Open Country know the names, basic household facts, and significant scandals of everyone they meet on the streets. Lacking the urbanites' protection of anonymity as they go about their public affairs, rural inhabitants generally tend to be more guarded in what they reveal of themselves. Even though I assured them that their real names would not be used and that accounts which would point to specific persons would not be written, I came to accept a general sense of distance in most Open Country people.

I gained initial access to Open Country through Quakers whom, as a Quaker, I had known for some time. One Quaker family offered me free use of an empty house on their property. I lived there during 1982, being joined at different periods by my husband and sons. From the core of Quaker friends and a few other personal links, I expanded my social circle, but most people continued to identify me as a member of the Norwegian Quaker community.

Beyond my personal welcome, I chose Open Country because it was clearly rural. Having no major city within commuting distance, I avoided the mixed country-city urban sprawl. Although some people commute 25 miles or more daily to factory jobs in three neighboring counties, this is not unusual in rural areas. With major employers and principal shopping centers outside the area, Open Country is typical of rural Iowa today and an excellent place to study rural Iowa women in their own social context.

I attacked the research in three ways, working concurrently on different projects throughout the year: first, I recorded extended interviews with 43 women and five men; second, I searched out and studied historical records of the lives of Open Country women; and third, I used the standard anthropoligical field technique of participant observation.

Interviews

The interviews gave insiders' accounts of the work and social patterns of Open Country women. Although I used a standard interview outline covering personal history, in the best interviews, these questions merely served to open extended accounts which the interviewees themselves shaped. Whenever possible, I interviewed subjects alone.[2]

The interviews began with childhood memories, through which older women provided rich detail of the early days of Open Country. All gave basic demographic facts and general descriptions of the way their families supported themselves, who did what, and what determined the situations. Information regarding the way a woman established her livelihood and household as an adult revealed segments of economic history, as well as the importance of kinsfolk and friends. A history of the different types of work done by a woman brought out distinctive patterns of temporary work, mosaics of different tasks (both inside and outside the home) that came together to support the household and absorb the economic and emotional shocks that characterized every household at one time or another. I explored various relations between and among women—what they did together, whether it was a chore or a relief, and what these relationships meant to them. The emotional content of these women's lives was especially important—how they felt, what they wanted, and whether they were satisfied with their rewards. Although I asked each woman about her perceptions of control and power, few provided much in the way of describing a sense of personal power. More often, this information came from other sources, which would point to a particular woman as being powerful in her home, church, or community affairs.

Rather than concentrating on a particular subgroup within the Open Country community, I selected the inverviewees as a diverse group. One woman was selected because of her family's long involvement with her church and 4-H; another was described as one who participated most fully in farm operation; another as the "fine old lady" of Center; another was a woman I met in a bar. Those interviewed ranged in age from 25 to 99, the age distribution shown in Table 1.1.

Table 1.1
Age Distribution of Women Interviewed*

Age	Number of Women	% of Sample	% of Women Older than Age 20 in County**
20–29	7	17	20
30–39	4	9	13
40–49	5	12	14
50–59	7	16	15
60–69	6	14	16
70–79	6	14	13
80 +	8	19	9

*In addition to the 43 women interviewed, five men, all older than age 80, were interviewed.
**Computed from federal census figures, 1980.

The age distribution of my sample shows more older women than does the 1980 county census, which reflects my interest in the past as well as the present. Of those who expressed an identification with one of the ethnic groups of early Open Country, nine were Norwegian, five were Hollanders, six were German, and three were Irish. Of the women, 38 were married or widowed and five were single; all five of the men were married or widowed. The group represented 35 lifetime residents and 13 who grew up outside of Open Country. Both full-time and part-time farmers were represented, as were nonfarm persons.

In selecting the people to be interviewed rather than drawing them from a random sample, I believe I found people with more interest in the project and with a broader range of experience. Because I was seeking personal, in-depth responses, it was not feasible to interview complete strangers. Much of the questioning and data gathering that could be done through random sampling had already been done through the population and agricultural censuses, the crop and livestock reporting service, various community development surveys, and the recent national survey of farm women (Jones and Rosenfeld 1981).

Not everyone was willing to be interviewed, however, and one woman volunteered that she would not be interviewed even before she was asked. While assessing such refusals is difficult, I believe those who refused to be interviewed were more stressed, had less education, or had less connection with the world outside of Open Country than did those who agreed to be inteviewed. Any of these factors might logically have led to hesitancy regarding the interrogations. At least one woman was directed by her husband not to be interviewed. Refusing to be interviewed did not necessarily signal hostility toward me or toward the project. Three women who refused to be interviewed had long conversations with me at different social gatherings. Although they answered all of my questions on these occasions, I was forced to write down sketchy notes afterwards and was unable to record the data completely. As anthropologist Frank Miller once remarked, it does an anthropologist good to be turned down once in a while. People who knew about my work fully appreciated that they did not have to cooperate in it.

The women interviewed were probably a more confident, better educated, and more socially outgoing group than the community of women as a whole. Furthermore, because I presented myself as a feminist, they probably included a greater number of self-conscious feminists than would be found in a random sample of the community. However, not everyone interviewed was a feminist; I talked openly and honestly with some of the women who were instrumental in opposing the Equal Rights Amendment, both nationally and in the 1980 state referendum. Most women were indifferent and largely unaware of feminist issues other than the ERA.

Barring personal objections or logistical problems, I tape recorded the interviews, thus ensuring that the interview records would be as complete and accurate as possible. The interview flowed much more freely if I did not have to be taking notes. Some women were, however, clearly hesitant to speak into the tape recorder, undoubtedly concerned to some degree about their privacy and personal vulnerability. The use of the tape recorder had both advantages and disadvantages. I was able to assess the effect of the tape recorder by continuing to talk with the women after the formal interviews. I was often offered coffee, or a meal or a tour of the farm, and I gained different insights through this more informal conversation. As a matter of fieldwork ethics, however, the tape recorder helped to authenticate my scholarly interest in the women's lives. I was clearly unable to become intimate friends with all of the women, although as a nonjudgmental listener I could offer acceptance and respect.

Written Records

In addition to interviewing Open Country people, collecting local written records of women's work and social interaction was an integral part of this study. In the early years of extension work county extension agents, both farm agents and home economists, kept voluminous records of each year's work. Although the yearly records varied, a typical year's records contained the following: a narrative description of the general farm outlook; a description of all extension projects undertaken; number of members, and names of officers of the Farm Bureau (the organization which directed extension activities until 1955); a list of meetings held and attendance at each meeting; photographs of extension activities; descriptions of 4-H work, including membership lists, projects, and photographs; and some of the brochures that were distributed.

I examined records from five churches, churches having been major social and cultural centers in times past. These records consisted of financial statements, religious themes, information on women's organizations, lists of appointments to committees, photographs, and minutes from some of the meetings. In every case, having firsthand information from some of the women who had been involved in church activities was helpful, as this served to highlight the most important aspects and to establish a context from which to interpret the records. Finally, I attended services and/or meetings in all of the churches and this helped to put these records in perspective.

Other public records were sketchier and tantalizingly incomplete. Some records of secular women's clubs were available. Again, going to several women's club meetings and interviewing club members helped elucidate these records. Local newspapers were good sources of material on women's social and economic life. Although the front-page was generally devoted to men's news, women wrote what is called "women's news"—accounts of visiting, birthday parties, weddings, anniversaries, and women's club meetings. In addition to accounts of general activities, there were advertisements placed by women working as seamstresses and music teachers, lists of schoolteachers and salaries, popular stories, and advertisements for various food, health, and beauty products of particular interest to women.

Individuals kept a variety of scrapbooks, photograph albums, financial records, letters, and journals. Their usefulness varied. Some, such as a collection of newspaper clippings about World War

II, were significant in that they indicated the events that the people themselves wanted to record. Others, such as one woman's record of chicken, egg, and cream receipts and expenses along with an account of all the money she spent or gave away from 1942 to 1945, are unique records of family resource pooling and values. Although this record came from outside of Open Country, the area was geographically close enough so that the economic and social context was similar to that of Open Country.

Participant Observation

The third and final type of research conducted, participant observation, is anthropolgists' term for on-site study and recording of ongoing events. As a participant, I lived in Open Country and used local stores and services. As a resident researcher, I came to know approximately 250 households, recognizing them in terms of occupation, religion, household composition, length of residence, and general social presence in the community. I regularly attended Quaker meetings, sports events, celebrations, and land auctions. I drank beer with the "regulars" at a bar, played in a summer tennis tournament, took a part in an amateur theater production, weeded soybeans, regularly quilted with a group of church women, made pies for community dinners, cleaned chickens with a group of women, sold hot dogs and pie at the Farm Bureau Women's fair stand, and visited in homes. Being invited to speak about my work at seven local women's club meetings, I was able to present my preliminary conclusions to the women and evaluate their responses. For a centennial project, I was cochair of a committee that put on a series of programs on the ethnic heritage of Farmtown. In short, as an outsider I received the hospitality of the people of Open Country and joined with them in some of their activities.

Although I appreciated the generosity of Open Country people, representing myself as anything other than an outside observer is misleading. At times people would break action and offer me special explanations of what was happening. Thus, my presence definitely altered the flow of events to some extent. My status as wife and mother was an asset and people were eager to greet my husband and teenaged sons, but my living apart from them during this time was considered bizarre. My permanent residence is in Ames, which Open Country people recognized as the site of Iowa State University, the state land grant institution. Although I had no official connection with the university during the research period, my interest in rural life and extension connected me to the school in the minds of Open Country people. This, together with having more formal education than most people in the county, undoubtedly had both negative and positive effects on my acceptance. Beyond this I found some understandable protectiveness about local customs and social groupings that only seldom erupted in overt behavior or pointed remarks.

In short, I wanted to feel a part of the community as I did my work. I wanted them to like me, and I believe for the most part they did. But I also sense that it was easy for me, as an anthropologist immersing myself in the social life of Open Country, to imagine that I achieved an intimacy and a depth of understanding that actually lie beyond the grasp of an outsider. The people of Open Country have unstated, shared secrets that they keep for themselves.

Plan of the Book

What follows is a description of Open Country as I observed it in the actions and accounts of women. Beginning with an examination of family relations in the early years of settlement, I proceed to assess women's work and woman-to-woman interaction in the period before World War II. Viewing the World War II years as a major turning point, I examine the impact of U.S. government policies on the lives of rural Iowa women. To present a longer-range view of one thread of change, one chapter is devoted to a study of change in the egg industry. Women's work and their positions within the Open Country community in the post-World War II period are then described. Finally, some of the parallels between the process of change undergone by Open Country women and that undergone by women in other parts of the world are explored. I argue for the infusion of a feminist perspective in rethinking basic concepts of development in rural areas.

CHAPTER 2

The Family in Open Country Before World War II

Elsa, born in 1901, had taught country school for two years before her marriage to a farmer in 1921. When interviewed in 1982, she spent a long afternoon describing her work as a schoolteacher and a farm woman, but she was hesitant and equivocating in her account. Clearly, she did not place the same values on her work experiences that I did. After the interview, she seemed finally to understand our different perspectives. She said that women did not work when she was young. A woman who would work was thought to be not quite decent; working would just not have been right. A woman interacting with strangers in a public place like a bank was unseemly. Then she qualified this: if a woman worked for someone she knew—like a family member—that work was acceptable. In other words, if she were under the protection and watchful eye of a family member, she was allowed to do things that would otherwise not be open to her, and she could do them without being scorned by others. Work within the context of a family meant something totally different from work done independently.

After this interview, I formulated "Elsa's hypothesis," which was that a woman lost social favor by engaging in any economic or political activity outside the context of the family, but almost any degree of crossover into male roles was permissable if done within the family's system of control. This hypothesis explained a surprisingly wide range of what I was discovering about women's work both in the past and in the present: while it was a disgrace for a woman to

19

be hired as a field laborer, doing that same work as part of a family farm operation earned admiration and respect. A woman was considered brazen if she applied for a position in a lawyer's office meeting strange men and engaging herself in their affairs, but an efficient and clever wife who managed an office for her lawyer husband and provided shrewd commentary on his legal cases over the dinner table was a prize. Most women who worked outside the family environment worked only with women (domestics), children (teachers), or the sick (nurses). Keeping house, socializing children, and caring for those in need were extensions of work done by women in the home. Before World War II, almost all of the socially approved interaction between men and women occurred within the family.

Family has diverse meanings. In certain contexts it has been equated with a nuclear grouping of husband, wife, and children; it has also been used to denote an extended kin grouping. Rather than attempting to solidify a definition of family as a concrete "thing," I follow some analyses of feminist anthropology in considering family as a moral construct, a way of thinking about connections among people (Collier, Rosaldo and Yanagisako 1982:37). In Rayna Rapp's words, family is

> . . . the normative, correct way in which people get recruited into households. . . . Families organize households, and it is within families that people experience the absence or presence, the sharing or withholding, of basic poolable resources. . . . "Family" . . . is conditioned by the exigencies of household formation, and serves as a shock absorber to keep households functioning (Rapp 1982:170).

Family connected men and women at the same time that it divided their worlds and imposed separate meaning on their lives. Not only did family constrain the activities of women, family relations also determined how people defined and valued what they did. Moreover, the working definition of family could be ambiguous: what the state understood by family was not always the same as what family meant for women in their daily lives.

Open Country women's sense of family grew out of the need to extend their worlds beyond their households. For them, family included a broad range of kinsfolk. Elsa's use of the word *family* was broad enough to have allowed her to take a position in a bank while operating within family boundaries. To understand the pervasive but ambiguous meaning of *family* in Open Country in the early twentieth century, it is necessary to review some of what was behind the westward expansion that populated Open Country.

Westward Expansion

Northwestern Iowa was part of *The Farmer's Last Frontier* (Shannon 1945), which Caucasians finally settled and farmed in the years between 1860 and 1897. Unlike farming areas which had been settled earlier, Open Country developed in the context of a world market in agricultural commodities. Native Americans living in Iowa before the European invasion had practiced an independent subsistence-oriented agricultural adaptation, but such a pattern was never adopted by the white farmers. The terms by which white settlers acquired and kept their land depended on their articulation with the economic structure of the eastern United States. That Open Country flourished as a farming community only after the completion of the railroad in the early 1880s underscores the importance of trade relations in the developing Open Country farm economy. The railroad transported livestock and other products to the major farm markets of Chicago and delivered manufactured goods to Open Country. Farmers had to sell farm commodities to pay for land, equipment, and taxes. The terms of trade, however, kept most farmers in a precarious position. Boom and bust cycles have marked the American agricultural economy since the Civil War, and there has never been a sustained period of economic stability to provide the basis for effective planning and orderly development. Settlers coped with an unpredictable farm commodity market from the first days of settlement.

There was also a well-developed land market. Although the Hamiltonian and Jeffersonian factions in the federal government disagreed with regard to the policies that governed the disposal of public land, cheap land was transferred to private interests by a number of land acts in the late eighteenth and early nineteenth centuries (Cochrane 1979:44). In the absence of a publicly debated and articulated plan, these measures worked to the advantage of specific private interests rather than that of a broad-based public. In a discussion of U.S. land disposal practices, Willard Cochrane (1979:181) concluded, "Personal greed, corrupt practices, and speculation pervaded the entire [land] disposal process and in-volved the whole citizenry from presidents down to the lowliest pioneer." While popular sentiment favored the claims of the settler who would work on the land, Congress was not always partial to this group. In the Panic of 1857, for example, thousands of Iowa settlers lost their land, and Congress declined to intervene (Gates 1964:72). Five years later, in 1862, it passed the Homestead Act, which gave 160 acres of public land free to farmers who would live on and work their farms for five years. By this time, however, millions of acres of Iowa land had already been transferred to railroads, speculators, and the state of Iowa; little was left for homesteading. Robert Swierenga (1968:45) estimates that by 1862 approximately two-thirds of the privately owned property in Iowa could only have been held for speculation. In Open Country, preceding the full-scale in-flux of white settlers in the 1880s, landowners held operations of thousands of acres, which they attempted to work with hired laborers (Peck, Montzheimer and Miller 1914:190–93; Gates 1964:70).

Although they opened up the country, the large-scale land-owners who amassed property in Open Country in the first acquisi-tions of public land actually managed their holdings as agricultural properties for less than five years in the 1870s and 1880s. They then divided and sold them in smaller farm units (Peck, Montzheimer and Miller 1914:191). Railroad companies, recipients of extensive land grants, also profited by selling their land in smaller parcels in Open Country and beyond. By 1890 the average Open Country farm was 185 acres, only slightly larger than the household operations of 160 acres which the government was parcelling out under the Homestead Act (USDA 1940:37). Land companies and railroads constantly recruited Open Country residents to continue the westward expansion by investing in yet more inexpensive, untilled land and moving again. In 1897 a railroad company placed adver-tisements in the local newspaper to sell Minnesota farmland for $3 per acre (Open Country Bulletin 1897). As late as 1924 adver-tisements appeared for the sale of inexpensive railroad land with long-term, low-interest payments (Open Country Bulletin 1924). A number of Open Country people did leave to try their luck in farm-ing in South Dakota, Minnesota, and Nebraska.

The constant westward pull on the thin population took badly needed farm labor, and the consequent lack of adequate wage labor undid the early agricultural developers (Pfeffer 1983:557). While there was never enough labor to meet all the farming needs, smaller farms could operate with the intensive use of household labor. Even with the smaller farms and household labor, farmers constantly sought hired hands, but older Open Country farmers all noted the difficulty of hiring laborers for their family operations. Some recruited immigrant laborers from Europe, but the continuing availability of even marginal farm land in the West lured the most energetic and capable of these workers away. Thus, the land market of the latter nineteenth century made hired labor costly and scarce.

But, as Harriet Friedmann (1978:582) noted, "The availability of land was not a 'natural' fact, . . . The actual availability of land for colonization was a social consequence of territorial expansion organized by national states." With the expansion of national states, characteristic of the nineteenth century, the territory of the United States was not secure until it was populated with individuals who were tied to the institutions of the eastern seaboard. Canada competed with the United States for control of the central area of the continent. The cowboys and itinerant farmhands who had worked on the large ranches and farms of the West had done little to establish a stable population base. Claiming this land and directing its use involved an active policy. In 1865, after the passage of the Homestead Act, President Andrew Johnson made clear that more intensive farming of the western lands was in the best interest of the country. He said:

> . . . the lands in the hands of industrious settlers, whose labor creates wealth and contributes to the public resources, are worth more to the United States than if they [the lands] had been reserved as a solitude for future purchasers (quoted in Fite 1974:16).

The United States sought to populate the region. More money might be realized from land sales by holding the land off the market until higher prices prevailed, but value was lost when the land was not put into production. It was people working the land as commercial farmers that would benefit the United States. Commercial farming on the scale of household operations, although it superseded agrarian capitalism, did not run counter to the development of industrial capitalism (Buttel 1982:35). Family labor was productive: it offered the possibility of more intensive cultivation with cheaper labor costs, thus providing low cost food for export on the world market and for consumption by industrial workers.

The family-based household was an ideal unit of intensive pro-duction given the shortage of labor. Labor requirements were especially critical in the early years of Open Country settlement, and a single person could not provide the necessary labor on a farm of 160 acres. Breaking the sod, even with a moldboard plow, was a slow process. Barns, sheds, fences, and houses had to be built. Construction went on continuously for years, in addition to the ongoing work of raising crops and tending livestock. Within a family, children, older people, and women were all recruited to the workforce along with the working-aged men. Where capitalist farmers had to pay their laborers in cash just to try to keep them, this was not necessary with family workers. A small part of the pay-ment family workers received was in cash, but the major share came in the form of in-kind benefits, such as food, clothing, hous-ing, and love. Money was needed for investments in building materials, farm equipment, and livestock, and the family minimized the labor expenditures.

Most of the earliest western explorers and adventurers were male, but the fertility of women as wives was crucial in establishing a securely rooted, household-based farming system. Unlike itinerant farmhands, a husband-wife family reproduced itself as a unit of production. Thus, government policy included selectively encouraging the immigration of married couples. Although the Homestead Act allowed both men and women over age 21 to claim 160 acres of land, it was soon prohibited for husband and wife to homestead separate plots (Cochrane 1979:81). A plot of 160 acres was considered suitable for a family comprised of a husband, a wife, and their children (Fite 1974:21). Records document the existence of single women homesteaders in the Dakotas and Wyoming (Myres 1982:258; Stewart 1914), but the United States Department of Agriculture (USDA), established in 1862, clearly promoted the ideal of the farm woman as a wife and the farmer as a husband. In its first annual report, for example, the USDA urged farmers to cultivate good working relationships with their wives as a means to a smoothly run farm system:

> The indisputable truth is, that there is no other item of superior, or perhaps equal, importance in the happy and profitable management of any farm, great or small, than that every person on it should be made to understand that deference and respect and prompt and faithful obedience should be paid, under all circumstances, to the

wife, the mother, and the mistress; . . . An illustration: A tardy meal infallibly ruffles the temper of the workmen, and too often of the husband; yet all the wife's orders were given in time; but the boy has lagged in bringing wood; or the girl failed to put her loaf to bake in season, because they did not fear the mistress, and the master was known not to be very particular to enforce his wife's authority. If by these causes a dinner is thrown back half an hour, it means on a good-sized farm a loss of time equivalent to the work of one hand a whole day; it means the very considerable difference between working pleasantly and grumblingly the remainder of the day; it means, in harvest time, in showery weather, the loss of loads of hay or grain (USDA 1863:463).

A woman farmer would not have had a wife to manage her household, but the Department did not address this situation, or that of any other unmarried person who had to develop different personal arrangements for farm life. As Joan Jensen (1981:103) notes, the ideal of the husband-wife farm unit, as put forth by the USDA, militated against Mormon polygyny as well as the communal farming practices of the Native Americans and some religious sects.

The USDA addressed the woman herself in terms of her sexual attractiveness, assuring her that, if she had the support of her husband, farm life would not turn her into an "Amazon." On the contrary, sharing farm work with a husband would keep a woman youthful, graceful, and charming (Davis 1867:437). Just as surely as a farmer would have a wife, a farm woman would have a husband. Being first and foremost a wife, she was to be concerned about her romantic appeal to him, and this is the way the USDA addressed her.

The reality of Washington, however, was not always the reality of Open Country. The family household placed a great responsibility on the shoulders of the Open Country farm woman. Maintaining a houseful of workers and children without the retail establishments, medical services, and informal support that many urban women took for granted, they found that staying youthful, graceful, and charming for their husbands was the least of their worries. For these women, *family* meant an extended family, with a network of supporting female kin. Ruth, born in Open Country in 1892, told of the way her extended family helped to absorb the shocks and to meet the needs of early settlers.

I was born on a cold winter night on a farm. . . . At five weeks old, we moved to a larger farm which Uncle John had rented with Father. Uncle John's [family members] were moving to Iowa with their three oldest children, . . . Ella [a fourth] arriving in November of that year. Father had been in Iowa for four years. The house was divided and the partnership lasted for three years. Then Father bought 80 acres one and one-quarter miles east, and Uncle John 15 acres . . . for a truck garden. The place where we had been living was located across the road from my grandparents. . . . In 1901, Father built an addition, for our family had increased to seven by then. When it was finished, my grandparents came to live with us, and by 1908 three more children had arrived. During this time, after my grandparents moved in, Aunt Alis spent many weeks with us while her son was building his house.

Ruth's household was growing and flexible, with people moving in and out according to their needs and opportunities. The household served as a refuge for kin in time of crisis:

In 1898, Aunt Anna P. [John's wife] died for pneumonia having six children. We were very close to the family and felt it keenly. However, we were glad to welcome [two of the children] to our family until it was arranged for their unmarried Aunt Martha to come . . . and care for them.

Ruth's household personnel changed continually. Her uncle, aunts, cousins, and grandparents all lived in her household at various times while she was growing up. Ruth lived and worked in the same household as her parents until 1917, when she married Harold, who had come to Open Country to rent land and farm, his sister keeping house for him. With the financial assistance of her Aunt Alis and her parents, Ruth and Harold purchased and moved to a small farm that was contiguous to her parents' farm. Ruth recalled that in 1920, in addition to their two children, Harold's sister and a teacher were living with them when Harold died of typhoid fever. Harold's mother then moved in to help run the household. Ruth continued to board teachers until she moved back to her parents' home in 1928, finally losing her farm in 1931. For Ruth, extended family provided credit, household help, and emergency shelter, things which neither the nuclear family nor the society at large afforded. In this context, *family* meant not the nuclear family envisioned by the USDA, but an extended family of kin which would, in Rapp's (1982:170) words, serve as a "shock absorber" to keep people going.

In general, women did not experience the exhilaration that men had at the prospect of coming to the prairie to farm (Schwieder 1980:152). Although, as with Ruth and Elsa, groups of kin migrated and settled together, the women were still uprooting themselves and probably leaving some of their supportive kin network behind in the eastern United States or in Europe. The families that they did have in their new homes helped them to meet the challenges posed by life in an undeveloped area. Kin who were geographically removed were often lost as functioning family members. Major moral or economic differences could also separate kin even within a community so that they did not consider each other family members, although this was rare. Most Open Country people had a number of local kin whom they considered to be family. The category of family defined the pool of kin which could be brought into a household economic operation without the formal exchange contract required by nonfamily members. Family connections served to define rights and responsibilities and to legitimate power relationships.

It has been claimed that the idea of the extended family of rural America is merely a "popular myth," insofar as census records have never shown a significant number of non-nuclear family members living under one roof (McNall and McNall 1983:19). The record of Open Country points toward a modification of this assessment. *Household* and *family* are two different concepts: census records count people in terms of household membership, with a household being a physical structure in which a group of people live. People living in the same household typically use the same kitchen and, to some extent, pool their resources. A household does not necessarily define a family, as nonfamily persons may be living in a household and family members may be living elsewhere.

Equating household and family means that the kinship connections of key importance in the lives of Open Country people are not part of the analysis of family. Ruth, for example, maintained a number of important kinship connections that went beyond her household, and these connections were essential to ongoing social and economic life. In the 1900 and 1910 censuses, the census takers listed a male head of household (if any adult male was present) and then listed the household members as they related to him, but they did not delineate the kinship networks of a community. Open Country's 1900 and 1910 census schedules show clusters of households whose inhabitants had the same surnames, but reading extended family connections from census forms in a systematic way is not possible. The only family relations recorded on these forms were those within a household. Since the USDA promoted the ideal of the nuclear family unit, those who designed the federal census procedures might have believed that households with nuclear families would be the rule and that kinship delineation of households would record the most significant family connections. But this assumption cannot be directly tested in the census schedules themselves.[1]

The census schedules do not show a preponderance of nuclear family households in Open Country in 1900 and 1910. Considering the population of two Open Country townships, we find that in 1900, 49 percent of the households had individuals other than the wife and unmarried children of the household head living in them; in 1910, 41 percent of the households had non-nuclear members.[2] These "others" included boarders, hired hands, servants, business partners, and extended family members. More than 20 percent of the households were listed as having kin other than nuclear family members (see Table 2.1).[3] Although this was not a majority of households, it does represent a substantial minority. These non-nuclear kin, listed in terms of relationship to the head of household, included siblings, parents, grandparents, cousins, aunts, uncles, nieces, nephews, in-laws, grandchildren, and stepchildren.

Table 2.1
Non-nuclear kin in the households of two Open Country townships, 1900 and 1910

Year	Number of Households with Non-nuclear Kin	Number of Households	Percentage of Households with Non-nuclear Kin
1900	49	239	21
1910	59	253	23

Source: U.S. census schedules for Open Country, 1900 and 1910.

Household membership was shifting. When many working age children lived in a household, the teenagers would frequently live with neighbors or relatives, for whom they would work. For example, a woman with two daughters shared one with a sister who needed summer help. At other times, special educational or medical needs required a shifting of households. For example, one summer Ruth's ailing uncle came to her home, where he was cared for until he died. By living with her aunt, Elsa was able to attend high school. Sophie lived with her grandmother after her own mother died. These arrangements, often temporary and encompassing approximately 20 percent of the households at a time, involved a greater percentage of the population at some time in their lives.

Thus, extended family relationships have been important connections. Family was important not only because the group lived together, but often because of the potential help from those in a local kinship network. An extended family was more permanent and secure than was a nuclear family. Not everyone married or had children. Once formed, a nuclear household like Ruth's was splintered by death or economic misfortune. A family was a means of adapting to these misfortunes. A large family, at its best, provided a set of choices for a woman in deciding where to go and what kind of work to do. The varied needs of households in the early period of settlement called for a flexible, large family grouping.

While family afforded women openings, it also constrained them. The legal system granted women rights in terms of family membership. Their status within a family determined the way that laws applied to them, but no woman had legal rights that equalled those of men.

Anna was born on a farm in 1914 and lived in Open Country her entire life. Her limited exposure to feminism was filtered through the teachings of the conservative Dutch Reformed church, and she did not consider herself a feminist. When interviewed in 1982, she talked about her granddaughter whose husband had left her and ended their marriage. The granddaughter, finding herself without a means of support, had a difficult (but empowering) period of transition and re-education. Anna seemed proud of her granddaughter's grit and determination, even though she resented the divorce. Then Anna reflected that if her own marriage had dissolved—which she never even dreamed would happen, but *if*—she could not have supported herself.

> It was more a man's world. . . . Like, for instance, if a couple would separate in the time I grew up, I don't know what a woman would do to earn a living. . . . I don't know many women who would have wanted to go on their own. I don't know what you would have done. Your whole living was the farm. You couldn't go off the farm. . . .

In that time, too, the laws belonged to the man. A farm was in the man's name. . . . I think everyone felt it was hers [too], but legally it wasn't. (Emphasis added.)

Anna's comment that the laws and property belonged to the man reflects the pervasiveness of English Common Law in America. Under the precepts of English Common Law, a woman lost her legal personhood at marriage, when she merged with the person of her husband, and the husband was henceforth the legal entity. The law's application to a woman derived from her affiliation with a man. Furthermore, Anna perceived this to be connected to the impossibility of a woman supporting herself outside of this affiliation. The farm was the man's because this was the way it was registered at the courthouse. Although Iowa law granted women title to their own earnings in 1886 and control of their own property in 1897, men still retained control of joint property (Gallaher 1918:92–93). Moreover, not all women or men understood or appreciated the implications of the new laws as well as they understood the customs that assigned financial affairs to the sphere of men. In practice, the only way a woman could achieve significant wealth was by default—if she inherited property from her husband or if she had no brothers to inherit property from her parents. Furthermore, whatever she inherited from her husband was held only until she could give it to her sons. A woman attempting to function outside the boundaries of family, without a man to represent her interests, was forced to operate within a system that was alien to her and that did not afford her full status. As Anna said, "I don't know what a woman would do to earn a living." The USDA was little help to an unmarried woman in her efforts to organize a farm operation. Earning a living meant having recourse to the recognition and protection of a legal system, and Anna did not believe that women had this. The practical effect of this was that most women sought security in family rather than in independence.

Family was particularly significant for women because of their exclusion from the public, nonfamily world of business and politics. Americans, unlike many nonindustrial societies, have defined a boundary between public and private, and this split shapes the ideology of the family in America (Collier, Rosaldo and Yanagisako 1982:34). *Family* has been conceptualized as a set of personal relations in which human warmth and nurturing are more important than achievement and wealth. Ideally, family has been a man's retreat from the public world in which he must prove himself. In Open Country, as elsewhere in the United States, women did the major share of the work in maintaining family relations. They planned the birthday, anniversary, and wedding festivities celebrating and reinforcing family ties within a household and among different households. In the early days of settlement, it was the women who welcomed new relatives into a household, taught them English if necessary, and provided the warmth and hospitality that could keep them living in one house rather than moving on. And it was, of course, the women who bore and cared for the children that replenished the family.

Dual Economy: Household and Market

Ruth's losing her farm in 1931 resulted from the Great Depression of the 1930s, but economic swings had afflicted Open Country since the early years of settlement. The depression of the 1890s dampened the early optimism of Open Country settlers soon after their arrival. Farm prices recovered at the turn of the century, culminating with the Golden Age of American Agriculture during the peak years from 1910 to 1914, and these prices held strong through World War I and immediately thereafter (Cochrane 1979:100). In the end, however, this good economic period functioned primarily to increase land prices, to lure farm people into debt, and to set the scene for the disastrous price drop of 1920, which brought on the beginning of the depression for farmers. For example, corn fell from $1.50 per bushel in May 1920 to 35 cents per bushel in May 1921; eggs fell from 36 cents per dozen in June 1920 to 16 cents per dozen in June 1921.[4] Such low prices afforded little opportunity to expand the scale of farming: In 1900, the average Open Country farm was 185 acres; in 1920, 183 acres; and in 1940, 181 acres (USDA 1940:37; USDC 1942A:130). Although prices did rise slightly in the 1920s, farm people did not share in the general economic prosperity of the rest of society. Using farm commodity prices and the increase in the scale of farming as indices of profitability, farming was obviously not a good way to accumulate significant wealth.

The economic marginality of most of the households shaped a woman's particular place in the family's division of labor. Producing farm commodities did not afford a dependable subsistence to the farm household. While subsistence production (that is, production only to meet the subsistence needs of the farm household) was not the primary basis of Open Country farming, a subsistence component was part of the farming system. This involved production of poultry, dairy products, and garden produce for the family table; the processing and manufacture of food and clothing; and the sales of produce such as eggs, which provided for the trade of groceries and dry goods that were used within the household. While men organized and controlled the commercial farming operation, subsistence production and reproduction of the farm labor force were closely tied together in women's work. Both men's and women's work was necessary. If the production of commodities for profit overshadowed subsistence production in the years from 1897 to 1920, subsistence became the major concern from the start of the farm depression in 1920 until 1940. Women's subsistence production provided the flexibility that balanced the swings in the economy.

Diversified farming lent itself to a subsistence contingency more readily than did specialized farming. Besides being a hedge against the market failure of any one crop, diversified farming provided a wide range of food items. Major crops—corn, oats, hay, and barley—were mostly consumed within Open Country by livestock, including beef and dairy cattle, pigs, horses, poultry, and sheep. Pigs, known as *mortgage burners,* or *mortgage lifters*, were the most consistent sources of capital growth. Dairy farming was a close second. Many farms also had minor production lines such as bees, poultry, rabbits, and fruits and vegetables. A 1912 Butler County, Iowa, farm diary recorded sales of eggs, onions, radishes, asparagus, lettuce, peas, potatoes, turnips, cabbage, eggplant, tomatoes, cauliflower, cucumbers, and cherries made by women as supplemental sources of income from a grain and livestock farm (Gabelmann 1912). In addition to the income from farming, such a diversified farm supplied its own meat, milk, butter, eggs, and fruits and vegetables, thereby reducing the need to expend cash for food. The cash that was used within the household usually came from the "side" sources rather than from the major farm commodities.

Farm commodity prices, which rose slightly toward the end of the 1920s, fell again with the advent of the Great Depression in the 1930s. Yet Iowa did not experience a wholesale out-migration of its farm population during this depression. In fact, Iowa farm people enjoyed a degree of security not matched by the city-dwelling poor (Fink and Schwieder 1984). At least on the farm there was a place to live and food to eat. A farm woman who wrote for *Wallaces' Farmer* in the 1930s told of seeing a hungry, jobless mother in town and feeling a sudden surge of gratitude for her work and the subsistence production of her farm. She wrote

> Suddenly I thought of those jars of meat! Hallelujah! We had food! The coat which I had bought four years ago was still good. Thank goodness, I was sufficiently clad! The innumerable tasks which lay ahead of us with the opening of spring work looked big and beautiful to me. Glory be! We had a job! (Country Air 1936:297).

The *we* that had a job was her husband and herself, and the diversified farm, with the jars of home canned meat on the shelf, provided the security for which she was so thankful. Poverty such as that which occurred on Open Country farms in the hard times of the 1920s and 1930s seems to have reinforced the diversified labor-intensive farming patterns which had characterized Open Country farms for most of the years between settlement and World War II.

Like the farms, town businesses were family based operations. Reading the federal census schedules of 1900, one is struck by the number and variety of businesses in Open Country. With more than ten trains making daily trips to Farmtown, the railroad was the largest single employer, but grocers, druggists, watchmakers, carpenters, restauranteurs, seamstresses, tailors, bakers, milliners, doctors, printers, and photographers were also present. Farmtown, with a population of just over 1,000, had three hotels and three doctors in 1915 (Farmtown 1983:8; R.L. Polk and Company 1918). As late as 1940, it had seven grocery stores. Given this number of businesses, the volume of any one was necessarily small. With small businesses, the demand for labor was fluid. A manager, for example, hired someone to unload a boxcar, but would not maintain a permanent loading crew, thus creating many part-time or one-time workers. In such small towns, no one lived far from anything, and in some cases the family actually lived in the same building from which their business was run. Moreover, the line between what was and was not a business was thin. Enterprises such as keeping boarders, sewing, and laundry services—things that women did for money—were not always considered occupations, particularly when done at home. Although successful town businesses tended to make more money than did farms (at least before the Great Depres-

sion), townspeople shared many of the same conditions that promoted family farm economies. Like the farms, Center and Farmtown businesses were small-scale, diversified family operations.
Although equating the experiences of farm and town rural women is
misleading, both groups participated in family economic operations that were similarly structured in terms of the division of labor
by age and sex. However, the majority of Open Country people were
farm-based before World War II, as illustrated in Table 2.2.

Table 2.2
Population of Open Country, 1915–1940

Status	1915	1930	1940
Rural	15,259	15,089	15,525
Farm	9,643	9,156	8,883
Nonfarm	5,616	5,933	6,642

Sources: U.S. population censuses.

Women's work, whether in farm or nonfarm households, was
conditoned by their nearly total responsibility for the reproductive
sphere. *Reproduction* in this sense was not just biological reproduction, but included the daily reproduction of the labor force and
social reproduction. *Daily reproduction* included food preparation,
household maintenance, and laundry and other tasks which were
necessary in order for workers to be physically and psychologically
able to do each day's work. *Social reproduction* involved teaching
children the moral responsibilities that would maintain the system.
Women also upheld the necessary moral norms for adults.

Not only did women work within a family economy, they occupied a specific place within this system. Women's work had a
distinct meaning that was different from the meaning assigned to
men's work. Not everyone in the family was the same.

Furthermore, a difference between the work actually done and
the way this work was evaluated was evident. Within a family
economy, people readily lost track of the importance of women's
work. Many, like Elsa, at once affirmed and denied women's work.
She had milked cows, raised poultry, and kept house for six people,
yet claimed she had not worked. Again and again women said that
they or their mothers had not worked—after describing the substantial work performed. Frequently, I would hear of women who *helped*

rather than *worked.* Gladys, who farmed with her husband from 1927 to 1942, made typical statements about her role on the farm:

> I did just about everything there was to be done. I did very little working in the field with the exception [that] I would help make hay and would help pick corn. As far as the actual farm labor was concerned, I didn't do any of that . . . [I would] milk cows and help take care of the hogs. At that time we had horses, and I would help take care of the horses. . . . I took care of 300 chickens. . . . As I said, I really didn't do any labor on the land except with helping pick the corn and make the hay.

Nor was it only on farms that women's work got lost in the telling. When asked if his mother had worked, Charles, whose family operated a general store before World War I, said, "No, she was just help." Asked for more specific information about what she did, he said

> [She helped] any place at all, Mother did. . . . One thing Mother did, she sold more linen tablecloths than [anyone else]. The man we bought the dry goods from, he said, "You sell more linen tablecloths than any store in Spencer [a small city approximately 40 miles from Open Country]." . . . I don't know why, but she always had quite a good way with dry goods. . . . She took care of that.

How does one assess reports of women who picked corn, made hay, milked cows, and tended hogs, horses, and chickens, yet did not do any farm labor? How does one understand a report of a woman who managed a dry goods department well, yet did not work in the store? Obviously, the people operated under a different conceptual system from that of today. Woman did specific activities that we tend to call work, but that, within the family economy, were not considered work. Had nonfamily people been hired to do the same tasks, they would have been called workers. Women's work might have been invisible in the family economy, but it was a factor of production and it shaped relations both within the household and among households.

Women provided a significant part of the daily economic support of a farm household. Alice's parents were married in 1922 and her father's parents moved from farm to town, leaving the young couple alone on the farm. After five years, Alice's grandfather died. Settling the estate involved transferring ownership of the farm to her father and paying her grandmother for her part of the estate. What they discovered was that Alice's father had no money. In the five years her father had lived and worked on the farm, his father had collected the proceeds of the farm, managed the business, and never paid the son for the work, other than by allowing his family to live on the farm. How had the young couple (and a baby daughter) survived? Alice said, "Could you believe it? My mother had been supporting the family for five years with her eggs." Her mother had raised chickens and marketed eggs, and it was she, rather than Alice's father, who made the only money that they saw within the household.

This case of a woman providing the daily support of the farm household is consistent with what has been written of nineteenth century farming. Joan Jensen sketched a model of a dual economy on U.S. farms in the earlier period:

> On many farms there was a dual economy—women and children providing for living expenses and keeping the expenses on a cash basis while men did field crops, using the income to pay for mortgages and new machinery and capital improvement (Jensen 1980:18).

Alice's grandfather kept these expenses separate by maintaining the farm accounts from a different household. Her mother's egg income was kept apart from the rest of the farm accounting; it was considered to belong to her rather than to the farm. In actual practice, most farm people did not divide the separate spheres as neatly, but the separation existed. Expanding Jensen's formulation by including reproduction of the workforce and production for home consumption as part of the woman's economy, the dual economy is a framework for assessing the varied inputs of farm women.

Glenda Riley (1981) and Dorothy Schwieder (1980) provide historical support for the dual model in their accounts of nineteenth century Iowa farm women's work. Farm women made cloth, clothing, candles, and soap; nursed the sick and delivered babies; cared for children; cleaned and laundered; and produced food. While labor shortages sometimes brought women into field work and farm management, this seems to have been a matter of crossing over into the male sphere. On the other hand, women routinely generated income by selling eggs or butter, keeping boarders, or teaching school. According to Schwieder (1980:153)

> . . . [T]he wife who did not bring some cash into the home or at least

reduce cash outgo by bartering for necessary goods and services, appears to have been the exception rather than the rule.

Women provided a large part of the household income and the manufactured products that were used in the home.

As the example of Alice's family suggests, the pattern of women producing for daily household maintenance persisted into the twentieth century. Men and women had separate spheres within the family economy. Although a woman might cross over into men's work if needed, most of her work was in maintaining a household production system that enabled the reproduction of the farm labor force. This work connected her to other women who were doing the same kind of work and with whom she exchanged her goods and services, but these exchanges were coordinated in an informal, decentralized way. The point of a woman's production was to meet the needs of people. Even when women realized cash from the sales of their produce, this cash would be converted into something usable within the home. *Value,* within the household component of the family economy, was *use value.* Measurement and quantification were only minor aspects of women's production. In the household sphere, social relations determined a person's rights to goods and services.

The male sphere of the family economy was commodity production. The products of men's work became commodities channeled into the public market system. Impersonal relations dominated market transactions, as buyers and sellers conceptualized value in terms of exchange rather than use. Money was the medium of exchange. The competition of the market promoted impersonal relations and profit maximization. In the public male world, the market dominated social relations.

The household and market spheres complemented and supported each other. There is evidence that women acknowledged and sought to enhance the household economy. In 1914 the Smith-Lever Act, which established the agricultural and home economics extension service, was pending before the U.S. Congress. In preparation for implementing this act (which became law the same year), the USDA sent an open-ended inquiry to the "housewives of 55,000 crop correspondents" (USDA 1915B:3) asking them how the USDA could be of service to them. Since the questions were open-ended, the replies varied and addressed diverse concens. They were not tabulated statistically. The samples that were published probably represented the ideas of the most educated and articulate wives of the most progressive farmers. In light of this probable skewing and the general prosperity of the period, it is particularly noteworthy that many of the wives complained that their husbands were inclined to put their money into farm operations rather than into the support of the households. One woman wrote

> . . . I would work to have a law passed whereby no man should be allowed to own a farm unless he would provide for his wife as well as he did for his stock—plenty of water, and easy to get, good drainage, and other sanitary conditions about the farmhouse (USDA 1915B:8).

Some asked that the USDA help them to enhance their own income potential. An Iowa woman wrote that she would like some kind of work to do in the winter

> . . . such as addressing envelopes or some such employment which would give a little pin money which I could spend for different articles which would make housework easier. . . . You, of course, know that no allowance is ever made for the wife of the farmer (USDA 1915B:18).

In this reply, as in several others, the woman used the term *pin money* to describe what she needed to run the house, thus indicating that she perceived the house to be of secondary importance. *Pin money* seems to have been a euphemism that distinguished women's money from men's money, which was used for the important business of running the farm.

Another woman asked that a portion of the farm profits be allocated to the woman:

> There is one thing I think causes farmers' wives to be unhappy. The wife naturally feels that she helps to make the income, but she has no claim to anything. I have always thought there should be a law requiring the husband to divide the whole income with his wife so she and her children would be sure of their rights under any conditions (USDA 1915B:17).

The point comes through that, even on presumably affluent farms during a golden period of agricultural profits, the wives were not substantially supported by their husbands on a daily basis. Wives wanted their own money, either as payment for their input into the general farm operation or for their own independent enterprises.

They consistently reported that their money went into their households, while their husbands' money went into the farms.

Family & Society

By establishing the extension service in 1914, the state reinforced the structure of the husband-wife family farm unit. Extension provided the framework for a network of federal, state, county, and local workers who would extend the latest developments in agriculture and home economics from the USDA to farm homes. The 1914 survey of farm women's needs elicited responses only from "housewives of crop correspondents" (USDA 1915B:3) and extension addressed farm women only as wives or future wives. Women's expressed need to earn money was never really addressed. Extension did not, for example, address the particular problems in credit and labor that a single woman might experience as a farmer, because the question of women's emergence into the public world was not part of the format of extension work. Moreover, extension did not seek to educate women to be farmers even within a family farm operation. The division of labor within the extension service assigned agriculture to the male sphere and home economics to the female sphere. Extension officials designed all extension work for women operating not just in a family context, but in a specifically structured nuclear family context, in which their most important role was that of a wife.[5]

A county tapped into this service by organizing a Farm Bureau, which would hire and direct the work of county extension agents. Because of this tie to government resources, the Farm Bureau became a powerful, quasi-public organization with a broad membership base. Membership in the Farm Bureau, however, was by nuclear family, and organizational parallels with prescribed nuclear family economic roles existed. A woman was automatically a member if her husband joined as a farmer; she did not join alone. While a women's committee directed the women's extension activities, the governing body of the Farm Bureau was male. Although the hired home economists reached more people than did the agricultural agents, their pay was always less. Thus, in structure as well as substance, the extension service mirrored and reinforced the nuclear family ideal.

The picture emerges of a system in which field work, large animals, legal matters, and farm capital were properly handled by men, while women were responsible for the everyday support of the farm household. An 1894 Open Country Farm Institute speaker stated that the two heads of a home should be equal, but "not in the absolute sense of woman's rights" (Open Country Bulletin 1894). He seemed to be saying that a man and a woman were not the same, but they should be deemed equally significant to the operation of a farm. In the Institute speaker's words and in Alice's family there is indication that the dual spheres of a farm operation were at last implicitly understood and accepted as the people themselves organized their activities. Whether or not they actually were equal, is debatable. The Institute speaker was exhorting men not to disregard the significance of their wives. No record was found of a contemporary woman speaker telling an audience of women not to underestimate their husbands' importance.

Ethnic groups within Open Country identified themselves according to the country of origin and had separate churches. Church memberships were, in essence, large extended family domains. Any two Open Country adults of the same ethnicity would almost certainly be joined by multiple kin ties. Many of the kinship diagrams became very complicated as sisters and brothers of one household married brothers and sisters of another. When two sisters married men who were cousins, their children were simultaneously first and second cousins to each other. The complex interlinkages as well as the vagueness of the outer boundaries of the kinship domain made the system flexible and well-suited to the needs of a family economy. Women, while remaining within a family, could interact with a number of different households. The groupings within large family domains came together in the membership of a common church.

Church membership was by family, a baby being baptized into the family church at birth. Household or family members rarely had different religious affiliations. Family members strongly urged young people to marry within their own ethnic/religious groupings and those who married outside would usually either leave the church or bring their spouses into the church. Since Open Country congregations had no more than 250 adult members (and many had substantially fewer), the people in a given congregation who were not related initially soon found themselves related by marriage.

Operating like a large family, church was the setting for Christmas programs, Easter festivities, and Thanksgiving dinners as well as the baptisms, weddings, confirmations, and funerals that celebrated important transitions for the individual and the family. The particular role anyone played in one of these events depended on family and that person's position in the family. Not only were major events held in the church, but the church also solidified a structure of meaning by which to interpret both the ordinary and extraordinary events of life. It controlled inner thoughts as well as outward behavior.

The church replicated the social organization of the family and, in turn, served as a model for its dual organization. Women, responsible for social reproduction, were the backbone of church membership, and their dedication to church life kept it a vital part of the community. Although men had less overall involvement in religious life than women did, men were the public face of the church, its formal leaders. Protestant churches were led by a (male) pastor or minister and were governed by a board of (male) deacons, elders, overseers, or presbyters. An exception was the Quaker Meeting, which had a Men's Meeting for Business and a parallel Women's Meeting for Business, but the women did not deal with any financial matters in their business meetings, thus leaving at least the formal control of an important segment of Meeting business in the hands of the men, just as it was done in the home.

Reinforced in the home, in the church, and by the government, the most salient organizing unit of Open Country was the family. Families controlled the local distribution of labor and the distribution of vital social assistance. Family determined a person's social boundaries. Notwithstanding the differences of national origin, the population of Open Country was largely homogeneous before World War II. Many Open Country people owned their own businesses and hoped to achieve independence and control of their own working conditions; but all shared the experience of being subordinate to the class of capitalists, including those who operated the railroads, the credit institutions, and the meatpacking industries. None of the individuals of this class lived in Open Country. There were a few blacks, but the local Ku Klux Klan kept them (as well as the few Catholics) from establishing a cultural base.

Differences in wealth existed, but most settlers had come with little and were hoping to get rich by developing cheap land into valuable land or by trading goods and services with a prospering farm population. From a male perspective, there was no incentive for a hired laborer living in the East to make the costly and uncomfortable trip to the West without at least the expectation of sometime in the future controlling his own economic operation. This was the magnet that brought settlers to Open Country. Poverty was more often a stage of development than a station of life. Children of poor or shiftless parents hoped to pull ahead with hard work and thrift, and there are numerous stories of people who started with nothing and accumulated modest estates for their descendants. Differences in wealth did not, for the most part, mean that people went to different churches or schools or did not associate with each other. Within the family structure everyone could usually pull together and rescue kinsfolk who had bad luck.

Family charity did, however, have its limits, particularly with the farm depression which came to rural Iowa nearly 10 years before the rest of the country. Cheap land to the northwest, advertised as late as the 1920s, was ever more difficult to purchase. The incidence of tenancy rose (USDC 1942A:118). After 1920, increasing numbers of farm people would have no realistic chance of becoming landowners. Most of these, like Ruth, were well-respected people hit by bad luck, but by the 1920s, there were other people whose conditions were increasingly hopeless and to whom the normal social rules did not apply.

Curtis Harnack (1981:92) told of the benign contempt his family felt for their hired hand in the 1930s:

> We took his second-class status in our household as matter-of-factly as Southerners might regard Negro servants. No matter how badly we were jumped on or humiliated by a sibling or scolded by a parent, Barney was handy to feel superior to, for he was a foreigner and knew it.

Hired hands and tenants who would never own land could be pushed around and had to accept whatever they were given.

Ruth Suckow, a writer who grew up in rural Iowa in the late nineteenth and early twentieth centuries and lived for a short time in Farmtown, wrote a short story, "Renters," describing an Iowa woman's bitter feelings when she was forced to leave the rented farm she and her husband had toiled to improve:

> She felt herself going back, back into dark depths of old

hopelessness that she had known before. She needn't have hoped; she might have known. Why should they have anything? She could smell the rich ripening corn in the hot night. It swelled her bitterness. The farm belonged to the others. They could send her off if they chose. She had nothing, was nothing. Work didn't matter (Suckow 1926B:131).

An *underclass*, as a group of poor who did not own their own means of production and never would except under extraordinary circumstances, did not appear before 1940; but seeds of hopelessness had been laid earlier. The signs of unaddressed poverty belied the security of family and kinship ties, but they did not erupt as a widespread reality until after World War II when local differences in property ownership that qualitatively affected the lives of succeeding generations became increasingly obvious.

Conclusion

Pre-World War II Open Country women functioned largely within the context of family. Lacking direct access to the public world of commerce, religion, and government, women experienced their rights and responsibilities as mediated by the men of their families. Although legal, economic, and social conditions prevailing in rural Iowa before World War II buttressed the family unit, the family was a large and flexible body of kin rather than a small, well-defined household. While family served to constrain women's activities and aspirations, it was not totally restrictive. Family businesses depended on women as strong helpers. Women also found places in religious and community life. There were compelling reasons for men as well as women to benefit from the education and personal development of women, as long as this development occurred in the context of the family. The following chapter discusses the scope of women's work and its significance within the family economy.

CHAPTER 3

The Scope of Women's Work Before 1940

A woman's family—its wealth and its means of livelihood as well as her status within the family—determined, to a considerable degree, the kind of work a woman did and the rewards she received from that work. A woman married to a merchant had a different set of rights and duties from those of the merchant's unmarried sister, even when they lived in the same house, were the same age, and did similar tasks. The wife of a teacher and the wife of a farmer were in the same structural position within the family and each expected to provide support services, but each had a different work situation and a different position within Open Country society. All Open Country women had their lives defined in terms of their connections to the men in their families. To a limited extent, a woman exerted control over her choice of husband, her choice to remain single, her choice of which kin to call family, and her choice to remain or leave Open Country; but once these issues were settled, her future development, to a large extent, occurred within the limits set by her family.

Within these family limits, the work of Open Country women before 1940 included housework, subsistence production, production for exchange, and personal care of the members of the household. While farm women were the most numerous, farm and nonfarm women were in structurally similar positions in family businesses. Only a minority worked outside of family business operations. Although there was a division of labor by sex, women spanned what is usually called the private sphere (home) and the public sphere (commerce).

Subsistence Production

> Those were hard times in '29. We had a big garden and my mother would can. We used an awful lot of milk and eggs and butter and potatoes.—Alma, born 1915, Open Country.

Hard times or not, a great deal of what was consumed in a farm home was produced on the farm. Precise figures of farm production for home consumption appeared for the first time in connection with the Depression recovery programs of the 1930s. Although there were methodological problems in collecting and reporting of statistics on production for consumption, particularly those gathered by the government in its attempt to promote rural change, the figures are suggestive. Iowa studies were done only with specifically defined sample groups of farmers. Mildred Stenswick (1939:30, 38) found that among a group of Iowa farmers seeking financial assistance through the Farm Security Administration in 1938, the annual value of home-produced fuel and food was $352.63; outside the farm they spent only $325.67 for purchased household goods. A group of more prosperous farmers, those using the services of the Home Management Specialist of the Iowa Extension Service, spent an average of $933 on living items not produced on the farm; the percentage of production for consumption was predictably less. A national study concluded that farm families with yearly living expenditures of approximately $1,000, slightly above the national average, realized about 45 percent of their consumption from in-kind production on the farm between 1935 and 1936 (Monroe 1940:85).[1] Self-sufficiency was a decided advantage for farm households during the Depression years when there was a shortage of cash, and farm people probably intensified their home production for consumption in order to survive. However, with the increasing industrialization of America, the overall trend was toward lesser, rather than greater, home production; and earlier statistics would probably have shown more, rather than less, home production for consumption. Although no valid and reliable numbers on its dollar value and its pattern of change are available, home production for consumption may safely be considered to have been an integral part of the total task of providing a livelihood on farms.

Farm women's work, whether in the farmhouse, the garden, or the barn, consisted largely of this home production of goods and services for the maintenance of the farm household, that is, the farm labor force. Some brief comments on the material working conditions of farm women will help to establish a setting for this work.

Compared to the urban homes of that period, the facilities in most farm homes were primitive. The addition of electricity and indoor plumbing in farm homes eased women's work, but these conveniences were slow in coming. The Rural Electrification Act, which provided low-interest loans for rural electrification projects, was passed in 1936. It eventually brought electricity to all rural areas in the United States, but it did not immediately or automatically put electricity in every home. In 1920, 21 percent of Iowa's farm homes had electricity; by 1940 45 percent had electricity (USDC 1942:119). In 1940, 75 percent of Open Country farm homes lacked running water, 82 percent had no indoor toilets, and 38 percent still had no electricity (USDC 1943A:495). The absence of amenities in rural homes greatly increased women's work. Joan Jensen (1985:16) estimates that the average New Mexican farm woman saved 260 miles of walking per year when indoor running water was installed. Even assuming that Iowa women had a closer source of water, they still made many trips to the pump with water buckets in hand. Indeed, Iowa farm women's situation must have approached that described by Jensen.

Farm women eagerly anticipated the upgrading of facilities in farm homes. In 1937, one Iowa farm woman wrote to *Wallaces' Farmer* stating that electricity brought "the equivalent of a houseful of servants—servants that carry water, sweep rugs, [and] help with washing and ironing and preparing of meals" (Servants on the Farm 1937:754).

In the meantime, many others did without. Anna, who married an Open Country farmer in 1936, said:

> It was quite a step when we were first married. I came from town where we had a modern house, running hot water, electric washing machine and iron, then moving to a farm and not having running water and no electricity. We had our oil lamps. That was quite different. . . .

What Anna called "different" in farm homes permeated nearly all areas of women's work. From changing diapers to baking cakes to tending chickens, things took longer and were more complicated without the running water, electric stoves, and heaters that post-World War II Americans have come to take for granted.

A big part of the walking, stooping, lifting, transporting water, and cooking centered around gardening. In terms of both the quality and the quantity of food consumed, the kitchen garden was basic. As one older person stated, "You didn't buy no cans of peas then." While the variety of garden produce was limited, the garden was often the only source of vegetables for farm people, and the farm women managed the gardening. Potatoes, relatively easy to grow, store, and cook, were the major garden crop and have always been the basis of any real dinner in a farm home. They were also a hedge against food shortage when money, time, or energy ran low. One woman remembered harvesting 100 bushels of potatoes one year; another reported that they would haul three wagonloads of potatoes to store in their basement in the fall. Besides the basic potatoes, most farm gardens had cabbage, onions, cucumbers, corn, squash, tomatoes, and peas. On many farms, various members of the households also tended apple, plum, and cherry trees as well as maintaining rhubarb, strawberry, and raspberry plantings.

Harvesting this produce was only the end of the beginning of the work. With their own fruits, vegetables, and meats as raw materials, farm women spent many hours washing and chopping up the foods and making pickles, relishes, sauerkraut, applesauce, and jams and jellies, all of which they packed in glass jars and processed in boiling water. Home economics extension had taken on the task of improving the farm diet by teaching canning techniques, and pressure canners came to be widely used by the 1920s and 1930s.

Home preservation of food also included canning and curing meat and rendering lard. The most time-consuming of the food processing chores was the meat, the centerpiece of the farm diet. A butchered steer translated into hundreds of jars of meat; a hog entailed additional curing and handling. Ruth, born in 1892, said:

> We canned corn and meat. . . . In late winter or early spring, we usually butchered a steer and two hogs, our year's supply of meat. . . . [M]ost of the time the next two weeks was spent caring for it. Canning many quarts of the beef, grinding a tub of sausage, frying it and putting it in jars, and then covering with lard. Pork chops were stored in this way, too. There were the hams and shoulders and bacon to put in a brine solution, then smoked and the lard to render.

Alice, born in 1931, remembered:

> She [Mother] also canned all the meat. When they would butcher, Dad would butcher the beef or pork and on the farm they had doors they could shut into the living room. In the winter they would usually have the doors shut. It would be a real cold room and that's where that meat would go. . . . We canned in a boiler. These copper boilers that are antiques now. They will hold sixteen quart jars at a time, but you have to boil it three hours, and it takes an hour to come to boil. That's four hours. It went that way for days. Then you made sausage. You had to grind all that.

Even houses that had running water were, for the most part, using corn cobs and wood for their cooking fuel and lacking refrigeration as well as freezers. In the absence of these labor saving amenities, women used their own labor liberally.

Raising the large livestock, beef and hogs, was usually considered men's work, but women had charge of almost all of the poultry operations. A 1929 Iowa State Extension flyer reads:

> Practically all the eggs produced in Iowa came from farm flocks. The farm flock is cared for and managed by farm women. The poultry industry of Iowa is a farm woman's enterprise . . . (ISES 1929).

Or, as Ora said

> Part of the farmer's wife's usual duties was to have chickens. The men didn't pay much attention to chickens.

So completely were chickens associated with women that older Open Country people frequently categorized chicken chores as housework. Chickens were the classic bane of men, but this did not keep them from being the most common enterprise on pre-World War II Iowa farms. A typical poultry flock was composed of approximately 100 chicks, which were purchased early in the spring. The more ambitious poultry raisers kept several hundred birds; the smallest flocks had as few as ten hens. Roosters were butchered and eaten or canned throughout the summer, hens were kept to provide eggs.

Although poultry raisng was a common enterprise, it was by no means simple or straightforward. The experts recommended that, in order to have hearty laying hens in the fall, the young chicks should be started as early as possible in the spring. At first, the hatching of eggs was done by collecting eggs and setting hens on them; by the early years of this century some of the women bought kerosene or hot water-heated incubators to keep the eggs at a constant, warm temperature. But done in the cold winter months without the benefit of electricity or thermostats, hatching chicks was tricky. By the 1920s, most women purchased chicks which had either been hatched locally by another farm woman, hatched in commercial hatcheries in town, or ordered by mail.

Once the small chicks arrived, keeping them alive was not an easy task either. The baby chicks required a constant warm temperature and many women kept them in the kitchen by the stove at first. Since the stove was usually fired only with corn cobs or wood, maintaining a constant warm temperature in the winter was difficult, and it had to be monitored continually. As the chicks grew, they were placed in a warm brooder that was heated with kerosene—when it worked. Several women reported instances of checking on chicks in the morning and finding them all dead from overheat, cold, or faulty ventilation. The brooders were primitive and unpredictable.

Nor was the danger over when the chicks emerged from the brooders. Because the presence of weasels and foxes (the natural predators of fowl) the chicks had to be housed and tended in clean quarters. Not being native to the midwest, they had no natural protection or instinct to save themselves—they could not even be relied upon to seek shelter during a storm. Hans, a farmer who was married in 1922, told of his wife's losing a flock of nearly grown chickens:

> [W]e had it happen too already that we was to church and a thunderstorm come up. . . . If those chicks got wet once they were goners. I know Sharon [his wife] felt pretty bad about that sometimes. We'd have to stay home all the time, she said. You did all that work and had them that far and then you'd lose them.

Daily chicken chores consisted of feeding and carrying water and gathering eggs. Once or twice a year the chicken house had to be cleaned, but a hired man, husband, or older son usually did this. Farm women did the work of cleaning and processing the chickens which were to be consumed on the farm. Sometimes men would do the unpleasant task of actually killing the chickens; but plucking, cleaning, drawing, and cutting up the butchered fowl were women's tasks. Dressing chickens went on continuously through the summer. The spring supply of roosters matured in the summer and since chickens were small enough to be eaten before requiring refrigeration, fried chicken was the most common summer meal. Women cut up the older hens and the chickens which were not eaten (or sold) and processed them in glass jars like beef or pork.

Turkeys, ducks, and geese were less common than chickens. Maintained primarily for family consumption and casual sales, these fowl also required careful attention if they were to survive the first days. After the initial stages, however, they needed little care beyond daily feeding and watering until they were butchered. Women and children did most of the work of raising these birds.

Dairy products were also important on the farm table. Women did varying amounts of the actual milking of the cows, but handling the milk for home use was largely women's work. Workers on the farm took the unused whole milk and separated it into cream and skimmed milk, with the skimmed milk frequently being given to the pigs. Regardless of who did the milking and separating, the women performed the tedious tasks of cleaning the milking equipment and washing the blades of the centrifugal cream separator. Farm households consumed a great deal of fresh cream and milk, but women also churned butter until the 1920s, at which time creameries and commercial butter came to be more readily available.

Women were not finished with food preparation once the eggs, milk, cream, butter, lard, and canned and fresh vegetables, fruit, and meat were produced for the table. Farm people ate three hearty meals each day all year. During the summer, when the work was harder and the days were longer, they ate mid-morning and mid-afternoon lunches that would today be called meals. Ruth said:

> [We ate] a hearty breakfast, no citrus fruit, mostly oatmeal, hot biscuits and honey or pancakes and sausage gravy, plenty of rich cream for the cereal. . . . In those days there were no packages of mixes; everything was made from scratch. When we served chicken to thrashers or were filling silos, we had chickens to dress, pies to make and sometimes bake bread. There were always potatoes to peel and then vegetables, too.
>
> . . . Our groceries bought were the staple things, perhaps a barrel of oatmeal, one-half ton of flour, one hundred pounds of sugar, and other small items such as salt, spices and so forth. We ground our

own cornmeal and usually a batch of hominy a winter. . . .

Mother made good bread. We baked as many as 36 large loaves each week.

Emma, like Ruth, was born in 1892, and she remembered making 10 loaves of bread each day when she had a threshing crew to feed. These crews, consisting of approximately 10 hard-working men with enormous appetites, spent up to a week on a farm at harvest. In addition to the large meals of meat, potatoes, vegetables, bread, and pie, women prepared daily lunches consisting of homemade bread and sausage sandwiches, freshly baked cake, and coffee or beer. Emma remembered lining a laundry basket with linen, packing it full of sandwiches and taking it out to the workers.

Lacking dishwashers to do the kitchen cleanup, the women had to heat the water and wash the dishes by hand. During the heaviest periods of farm labor, kitchen work continued from early morning until bedtime.

Although food production and processing were the central tasks around which other work was planned, doing laundry, and sewing and mending clothes were also part of women's work. Although women could schedule this work with more flexibility than they could schedule food preparation, they could not avoid it.

Monday was washday. Without hot running water and electricity, washing clothes could be a full day's work. In the first part of the twentieth century, women made their own laundry soap with tallow and lye. When the wash was ready to be done they carried or drew the water and added lye, which brought the minerals to the surface to be skimmed off, thereby softening the water. They then heated the water over a fire which they had prepared with corn cobs or wood, agitated the clothing and linens with a hand crank or lever, wrung them, rinsed them in clear water, wrung them again, starched some of the items, hung them out on a line, and brought them in when they were dry.

Before the advent of electric irons, women either heated irons on the stove or filled them with hot coals to keep them hot. In many homes, ironing took all day Tuesday to complete. Carla, born in 1930, described her mother's ironing:

In those days they ironed. She [Mother] had the kind of iron that you put on the stove. The pillowcases and dresser scarves and shirts were all starched. I grew up with that. She always ironed the top part of the sheets. . . . She would have two or three baskets of clothes. Well, Tuesday was ironing day all day. In those days there was no perma-nent press. You ironed everything. The handkerchiefs, all the dresses, the blouses had to be ironed. The overalls had to be flattened at least. She'd even sprinkle all that stuff and roll it up and pack it in the basket. That's the way I grew up.

Sewing, particularly for daughters, was a further responsibility of women. Clothing was made and remade. Again, Carla's memories:

[Mother] sewed everything that she could possibly make. She would sew us coats. She didn't sew for the boys. She made all the dresses that my sisters and I and she wore. . . . I don't know who taught her to sew.

Women also darned socks, patched overalls, and mended clothing.

Beyond food preparation, laundry, and sewing and mending, keeping a house clean represented a considerable effort. The work of house cleaning was complicated by the lack of electricity and running water. Farm workers, with their work in dirt, mud, and manure, gave farmhouses, especially the kitchens, hard use. Women had a continuing battle with mud and dirt on the floors. When kerosene lamps were used, the lamp posts had to be cleaned regularly, as the fire produced soot which then blocked out the light.

The way houses were kept clean and how much time was spent doing so varied greatly among households. While women might minimize housekeeping chores by not being too fastidious, a farm-house full of people required a substantial amount of unavoidable maintenance. Like people everywhere, farm people liked their living quarters to be pleasing. Papering walls, hanging curtains, and paint-ing made a home more livable and gave a sense of purpose to the daily hard work. A good farm woman provided this sense of purpose as she made people comfortable and reasonably contented.

Farm households were large. Historically, farm women have had more children than women in either small towns or cities (Baker and Taeuber 1940:836). Comparing the birthrate in the county in which Open Country is located with that of Black Hawk and Polk, two predominantly urban Iowa counties, the birth rate in Open

Country is significantly higher in the early years of the twentieth century, although the difference decreases over time.

Table 3.1
Number of Births Per 1,000 Females,
Ages 20–45, in Three Iowa Counties, 1890–1930

County	1890	1900	1910	1920	1930
Open Country	14.9	11.7	10.5	15.9	10.3
Black Hawk	4.4	2.8	3.3	7.5	8.6
Polk	4.7	2.0	2.7	7.9	8.1

Source: *Statistics and Data for Iowa*, Iowa State Planning Board (1952).

In Open Country in 1930, 11 percent of the farm population, as compared to 7 percent of the nonfarm population, was younger than age five (USDC 1932:779). The higher farm birthrate has often been attributed to the heavy demand for farm labor, but it has not always been recognized as a specific contribution of women to the farm economy. Women gave birth to children, nursed them, and cared for them during their most demanding years, those from birth to age five, during which time the household could realize no economic benefit from their presence. In addition to the large number of children, nearly one-half of the households had members from outside the nuclear family.[2] Many of these were hired laborers for whom women's housekeeping goods and services were a significant part of their pay.

The Depression of the 1930s seems to have held people on Iowa farms, thereby sustaining women's role in household production. Curtis Harnack (1981), who wrote of his experiences growing up on an Iowa farm in the 1930s, was one of those who fell back on the extended family in times of adversity. When Harnack's father died, his mother took her four children to live with her sister, who was married to her husband's brother. The new household had two men (one of them a hired hand), two women, and seven children, forming a farm household/labor crew/survival system of eleven. In a similar situation in Open Country, Ruth took her two fatherless children home to live with her parents in 1928.

Arlene, born on an Open Country farm in 1922, also saw members of her family compressed into a single household during the Depression. Her immigrant grandparents had established large and well-tended farms and had passed this property to the succeeding generation. Although shaken by the hardships of the 1920s, it was during the 1930s that Arlene's family, like many others, fell critically short in meeting their financial obligations. In protecting its interests, the bank stipulated that Arlene's two older brothers could not leave the farm. If the bank was to carry the family through, the boys had to stay home and work. Women's input was in keeping them fed and doing their laundry after the time when they would otherwise have left the home.

Even if the bank had permitted Arlene's brothers to leave, the difficulties in finding jobs outside the farm might well have forced them back to the parental home, a place of refuge for many when times were rough. James Hearst, an Iowa writer, wrote that his family even took in a former hired man who was down and out during the Depression:

> One day Chuck and I received a phone call from a man who had once worked for us. He was working in the John Deere factory in Waterloo. John Deere paid better wages than a farmer paid. Now he felt the abrasive touch of unemployment. "Come and get me," he said over the phone, "I'll work for just my food. I ain't going on relief."
>
> Already our two hired men worked on pretty slim wages. They each had a house to live in and food to eat. Chuck said, "What will we do; we haven't work enough for another man."
>
> But we cranked up our Model T Ford and drove to Waterloo. . . . We took him home, fed him, and turned him over to Mother (Hearst 1978:70).

Willard Cochrane (1979:123) writes of the "large, redundant, or underemployed labor force in the farm sector" of the 1930s. Farms were still being run as personalized, family operations and were, therefore, under some obligation to absorb the surplus labor returning from the cities.

In Open Country, some hired farm laborers worked for no more than board and room. Carla's description of farming during the Depression reveals the importance of her mother's housework:

> You couldn't hardly sell anything in the middle thirties and then in '36 they dried out. And they always had that hired man. Overalls cost $1.98 and they bought his overalls because they didn't pay him that much. He got his laundry, food and she [Mother] darned his socks, patched his overalls. That was part of the deal.

Women's farm work, for the most part, enabled this increased carry-ing capacity on the farms. Had farms been dependent on the income from corn, dairying, or hogs they would have been as helpless as their city cousins. The milk, potatoes, eggs, and chicken that farm women raised fed the people like the five Harnacks, Ruth and her children, Arlene's brothers, and the Hearsts' hired man. The houses that women cleaned and decorated made places for the workers. Carla's mother's cooking, washing, darning, and patching kept their hired man on the farm when they were not paying him enough to buy his own work clothes.

A farm woman was not usually doing all of this "housework" alone. The wife or mother of the primary male farm operator was in charge of women's work on the farm, but older daughters, hired "girls," and other female family members helped her. Because of the flexibility of the family system, a woman could "borrow" a niece for a summer or prevail upon her mother or an aunt to spend time with her when she was saddled with the most intense work either with raising small children or with feeding crews of men. In times of extreme emergency, such as a grave illness or death, neighbors and family women would all join in to do the most pressing chores. For example, in 1910 Ruth's household had 14 people, which represented an enormous output of energy to feed, clothe, and bed. But these 14 people included four working women—Ruth's great-aunt, her grandmother, her mother, and Ruth (age 18). Her younger sister, Laura, was also doing substantial work. The person respons-ible for the operation of the household, Ruth's mother, had help from the ascending and descending generations. The family system of the early twentieth century did not isolate women. It made in-creased housework for them, but it also made doing this work pos-sible.

Farm women's production of goods and services for their households may be considered part of a subsistence economy which subsidized the commodity production of farm men. Farm commodity production did not stand on its own or pay its own bills during much of the period from 1880 to 1940; rather, it was sub-sidized by a subsistence economy that has been ignored because it was women's work.

Open Country town women also did subsistence production, but to a lesser extent and under more favorable conditions than did farm women. Their work was lightened by the earlier acquisition of electricity and indoor plumbing in the early twentieth century, as well as by a readier access to food stores and other services, and they had a closer proximity to women outside their households. While some town women purchased their produce and hired other women to do some of their housekeeping, many had gardens and a few kept chickens and possibly a dairy cow or a few pigs. Like the farm women, their work in food production and processing, together with other housework, supported the business operations of the men by providing the services that nourished them physically and psychologically. Their work in the home was similar in kind to that of the farm women.

Women's Production for Exchange

Women's work went beyond providing food, clothing, and housekeeping services for their families. Before World War II, women, in addition to doing these "feminine" housekeeping tasks, were reaching outside the home to exchange for what could not be produced at home. Some women had occasional business transactions outside the household; others had steady incomes. Some bartered their work or produce directly for goods and services. Some traded for cash. Although none made large amounts, no one interviewed for this study cited an instance of a pre-1940 farm woman not trading outside the farm; many of the town women were also making money.

Open Country women turned their cooking skills to monetary advantage in varying ways. Esther said that she and her sister had once made $75 worth of angel food cakes in one day for a church fund-raising effort. Her sister was an excellent cook and regularly received orders for baked goods for her own profit. Her culinary abilities also attracted boarders, who ate meals at the farm home. Road construction crews and other workers took meals in farm homes wherever they were. May established a small business that she ran from her farm home in the 1920s and 1930s: She made fresh ice cream, which she served with sweets and strawberries when they were available from the garden; she also sold homemade bread and other baked goods as well as garden produce in season. She was particularly successful with this endeavor because her farm home was located on a major highway. On a smaller scale, Emma brewed and sold beer from her home.

Schoolteachers found room and board in households, paying

small amounts into women's household funds. Other women were live-in practical nurses who spent several weeks in people's homes when someone was sick or when a baby was born. Many women sewed or did other special tasks, such as weaving rugs. No one type of work would have been possible for everyone, but within Open Country there was room for a variety of different housework-related enterprises.

Farm women continued to make butter up until World War II, although not to the degree that it was reported for earlier periods (Jensen 1980). Ruth's mother churned 40 pounds of butter each week in the early 1900s. She then packed it into a big tub and took it to town with a horse and buggy. Martin, born in 1900, remembered:

> My mother, all the time I was a boy at home, we milked ten cows and churned all that cream and we sold it for a little extra to special customers. . . . She made especially good butter. . . . There was quite a few of them [who did it] for a little extra income.

Charles, who worked in his family's general store before World War I, explained:

> Pretty near everybody brought in cream and butter. They'd bring that in and we'd put that in a barrel. When the barrel was full we'd ship it to Chicago. There were certain people that made extra good butter. Certain ones would come in and say, "Do you have any of Ella's butter here? If you have I want it." . . . A lot of people would come in just as fast as she brought it in. They would see her come to town and they'd think they would get some of that butter before it's gone.

Ruth, widowed as a young mother in 1920, continued to keep two or three cows, churning and selling the butter. She explained, "It wasn't so much money, but it was a little coming in."

After 1920, homemade butter was less common and most of the farms sold cream. While some farm people considered the money earned from the cream sales as properly belonging to the woman, others, including specialized dairy farmers, considered it as part of the general farm income.

In 1914 when the USDA asked farm women what they needed as services from the soon-to-be-established extension service, the women stated their concern that they be allowed to earn and control some money of their own (USDA 1915A, 1915B). This seems to have been a continuing concern. In the 1930s, it became even more critical. *Wallace's Farmer* sponsored a contest in 1933 asking how farm women were responding to the shortage of cash caused by the low prices for hogs and corn. More than 300 women wrote, describing a variety of goods and services to sell and trade. Ranking first was the direct sale of farm produce to town customers. Other products sold included braided rag rugs, quilts, Persian cats, canaries, doughnuts and other pastry, black walnuts, winter bouquets, goldfish, and water lillies. One woman sold prepared soup, beans, and stews from door to door in town two or three days each week (Swelling Family Incomes 1933:220).

The most common source of money for farm women came from eggs produced by the ubiquitous Iowa poultry flocks. Marketing eggs involved washing them (sometimes scrubbing them individually with steel wool), packing them in a carton or basket, and taking them to town. Women could barter or sell eggs at 60 sites in Open Country in 1931. Usually women took their eggs to a general store to trade for food and dry goods. Typically, no money changed hands and some women operated their households entirely on this barter system. Charles, talking about the general store, said:

> [E]veryone figured their eggs and butter had to buy groceries. Nobody paid cash. I can't remember anyone coming into the store and giving you a bill of goods and paying for it. . . . Maybe there was a little too much; they'd just get credit for it.

Furthermore, rural grocers gave a slightly higher price for eggs if the money was taken out in trade.

Buying eggs and offering a good price was a grocer's way of luring customers. A 1928 Iowa State College thesis stated that 90 percent of the money paid by local Iowa stores to egg sellers remained in the store and was taken out in trade (Termohlen 1928:43). Although the thesis decried the lack of records, the unscientific character of production, the selling of ungraded eggs, and the inefficiencies of marketing, extension experts were unsuccessful in stopping these practices. A 1940 thesis reported that from 70 to 80 percent of Iowa's flocks consisted of fewer than 200 hens, the average flock being 132 hens, a size generally sufficient to pay a farm household grocery bill (Dodds 1940:6). In one county, more than one-half of the egg sellers were selling to country stores, although a cooperative was purchasing substantial numbers of eggs. In addition to groceries, country stores sold hardware such as nuts and bolts, school books and supplies, overalls and other work clothes, and boots, all of which could be bought with egg trade. The still-common use of the word *trade* rather than *shop* in rural Iowa is a car-ryover from the time when barter for eggs was the most common means of purchase. A person will say, for example, "I trade at Ralph's Grocery," rather than "I shop at Ralph's."

With no money being realized from men's farm commodities, women's egg operations assumed an increased importance during the 1930s, even though the price went as low as six cents per dozen. The 1932 Poultry Record Report of Iowa State College had on its cover a cartoon of a large hen pulling a farm truck up a steep hill. The caption read, "Helping the Farmer over a Bad Stretch." A farmer was pictured as saying, "Not so bad for a depression year—after paying all expenses I still have 60 cents from each hen for my labor" (ISES 1932). In actuality, however, the women were running the poultry operations, not the men. Spent for food and small household items, even a small income could make a critical difference in the nutrition and well-being of the farm family. Several women remembered shopping carefully and putting back items if the total bill exceeded the egg money. One woman, married in 1931, did her food shopping for ninety cents each week in egg trade.

Secondary sources of poultry income came from the sale of hatching eggs, incubation of eggs, the sale of chicks, the handling of breeding flocks for hatcheries, and the sale of birds. Women sold surplus chickens and spent hens to town people or traded them at the store in the same way that eggs were traded. Some women sold turkeys, ducks, and geese for additional income.

A farm woman also used eggs and other produce like money when paying for household services. She might pay a dentist or doc-tor for services by delivering five spring chickens to his back door. Farm households gave clergymen frequent gifts of meat, milk, vegetables, and eggs, and this could well be considered a part of their income. Alma, who was born in 1915, said:

> In those years, I think back in '29 . . . they would butcher and bring potatoes, meat, and vegetables to our minister because there just wasn't enough money to pay for them. . . . People just didn't have the money so they would bring food and meat. More poor people who you knew just didn't have the money.

In the absence of money, the food, produced largely by the women, supported not only the farm households, but also other businesses and religious bodies.

All of the income generated—whether by baking, boarding, cooking, nursing, brewing, managing an ice cream parlor, churning, or keeping poultry—allowed women to provide the farm family with goods and services that could not be produced on the farm. Women consistently said that money from this work was theirs to use for family needs, while men reinvested their money in the farm operation. Although men indirectly contributed to the household income and contributed directly in varying degrees, the Open Country reports clearly indicate that most of the routine household purchases of food and clothing and some of the religious, medical, and social services were contracted and paid for by the women. But in spite of these unequivocal reports, I have located no quantitative data in the form of household accounts which would indicate exactly what constituted routine purchases and how much of this was actually covered by women's income. In the 1930s, yearly profits from the state extension record poultry flocks (which might well have been more profitable than the average flocks) ranged from a low of $160.72 in 1934 to a high of $469.30 in 1935, with an average annual net of $291.35 from egg sales alone (ISES 1930–39). The median income from egg operations represented slightly more than one-half of the money expenditures of the median income U.S. farm family between 1935 and 1936 (Monroe 1940:850). Joann Vanek (1980:425), in her report of U.S. farm economies, cites a 1915 Michigan study stating that:

> . . . 80 percent of the living expenditures, as distinct from the expenses associated with producing the principal product on the farm, were met by cash earnings of the wife.

There is some indication that women's incomes may have extended beyond the weekly food and incidentals commonly described. In *Wallaces' Farmer*, a series of advertisements for a cooking range was aimed squarely at tapping women's poultry incomes. One advertisement read,

> Farm Women Can Now Buy Monarch Ranges Out of Poultry Money—Only $6.25 a Month . . . At terms so low as this, most farm women can spare the money to make the monthly payments out of their own income, from poultry, butter, garden truck, or other farm produce sold throughout the year (Wallaces' Farmer 1935:299).

The advertisers spent their money believing that farm women could feasibly manage a one-year payment plan and buy major appliances with their own incomes.

The income from women's enterprise was not always limited to purchasing food, clothing, or items for the home. Hans remembered using his wife's egg credit to pay farm bills:

> Well, we even paid out vaccinating for pigs one time with credit at the grocery store. [To] the veterinarian, I said, "I ain't got much cash; we've got more credit in the grocery store than we'll use."
>
> We just transferred it to him.
>
> "Sure," he says.
>
> I went over to the grocery store and looked at his record and he had $400 charged there, and in them days $400 was a lot of money. That was in the thirties. That vet didn't get paid . . . so he was glad we paid off a little on his bill.

Carla told of her father using egg money as a downpayment on some cheap land in the 1930s:

> [We] sold eggs for groceries. . . . When my dad went round to get credit for the farm, there was the local general store that bought chickens and eggs. He had some credit there, he cashed in all his surplus on all the insurance policies that we had. Wherever he had any credit he went around and got all this together. I don't remember the amount but I do remember him doing that.

In the instances where women's egg money was used for men's farming expenses, it was men rather than women who seem to have taken control of the money. One woman, however, used her egg money to buy her husband a manure spreader in 1931, saying that it would save him some hard work. Such reports of major farm and home purchases made with women's income in the 1930s are tantalizing indications that women's sphere was significant not just in production for family consumption or for routine household money, but it was also assuming an increased share of what formerly had been solely men's financial responsibilities.

Women in Farm Commodity Production

Women also did "men's work." While both men and women

clearly understood the general separation of women's and men's spheres on the farm, they were by no means prepared to rigidly delineate them or to remain within them. Women, in fact, seemed to do work with crops and large livestock more readily than men did housework. Moreover, different subgroups divided men's and women's spheres differently. More prosperous farms were likely to employ hired men to do the fieldwork and chores. Besides meeting or easing the labor demands in the men's sphere of the farm, they created more housework for the women, who cooked meals and washed clothing for hired men. Thus, women of the larger, richer farms would be less likely to be working in the fields than would the poorer farm women. Larger households would likewise have more working men within the household and thus less need for women's help. Ethnic differences accounted for other variations: German women generally did work in the fields; Hollander women did field work frequently; Norwegian and Irish women typically were not in the fields.

With a clear understanding of whose work was being done, men and women often helped each other. Emma and Eddie, a German couple married in 1913, described their division of labor saying that Emma did the animal chores while Eddie did the field work, thereby dividing their work in such a way as to provide a wide work setting for Emma in tending cattle, hogs, and poultry. Pigs, aforementioned *mortagage burners*, were important to the cash balance of the farm and Eddie was in charge of the pig operation, even though Emma did the work. The line dividing his work from her work was flexible: Eddie helped carry water for the pigs and helped Emma turn the cream separator. Emma, in turn, shocked oats, picked corn, and plowed. A younger German woman told me that women absolutely worked in the fields; she could not imagine a situation in which a healthy woman would not help.

Jacob Van der Zee (1912:325), in his history of the Hollanders in Iowa, quoted a nineteenth century upper-class Dutch immigrant woman as saying, "I never worked in Holland for it was considered disgraceful for a lady to work, but in America I find it is thought to be disgraceful for a lady not to work." The three older Dutch women interviewed for this study all described substantial blending of male and female spheres of work. One told me that her mother had helped with the fieldwork, including picking corn. When asked if this was typical of Dutch women, she said, "A lot did, but not all. My husband's mother, she didn't do anything outside, so all farm women didn't."

Norwegians tended to place the dividing line between male and female work areas at the chicken house, but, again, this line was bent and crossed. Ora, born of Norwegian parents in 1922, said:

> Dad felt fairly strong that Mother was busy enough [without working in the male sphere], . . . that a woman's work was in the house and the man's work was to take care of the big livestock. Mother had milked cows at home before she married and maybe before we kids came she might have helped.

Carl, a Norwegian farmer born in Open Country in 1891, said that women indeed worked in the fields in the early 1900s.

Ruth, born in 1892 of a Norwegian mother and Scottish father, remembered her mother's field work in connection with the family's move to a new house in 1901:

> My first memory of our new home was on a full moon night when Father and Mother gathered up the hay along the roadside, we children in the hayrack.

As a girl, the oldest of eight children, she eventually drove a hay wagon, raked hay, and picked corn for her parents. Her brother explained that a girl did this only if no boys were old enough to work. When Ruth was widowed in 1920, she turned over her land to her brothers to farm while she kept charge of the cows, pigs, and chickens.

When women were in the fields, they usually referred to their efforts as *help* rather than as actual *work*. Ruth, for example, said:

> Women didn't do like they do nowadays—farm. . . . No, women didn't really farm. They helped, but they didn't go out and do farm work.

The use of the word *help* suggests that they were doing something extra for the men, rather than doing their own work. A man who picked corn with his wife in the field did not say that he helped pick corn. He said that he picked corn and his wife said that she helped.

But even with women in the fields, some work, particularly that deemed especially critical, was the job of men. Seeding was, without exception, a man's job. Corn fields were at this time *checked*: not only were the rows straight, the columns and diagonals were also straight so that they could be cultivated crosswise. Several men explained that women did not seed because it had to be done exactly right, the obvious implication being that no woman could do what had to be done exactly right. Seeding might have been a symbolically male function, but insisting that women could not do it reinforced the cultural and social norms that stated women could not farm without men. Although women could do nearly any kind of farm work, they were still doing this work only with men and only while denying that they were working. They were, in effect, denying their abilities at the same time they were crossing over and doing men's farm work. In the context of the family, they were doing work that they would not acknowledge or develop.

Town Women's Exchange Production

Like farm women, town women were often deeply involved in the small business operations of their families. In addition to doing the housekeeping chores that supported the business workforce, women pitched in, doing a myriad of tasks required to keep businesses functioning. Willa Cather gave an example of this kind of family business, The Gardeners' hotel, in *My Antonia*, a novel about the Nebraska town, of "Black Hawk" during the late nineteenth and early twentieth centuries. Cather, as she often did, stressed the acumen of the woman in operating the family business:

> It was Mrs. Gardener who ran the business and looked after everything. Her husband stood at the desk and welcomed incoming travellers. He was a popular fellow, but no manager (Cather 1918:182).

> He [Mr. Gardener] was an affectionate little man, and he thought his wife a wonderful woman; he knew that without her he would hardly be more than a clerk in some other man's hotel (Cather 1918:191).

In Open Country, hotels were often simply overgrown rooming houses in which the whole family worked together preparing beds and home cooked meals for the guests. Sally's parents, who ran one of the more substantial establishments, said that in 1982, more than 30 years after they closed the business, people still reminisced about the varied, well-prepared dishes served at the restaurant and the warm hospitality of her parents. Although her father was actually the proprietor, Sally, her mother, and her three sisters did much of the work, starting with growing potatoes in their garden and extending through cooking and serving guests. Her mother, she said, was a full partner. She spent the greater part of her day making pies and cooking at the restaurant, returning home at 3:00 p.m. to do her own cooking and cleaning and meet her children coming home from school.

The telephone company provides another example of a family business. Ardith and Vern assumed operation of Center's telephone exchange from their home in 1932, receiving a salary from Vern's parents who owned the business. Ardith was a telephone operator, and she received some help from her mother-in-law and a hired woman who worked mornings. Vern did the linework and answered the switchboard from bed at night.

Some widows ran family businesses, either taking over after their husbands' deaths or starting their own businesses. The informal rules seem to have permitted a widow to step outside the boundaries separating the sexes, particularly if this kept her from being a burden on other family members. Some widows ran small shops or cafes, or worked as waitresses or office help. However, their most common occupation was domestic service. Only an exceptional woman had a business that truly provided a living for a town household.

Anna, whose parents lost their farm in the late 1920s, found herself in town helping to run a mixed family business operation in 1932. Her father drove a Raleigh route, a business which peddled medicines and various sundries in rural areas. Her family also ran a cream station which bought cream and eggs. In connection with this venture, they ran a small ice cream shop that had a few tables and catered to the Saturday farm crowds, selling short-order items such as hamburgers and hot dogs. Anna worked in her parents' shop intermittently while holding a series of other jobs, including teaching, being a hired "girl," and reporting the local news for the town newspaper. The family operation was a collection of small, piecemeal enterprises that, when combined and with the help of everyone in the household, enabled the family to survive.

Anna freely identified herself and her mother as working; but women who were married to the more prosperous business and professional men said that they never had any involvement with business life. They stressed the importance of the mother in caring for the children and their reluctance to use babysitters. Hilda's stories of her life as the daughter of one successful businessman and the wife of another were about fashions, hairdos, and recreation. Yet there were important ways in which she, too, participated in the business operations.

In a small town where everyone knew each other, an entire family, by being friendly, contributed to the success of a business. Townspeople expected the wife of a prominent businessman to be gracious toward those who were less fortunate and to take the lead in charitable projects done by her church or community clubs. In addition, the more prominent the family, the more a husband's business or political office required of the woman by way of proper dress, elaborate household furnishing, and entertainment. By excelling in these displays, a woman enhanced the prospects for even greater achievement. But these activities required more time and energy than is immediately apparent. Hanna Papanek (1979:775) refers to such activity as *family status production*, a process by which women increased the upward mobility of their families, and which was possible only when the household existed above the subsistence level, thereby allowing some of the members freedom from subsistence production. Although these concerns with status achievement and maintenance might appear to be leisurely or relaxing, to the women they constituted a demanding job.

Going Out to Work

While the majority of women, both in town and on the farm, worked within the boundaries of their family operations, a minority worked at waged or salaried jobs. While employment statistics accurately record the incidence of this work, the early statistics, unfortunately, are not separated by urban and rural areas. But evidence of a trend is found: in the entire county, the number of recorded working women grew from 629 in 1915 to 1,190 in 1940, the latter figure accounting for 16.6 percent of all women older than age 14 (USDC 1943B:906; Executive Council of the State of Iowa 1916:567). In 1940 in Open Country (the rural part of the county), 518 rural town women and 171 farm women were listed as being in the nonfarm labor force, accounting for 20 percent of the town women older than age 14 and 6 percent of the farm women (USDC 1943B:924, 925). Women in the recognized labor force formed a small but significant and growing minority.[3]

Statistics indicate that many of these women were working in domestic service jobs (see Table 3.2). These were the hired "girls" working in farm homes or the housekeepers in town. In town, a significant number also worked in other service jobs, a category which includes restaurant and janitorial work. Town women had retail and clerical jobs in greater numbers than did farm women. The census lists 26 town women (or 5 percent of the total workers) as managing businesses. The category *professional* included the many women who taught, either in town or in country schools.

Table 3.2
Number of Employed Farm and Nonfarm
Women in Open Country, 1940

Employment Category	Farm	Nonfarm Rural
Professional	49	122
Managers, proprietors	5	26
Retail, clerical	18	123
Operatives	7	28
Domestic service	81	91
Other service	6	99
Other, unreported	5	29
Total women employed	171	518
Total women older than age 14	2899	2698

Source: U.S. Population Census, 1940.

Women's career planning was haphazard in that a married woman did not know where she would be living or how many children she would bear. I gradually stopped asking women how they had decided on their work. One woman said she had fallen in love with a farmer and his profession was unimportant to her. Another indicated that questions about career choice were inappropriate because a woman should be content with what was offered to her. Few claimed a positive choice. Nora, in explaining her first job as a teacher in 1921, emphasized that she had never pushed herself forward:

> Well, life's been very kind to me. Things have happened. A lady came to this school and asked about the girls who might be taking training and the principal of the school recommended me. So she came to me

and told me that she had done that. She helped me write the letter and application and everything. I think she even bought the stamp. I was hired.

The majority of Open Country women considered marriage itself as the most desirable career goal.

As the daughter of a wealthy Open Country family, Hilda was one of the first women to graduate from college in 1905. She then taught school for two years before her marriage to a local businessman in 1907. At this point she retired from teaching and proceeded to raise her four children. When I asked her if she had missed teaching, she said that possibly she had, but that she had enough to do without thinking about that; preparing a large noon meal would have been impossible if she had been teaching school. Few other college educated women followed Hilda's example of returning to Open Country for marriage. According to Mary Hargreaves (1976:118), until 1940 most of the college educated women left the rural areas, because there were no opportunities for them to use their college degrees adequately in the country. Since Open Country had no colleges, pursuing a college education meant leaving the area and few job opportunities drew them back.

Of course, a few women were determined to have educations and careers and this usually precluded marriage. In one family, two daughters received higher educations, became educators, and stayed in cities outside of Iowa. Esther left in the 1920s to take nurse's training in Des Moines, eventually spending her working life in California and Central America. Bella, another single woman, graduated from Iowa State College, became a dietician, and did not return to Open Country until she retired. In fact, I suspect that the method of local study may systematically miss some of the more determined and independent women, although articles about them did appear in newspapers and some of them have now retired and returned to Open Country. There are enough examples to indicate that educated, career-oriented women tended to remain single and to leave the rural area. Marriage functioned as a career alternative that often eliminated many other alternatives.

Ardith, born in 1899, was an exception. Her family had housed four teachers during her childhood, and she had decided that she not only wanted to be a teacher, but that she wanted to be a college-educated teacher. Allying with her, the teachers convinced her father to let her pursue her education. Forced to take two years out of her higher education to teach without a college degree, she eventually received her degree and teaching credentials and went to Center as the high school principal in 1925. One year later, she married the son of a local businessman and continued her work. She was either lucky or careful in her selection of a husband who lived close to her work and who did not object to her continued teaching.

Although some women were, in a sense, breaking barriers by working outside the home, the sense of family continued to affect their work patterns. The workforce was segregated, with women concentrated in the areas of teaching and service. Moreover, hiring was done on a personal basis, with family connections and social standing being major factors in getting jobs. Seldom, if ever, was a job open to all with impartial screening of applicants. Nora's account of getting her teaching job was typical in that women were chosen by the authority. Rather than seeking a job, a woman waited for an employer to favor her.

In 1917 Coral, for example, worked for a grocer without receiving any pay unil he decided to actually hire her. In 1929 after she was forced to close her own grocery store because of an infected leg, Mike, another grocer, decided to hire her. He saw her sister and asked her to tell Coral to come to talk to him. Coral said:

> I went down and he wanted to know if I would work a couple of weeks. I said, "Yeah, I'll work a couple of weeks." I started counting eggs and cleaned eggs and put up orders and everything. I liked it. I was there twelve years. I think they try you out that way. . . . Always do a bit more than you're supposed to. Bend over backwards a little bit. It pays out in the long run.

While doing "a bit more" was to a woman's advantage, it was even more advantageous for the employer to have an employee who would do "a bit more" for him. Employers had a direct stake in women assuming an ingratiating demeanor and they had no reason to encourage anything else.

This pattern of personal selection had the effect of enforcing conformity. Although a woman was never certain of what would please a potential employer, she was usually safe in assuming that it probably was not aggressive behavior or agitation. A woman would have no chance to plead her case if she was not selected. Employers valued women as workers who were friendly and easygoing, not troublemakers. Women like Coral who were among the first to cross into men's business spheres were especially careful not to damage their prospects by ignoring any more social customs than they already had. Male employers probably never consciously decided to require different personal characteristics from women employees; it was simply a part of their understanding of women as family people.

The small amount of money accorded women for their work further constrained their options. Income inequality was embedded in the different jobs done by men and women. A man who did manual labor during the Depression reported working for as little as fifteen cents per hour; Anna worked as a domestic helper from 5:30 A.M. until after the evening meal for fifty cents per day during the same time period, thus receiving between three and four cents an hour for her work.

The division of work and the relatively higher pay for men is seen in teaching as well. The lowest paying positions were grade school teachers, who were all women; the better paying teaching positions were high school teachers, administrators, and coaches, and it was among these positions that men were found. For example, in the 1933–34 academic year, the superintendent and the coach, the only two men employed in the Center school, averaged $115.50 per month in pay, while the twelve women teachers averaged $69.16 per month (Open Country Bulletin 1933). Women working in shops received less: Mike paid Coral $52 per month for her work in the grocery store; Nora earned $7 per week ($28–$31 per month) for working afternoons and Saturdays in a dress shop. By way of comparison, Ardith and Vern together earned $75 per month running the telephone exchange during the depression. Although Ardith supplemented this with income from boarding teachers, it was barely enough to support the two of them. She and Vern would be eating pancakes at each month's end.

Open Country businesses and schools of the 1930s seem to have remained open by keeping operating costs low; employing women was a saving, because employing women kept down the operating costs. The women were, in effect, bolstering an economic system that would in turn provide an economic niche for them. Women's low wages meant that their best chances for furthering their own economic interests were subsidies from the higher incomes of men, in other words, to operate within a family setting if possible.

Beginning in 1929 with the advent of the Depression, discrimination against women became explicit instead of being simply embedded in the social patterns of Open Country. For example, married women teachers lost their jobs. Although no specific policy to support the firing of married women was ever issued, the practice was commonly used by school boards. Ardith lost her job as principal of Center High School at the beginning of the Depres-sion; Nora and many other married women lost their grade school teaching jobs as well.

From a distance of 50 years, all of the women interviewed seem to have accepted the dismissals philosophically. Gert said, "They were only trying to be fair." Nora had first taught in 1921, married and quit her job in 1922, returned to teaching in 1924, and taught until 1933 (she is childless). She said:

> [T]he directors had their yearly meeting. While they were there they brought up the problem of married teachers. So they decided not to have married teachers. Then after one of the men out there in the district where I was teaching found this out he came down and asked me if I would reconsider if they would go to the board and try to get that rescinded. . . . Then they had their meeting and voted and it came out a tie. . . . The president refused to vote out the tie. . . . That was the end of my teaching days. I didn't especially care.

"The problem of married teachers" concerned only married women, who it was assumed could be supported by their husands. One of the directors that would have supported Nora's position was in the hospital when the vote was taken. When asked if she could have raised the issue at another meeting, Nora conceded that she could have, but people would have said she was the kind of woman who was not happy with her husband, and she did not want that to happen. The institution of the family, therefore, limited Nora's assertiveness and stopped her from challenging the given rules.

Depression relief came to Open Country, but in terms of jobs, the effort was directed toward men. A county employment office opened in Center in 1934. Of a departing employment office manager, the local newspaper wrote, "His records were at all times in fine shape, and he placed many hundreds of men during his term of office" (Open Country Bulletin 1937B). An unemployment survey of 1937 directed all potential workers to fill out cards, but then stated, "Housewives should not fill out cards unless they are able to do other work and are looking for work with pay" (Open Country Bulletin 1937A). At the very least, this did not encourage married women to think of themselves as possible wage earners.

The biggest relief project in the county was the construction of a state park and damming of a creek to create an artificial lake. A crew of over 300 Works Progress Administration (WPA) men worked on the project. The indications are that in Open Country, the women had not yet obtained enough of a foothold in the public economic world to accord their positions the much-deserved protection and enhancement by public expenditures. Women, so it was thought, always had the family.

In spite of losing jobs, few of the unemployed women stayed completely out of the labor market in the 1930s. Nora had already been working Saturdays in a dress shop and she expanded this work to afternoon weekdays. Ardith worked part-time in a store for three years before she and Vern began work with the telephone exchange in 1932. The number of women in the county listed as being in the labor force increased by 28 percent from 1930 to 1940 (USDC 1932:793; USDC 1943B:906).

The 1930s did not push the women out of the labor market; it depressed their position within it. Although the number of women working outside of family business operations was increasing, there was nothing particularly liberating about the process. Once in the business world, they found themselves without real power to establish an equitable working environment or to protect their jobs. Women working in the family might have had the collective power of their own kin to bring to bear on recalcitrant or exploitative men who were impinging on them, but women outside the family had no traditional lines of support.

Conclusion

Considering only those Open Country women who were working outside the family operation as workers is misleading. Services done in the home were, in fact, an integral part of the family economy and only the most tenuous, formal separation between the public and private spheres existed. This conclusion supports the finding of Mary Meek Atkeson (1929:189), who saw women as central to the farm economy of the 1920s:

Thus, most of the prosperity of American agriculture has rested squarely upon the backs of the women and children who worked without pay, and unless prices of farm crops advance greatly there it will continue to rest.

The statistical practice of acknowledging only women working outside the family operation as workers denies the considerable measure of work done by women within the family economy (which was also the site of most rural men's work, which *was* acknowledged by statisticians). Work and the identification of a person as a worker is basic to American values. American culture has confered respect and personal dignity on persons who are good, honest, hard workers; and for at least 100 years women sought to raise their status by carrying on trades and pursuing professions. It is ironic that in this rural area the status of worker was granted only to those women who worked outside the home, in a context in which they were extremely vulnerable. Conversely, a woman was almost never labelled a farmer, a vocation which was supposed to be the basis of rural wealth and property.

Even if an attempt is made to define work in some sense as being that production which was done for exchange outside the household rather than consumption within it, there were many farm women who were maintaining substantial poultry enterprises, marketing butter and other produce, working in the farm fields, or tending animals for the purpose of making money, yet who were not listed in the census as being workers. Including these women as workers would go part of the way toward developing an equitable statistical assessment of women workers.

Open Country had 1,986 farms in 1940 (USDC 1942:130) and each one of these needed at least one woman doing farm work. These women may be added to the published number of women workers for a more reliable estimate. In fact, many farms (like Ruth's) had more than one woman worker; therefore the resulting estimate is a minimum figure. In 1940, 689 women were officially listed as being in the paid labor force (See Table 3.1). If the many town women who were working in family businesses are not included, and only 1,986 extra farm workers are included, the resulting estimate is that Open Country had 2,675 women workers in 1940. With a total of 5,597 Open Country women between ages 14 and 65, this estimate suggests that approximately 48 percent of the working age women of Open Country were working in 1940 (USDC 1943B:924, 935), considerably more than the 13 percent reported in the census as workers. Twenty-seven percent of urban Iowa women of working age were listed as being in the labor force at this time (USDC 1943B:866). If this statistic is reasonably accurate, a substantially greater percentage of Open Country women than urban women were in the labor force before World War II.

Many women were workers, but what did this really do for them? What were the limits of Open Country women's horizons before World War II? Is it romanticizing the agrarian past to suggest that women doing hard farm work achieved power through their economic centrality? Slaves, after all, were economically central without being free or powerful. What difference did it make that "the laws belonged to the man," that a man was the formal head of the family operation, and that women had only indirect access to capital? Did the people of Open Country, perhaps, operate in a system in which the legal, hierarchical rules of the state did not affect their daily lives? The following chapter addresses this question by examining the relationships that women had with each other and the way they used these relationships to effect their goals.

CHAPTER 4

Woman to Woman

Open Country women, for the most part, did not have access to resources or power in the public, male world. There were exceptional women who entered the business world and there were undoubtedly women who exercised considerable power within the home, but on the aggregate the legal, economic, and political system was rigged against women. Attempting to delineate all the subtleties in which male-female power relationships were played out is difficult, but defining the parameters of these relationships is possible. Women's rights to food and shelter as well as to a means of earning a livelihood within a household economy were customary rather than legal. In such a situation, the weight of public opinion and the social support a woman garnered were crucial. In a social system based on family organization, a woman's interaction with other women, both inside and outside her family could consolidate her base of social power. In fact, women seem to have put significant time and energy into cultivating this interaction. Rather than assessing women's power by focussing on relationships with men, this chapter examines the interaction among them and the material context in which this occurred before 1940.

Open Country farm women got together over their work. On the farm the frequency and duration as well as the physical setting of women's interaction was dependent upon the demands of their work, demands that structured rather than precluded social contacts. Compared to farm women, town women had more leisure time and more opportunity for strictly social visiting. The direction of change brought farm women more and more into the cultural patterns and expectations of town women. Each woman's social space can be pictured as a series of concentric circles representing household, (extended) family, church, the farm or town community, and Open Country as a whole. The most intimate friends were located in each other's inner circles. While the center of a woman's interpersonal life was her family, she often reached beyond the family to establish ties with the women, but not with the men, in her church and in secular clubs.

American women have a tradition of intimate female relationships. Carroll Smith-Rosenberg (1982) described deep, lasting, and complex relations among women of the eighteenth and nineteenth centuries. She wrote:

> Central to this female world was an inner core of kin. The ties between sisters, first cousins, aunts, and nieces provided the underlying structure upon which groups of friends and their networks of female relatives clustered.

This intimacy was not limited to urban or eastern women. John Mack Faragher (1981:553) implied that a network of women united by kinship might have been a powerful, sustaining force for ninetenth-century rural women. Most Open Country women of the early twentieth century had this core of kin which could provide the structure for close relationships, but farm women had to contend with the isolation of living on farms which were geographically separated from their neighbors. How large did this isolation loom for Open Country farm women? From whom or what were they isolated? Living in the country both isolated and united women.

Writing about the settlement of the northern plains, Mary Hargreaves (1976) presented the popular image of the woman as lonely and oppressed by the hardship of frontier life. According to Hargreaves, the long hours farm women spent working left little time for socializing and relaxing or easing up on their work. In contrast to Hargreaves' image of women's lives on the northern plains, the women of Open Country seem to have socialized without relaxing. Although the farm women of Open Country worked hard and were largely isolated from urban life, the conditions on Iowa farms do not appear as bleak as those described by Hargreaves. The fertility of Iowa soil and the reasonably secure rainfall enabled a denser rural population to flourish than in Nebraska or the Dakotas, lying immediately to the west. Dorothy Schwieder (1980:153) found that farm women did work hard for the successful settlement of Iowa, but denied that this led to isolation during the period between 1840 and 1880. She documented accounts of neighboring farm women visiting each other for the day, friends dropping by for tea, women helping each other during times of crisis and entertaining large groups of people at Christmas. She concluded:

> [C]ontrary to the mistaken assumption that excessive workloads precluded social contacts, it is apparent that extended economic and labor roles precipitated and encouraged such relationships (Schwieder 1980:165).

The pattern of visiting and helping among farm families prevailed into the twentieth century. The farm diary that 24-year-old Bertha Gabelmann of Butler County, Iowa, began in 1912 described a steady stream of people coming and going in the course of doing work. Three adult women lived in Bertha's household—her mother, her unmarried sister Lydia, and Bertha. Her married sister Hulda called frequently and the women in the two households shared much of their work. The following random sample illustrates a typical 1912 week.

> July 3. "Hulda was here all day. Will got her in the eve."
> July 4 "[W]as by W. Biekerts in the evening. Will Stille's, Aug Stille's Jake Biekerts, Carl Witts, Arne Jackobs, Charlie Vetter, Will's and the Ministers were there."
> July 5. "Martha and Lorenzo was here."
> July 7. "Was to church. Mother and Father was to W. Stille's for dinner. Will was here after church. E.A. and H. Schalbachs and E. Hannamen whent to Mitchel Jake whent visiting to night. I brought Martha Lorence food this morning and some flowers."
> July 8. "Father and mother was to Nashua and stopped by Lizzie when they came home. . . . Will and Hulda was here we picked red and blackberries."
> July 10. "Mary had stomack cramps. Mother and father was over their. Will Biekerts butchered a pig by W. Stille. Lydia went over to help Lizzie fry the Meat down."

An Open Country farm woman's diary showed a similar pattern in which virtually every entry was about women visiting, often helping with work. In fact, during my fieldwork, older farm people frequently stated that they "neighbored" more in times past than now. While some of this may be discounted as nostalgia, these memories were too general to be dismissed. Nothing in the reports suggested that the lack of automobiles or the presence of heavy workloads precluded visiting among farm people. On the contrary, the lack of easy transportation may have promoted social relationships. Women who spent a long day working together may have come to know one another better than they would have by drinking tea together. If the difficulty in travelling discouraged short drop-in visits, it probably encouraged longer visits, which allowed for intimacy and support when visiting occurred.

Young women had parties, picnics, and sports events to attend. A young farm woman's letter to her brother in Des Moines, dated December 8, 1908, described an active Open Country social life for high school students.

> George and Ray had a party and Addie and I went out with William and Agnes. They had Uncle John's horses. That was Friday night. We stayed in at Agnes's and Saturday morning Esther and I went skating with about ten. My we had fun, the ice was fine. It's the first time I have gone skating this year. 2 weeks ago Gertie had a party for Lucile. You know she is going away. It was a surprise on her. Then Agnes had a party and Helen a party so that makes four. Papa said that's about enough. He hopes they will not invite us anymore. He says pretty soon there will be two buggies driving in the yard after us. And he said that he bet that we went more in a week than you did in a month. . . . The High School had a supper last night and they made $75. It was to raise money to help pay for the piano that we have at school.

Young men and women had dates, but sleeping overnight and ice skating seems to have been for young women only. This does not, of course, mean that every young woman had an equally rich social life; however, it does confirm that living on a farm did not automatically preclude social contacts.

While little suggests that farm life in Iowa was intrinsically isolating, the twentieth century saw an increasing discontent with some aspects of farm life, particularly when compared with life in cities and towns. A frequent complaint about farm life was isolation. Part of the discontent emanated from farm people who recognized shortcomings in their physical comforts and social opportunities when contrasted with those of town people (Schwieder 1983:104). Farm people were, in truth, isolated from city life. Insofar as they came to believe that the good things in life came from the city, they began to feel out of touch and disadvantaged when they saw the conditions of even the immediately visible rural towns. Farm children as well as adults sensed the hegemony of town life. Curtis Harnack (1981:173) described what growing up as an Iowa farm youngster among town classmates in the 1930s meant to him:

> In truth, I was a dumb farmer, rube, hick, hayseed. The illiterate junk dealer, the lowliest tradesman in town felt superior. His children mocked us because they lived under street lights and had a box at the post office, not R.F.D. Farmers seemed ludicrous to them, smelly and awkward, more familiar with animals than people, couldn't talk.

Discontent with farm life also came from urban America. Urbanites, vulnerable in their dependence on farmers, were becoming increasingly concerned at what they perceived as inefficiency and poor organization in the agricultural base (Danbom 1979:74). In the 1909 *Country Life Report*, urban experts on farm conditions came to conclusions similar to Harnack's. According to this report, written by a Presidential Commission appointed by Theodore Roosevelt to assess the quality of rural life, American farm life was backward and suffering from "social sterility" (Bailey et al. 1911:114). Farm people needed help in establishing the libraries, organizations, and educational institutions that would stabilize the rural population. The commission found that the deprivations of farm life were especially hard on women:

> [W]hatever general hardships, such as poverty, isolation, lack of labor-saving devices,may exist on any given farm, the burden of these hardships falls more heavily on the farmer's wife than on the farmer himself. In general her life is more monotonous and the more isolated, no matter what the wealth or the poverty of the family may be (Bailey et al. 1911:104).

Farm women contrasted their own situations with those of their town relatives and kin, only a few miles distant, who took for granted electricity and running water in their homes as well as the close proximity of grocery stores, doctors, schools, and playmates for their children. Compounding the situation, country roads were undependable, and these roads made it impossible for farm women to plan and carry out community activities in the same way that town women did.

When, in connection with plans for organizing the extension service, the USDA asked women about their social and labor needs, respondents from across the country expressed the need for more organizations for farm women. They wanted organizations that would provide social contact, intellectual stimulation, and relaxation and that would improve education opportunities in rural areas. One woman asked for education for cooperation "as you have been educating the men for years" (USDA 1915A:28). Yet a close reading did not indicate that they were asking for conditions which would match those of the towns. For the farm women who answered the questions, their work and social needs were not separate. Women showed an interest in having cooperatives for household tasks—laundry, baking, butchering, canning, and boarding and feeding hired hands. A letter from an Illinois farm woman stated,

> The only thing in sight to lighten the burden of the indoor worker on the farm is cooperation. We have arrived at a place where the individual effort in many things has proven to be wasteful in cash and human energy, and we are making new discoveries along that line. The thing that presents itself forcibly to my mind is a community plant for doing the laundry work, making the sausage, rendering the lard, canning and evaporation of fruits and vegetables for the farmers' use. Such a plant for the accommodation of from 25 to 50 families or, in other words, one for the convenience of the patrons in each school district would cost from $700 to $1,000 building included (USDA 1915A:63).

Charlotte Perkins Gilman (1909:121) had initiated the plea for cooperative housekeeping in rural areas, and these rural women echoed her appeal. They asked for help in establishing small collective work units. Such collectives would ease the women's work loads, but perhaps of equal importance, they would provide opportunities for shared work and interaction among women. These women felt that sharing work with other women was a key part of solving the problems of rural life.

As will be discussed later, when extension service was established, its agenda was somewhat different from that projected by these farm women. It did, however, fundamentally alter the lives of farm women by infusing a program of change specifically aimed at them. Open Country received its first extension home demonstration agent in 1933, thereby instituting a new network connecting farm women with the urban world and lessening the barriers between farm life and the outside world.

In addition to the home demonstration agents, by the 1930s, other factors set the stage for a change in the relative separation of farm and town people. As a result of a concerted effort to upgrade country roads, the number of Iowa farms on surfaced roads increased from 23,909 in 1925, to 57,358 in 1930, and to 121,863 in 1940 (USDC 1942:119). This, along with improved automobiles, facilitated travel, thereby helping bridge some of the social gap between town and farm. Radios became more popular, and farm people were able to follow the same sports, politics, music, and popular personalities as town folks. Moreover, when farm people went to town they no longer stood face to face with their economic superiors. The townspeople of the 1930s were suffering from Depression hardships which in some cases more than matched those of the farm people (Fink and Schwieder 1984:16). While this did not instantly nullify the enormous cultural advantage thought to inhere in town life, some of the material differences between farm and town living were dissolving, and along with these differences went some of the sense of isolation from the cultural mainstream.

Before 1940, an Open Country woman's world centered on the family. This included family members who were part of her household as well as those living nearby. As discussed in Chapter 2, household membership was fluid, with (extended) family members forming a pool of potential recruits for a household economy. Some members of a household came as workers and others came because, as family, they had a claim to the shelter and care of the household. Children went from house to house, visiting grandparents and cousins, and being fed and cared for wherever they happened to be. Ruth, born in 1892, said that by age nine the children of her family could hitch horses to a wagon and drive around the country neighborhood. Some children lived with relatives in order to attend school. Emma spent a summer with her mother's sister in 1908 because her own mother had plenty of help and her aunt had no daughters. In the absence of retirement homes, old people lived with their children or other relatives. This shifting household composition strengthened family ties. For a woman, the option of living in another household might have represented an escape route both in childhood and in old age, as well as a way to choose her closest friends among her family members.

Women of different farm households did not compete with each other for scarce material resources. While men's goals of prospering in order to buy more land put them in competition with neighboring farmers, some of whom were family members, women's egg, butter, and cream enterprises were not threatened by their neighbors' successes. Local produce buyers transported surplus butter, chicken, and eggs to the major markets; therefore, the success of any one farm woman had a negligible effect on prices. A woman expanded or contracted her operations according to variables that were unrelated to her neighbors' fortunes. This set the climate for cooperation among farm women.

A woman's first line of support outside her household came from the women of her own family. Bertha Gabelmann's diary entry of December 3, 1912, is typical of many instances of sharing work with her married sister: "I was by Will's. helped her wash to rooms and pick up wood. We carried the seed corn upstairs." The women undoubtedly offered moral as well as material support in these visits. Laura, born in 1901, told of her mother's visiting and sharing work:

> Mother used to go visit her neighbors a little more than we do now. I don't know why. . . . They'd go in the afternoon and spend all afternoon. Mother would drive over the team of horses. They'd just go over and have a good old family talk—everything from A to Z. . . . We used to go around a lot that way—just the women. . . . People would rush in and help with everything. They'd have threshing crews. Women would get the dinner ready.

Unmarried sisters, aunts, and cousins were part of the family fold. In 1930, one out of four of the Open Country women older than age 15 had never been married (USDC 1932:779). Emily, born on an Open Country farm in 1891, did not marry until she was 45 and she never had children of her own. She lived with her parents in close proximity to cousins, siblings, nieces, and nephews and formed intimate ties with her favorites. When asked if she had felt any stigma or loneliness attached to being single, she answered "definitely not." Her family had celebrations on Thanksgiving, Christmas, New Years, Easter, birthdays and anniversaries and often gathered for Sunday dinners. The women shared their work and their lives with each other. Emily taught school and later became a nurse. Her work and family left her too busy to marry. She had a chance to marry a steady male friend as a young woman, but he tired of waiting and married someone else. Interviewed in her nineties, she still maintained fond feelings for him, but she did not regret her decision to remain with her family rather than marry at that time. Being single had not excluded her from taking an active part in rural social life.

When a young woman was about to be married, family and women friends came to help her hem linens and to prepare her for married life by offering moral and practical advice. Young couples were not supposed to have extensive private interactions during the period of courtship. Even when this rule was violated, the courting woman did not have a chance to establish the kind of strong, socially affirmed tie with her future husband that women shared with each other. Thus, the women who gathered to sew and talk gave the support of their presence at what must have been a traumatic transition. If, as was the usual case, the woman married someone within Open Country, this supportive circle of friends remained available to her after marriage.

Through the network of women's relationships, a woman gained access to a wide range of persons within Open Country and this sometimes led to significant control in community life. Ruth's Great-Aunt Alis was the founding member of the Norwegian Quaker community. She came to Open Country as a widow in 1883 at age 51, purchased a tract of land that provided a farm for each of her three children, and spent much of the next 40 years living in various homes, seeing to the needs of the people, and gently guiding the household economics and the moral life of the community. An example of an Aunt Alis story is of a household in which the man had a drinking problem, the woman was sickly, and the children were unattended. Alis moved in for several weeks, got the woman out of bed, and began putting the house in order. According to the story, she managed to solve most of the household's problems in the weeks she was there. Ruth, who as a teenager shared her bedroom with her aunt during the periods when she was in her home, said, "She was able to give the young a sense of being equal, and many are the moral talks we had after the lights were out."

Alis died in 1925 and has become almost a legendary figure since then. While the stories about her may have been augmented, it is nevertheless significant that no one pictured her as interfering in a negative way. Ruth continued:

> She was a pioneer social worker, . . . a midwife of many baby cases, usually with no doctor present. She would spend weeks in a home before and after a baby was born. With one foot on the rocker of the

cradle she would quiet the baby as well as be mending or piecing a comfort top keeping her hands busy.

Alis's daughter's son said:

> She would stay with us when all of us younger kids were home, I know. Take care of us. . . . She delivered over 100 babies and never lost a baby. She had a remedy for all ailments. When someone had a cold, she'd give us a teaspoon full of dry mustard, make us sweat. . . . I don't think she ever had an enemy.

Laura, Ruth's younger sister, generalized about the type of service Aunt Alis yielded to the community:

> She was a worker. She did everything. She went everyplace and helped do up their work. . . . Neighbor helped neighbor a lot more in those days.

Alis came to Open Country and helped recruit Norwegians and Quakers to the area. In her later years, she helped establish a Quaker boarding school in central Iowa, which served not only the Open Country Quakers but also Quakers and non-Quakers from across the state. She left Open Country for a year to be the first matron of the school. Her model of independence as well as her ethic of community concern set its mark on all the women of the Norwegian community. A woman who was only distantly related to her said that Alis held the community together. She did this by having her primary interaction with women and children, not with men.

For those who, like Ruth and Emily, had large families, family members were sufficient to meet their needs both to share work and to enjoy companionship. Extended family was the essential core of their social life. Curtis Harnack (1981:106) wrote of the annual gatherings of farm neighbors that his household hosted to make plans for thrashing:

> Mother and Aunt Lizzie felt a trifle uneasy, for this was the only night of the year when our visitors were other than relatives. With so many dozens of kin on both sides of the family, we needed no further friends.

Expressions of anger or competition came most often in the form of avoidance or indirect hostility. More than men, women were required to refrain from open hostility and to smooth over disagreements as they arose. There were definitely hurts that have lasted through the years, undoubtedly the more painful for never having been expressed. This avoidance of overt conflict came at the detriment of relationships between particular individuals. Although it may have inhibited personal growth, it seems to have promoted family cohesiveness.

A young woman gained much from having a mother or an aunt in her household or in the vicinity as support during the early years of her adulthood and as help when her children were born, but older women achieved a greater measure of freedom as they matured. Sarah, born in 1904, lived with her grandmother after her mother's death, and maintained that her grandmother went visiting every morning as soon as she arose. As a teenager, Sarah learned to drive in order to take her grandmother on her daily visits. Younger women in a household also freed senior women's time, allowing them extended periods for other activities. Ruth remembered

> At the age of 16, I was left in charge of the household while Mother took a vacation with Aunt Alis, visiting relatives and friends in Stavanger, Le Grand, Norway [, Iowa], and Cedar Rapids.

Again, at age 19, Ruth was left in charge of the whole farm while both of her parents and another aunt left for "six to eight weeks" to visit relatives and friends in New England. Another farm woman made trips into Minnesota and the Dakotas while her younger women family members cared for her house. The ties to family were liberating ties for these older women who had cultivated relationships with younger women. The women who were too old or infirm to benefit from traveling, visiting, or sharing work were often widows. These widows and other people needing care found homes with family members, or younger family members moved in with them. A person typically died in a family home.

Paradoxically, the family organization that liberated women also restricted them. Young women felt the weight most directly. Parents, as well as the women themselves, expected the younger women to bend to the needs of the family. Although some women expressed regrets that this happened, none expressed bitterness. Ruth went away to boarding school but returned to meet family demands:

> I enjoyed one year at Stavanger School and wanted to spend the next
> year at Olney, but the folks felt I was needed at home. It seemed there
> was no further opportunity to continue an education except by ex-
> perience.

Similarly, Gladys (born in 1900) had a year of secretarial training
that she was unable to put to use:

> I learned to be [a secretary] but I didn't use my education until a
> number of years afterwards because I had to quit college. My mother
> became ill and I, being the oldest one in the family, went home to
> help take care of the brothers and sisters.

Coral, who worked for a grocery store in town, also quit her job
when her mother needed to be taken care of at home.

Ruth Suckow, the daughter of a minister, grew up in rural Iowa
in the early twentieth century. Her fiction portrays the people and
situations she knew in her early years. A recurring theme in her
work is of a devoted daughter who gave up education, marriage, or
personal plans in order to meet the needs of her mother. Although
this care consumed the youth of the daughter, the mother was
always presented in a favorable light, as a woman who was loveable;
frequently, her age and experience endowed her with personal traits
that younger women did not have and that endeared others to her.
The novel *The Kramer Girls* (Suckow 1930) and the short story "The
Daughter" (Suckow 1926A) are two of Suckow's many works with
this theme. Young women's care and sacrifice for older women is
consistent with the reports given by Open Country people. Like
Ruth's Aunt Alis, older women seem to have been cherished for
their wisdom and experience. While they consumed resources and
made demands on a household, younger women loved and appreciated them. Although having an aging or infirm person in the
household undoubtedly added to the work, it seems to have been a
burden that was sought rather than avoided.

As on the farms, family formed the core of town women's
worlds. Like the farm women, the majority worked in family
economies and their closest associations were with their families.
Coral (born in 1904) was an exception in that she was employed in
the grocery store of a nonfamily member, but she lived in her
parents' home all her life and maintained her closest emotional ties
with her mother and sister. They taught themselves music and in
1928 formed a trio that performed at local events and on the radio.

Living and working in town, Coral also came into daily contact with a number of nonfamily people. She considered her cheerful nature an asset to her work in the grocery store, and she kept track of people's health and fortunes as they shopped. As a single woman, she became good friends with other single women in town, friends who came to be "just like one of the family":

> [A] bunch of teachers always came to our house. The teachers came here from Minneapolis and Sioux Falls and Sioux City, and they still come to see me. They were just like one of the family. . . . We got teachers that came down and they didn't know anybody . . . and we got acquainted with them at the meeting in September when school started.
>
> They said, "Where do you girls live?"
>
> We told them.
>
> We said, "Where do you room?"
>
> Well, they roomed so and so and one another place.
>
> They said, "Come and see us sometime."
>
> We told Mom and Mom said, "Well, why don't you have them come over. They get lonesome. It'd be just like we'd go to another town and not know anybody."
>
> They had us come up. At that time I worked in the store and my sister in the drugstore. They were always in there after school getting something. They invited us up for certain nights and then we had them over. Mom made hot rolls. They'd come in the back door and have hot rolls and butter. They had dinner with us on Sunday. . . .
>
> They liked to dance. . . . They'd come up to the store after school and say, "Are you girls going to Farmtown to the dance tonight?"
>
> I said, "Well, we haven't said much about it. Ask Lucy [her sister] at the drugstore."
>
> "Yeah, we'll go."
>
> Four or five of us would go. We taught some of them to dance. We'd get a booth and popcorn and pop and start to dance.

The earlier acquisition of electricity and running water freed town women from some of the housework that farm women did, thereby allowing them more time for strictly social interaction.

Furthermore, with more disposable wealth in town, some of the town women separated themselves from material production to a large extent. Hilda, born in Center in 1883, told of afternoon visits with women friends and card parties but had no recollection of women working together. Her mother and unmarried sister lived less than two blocks from her house in town throughout her married life, but she could not recall that they had ever helped her in any material way. When Hilda's children were born, she hired a "girl" to help her in the house, but her mother and sister did not help. As some of the richest people in Center, their activities centered on management of their economic and social position. Although Hilda was in the minority, she was influential as a model that other town women attempted to emulate. While Coral, with close cooperative family relations, was more typical of Open Country than Hilda, Hilda was more widely known and admired.

A farm woman's circle of friends could also include those outside the family who lived in close proximity to her. These friends got together to sew or to help each other. Emma, married in 1913, was part of a close circle of four women who gathered to quilt and sew as frequently as their farm work schedules allowed, there being more opportunity in the winter and spring than in the summer and fall. Even with the many women in her family, Emily's mother had her closest friendship with a nonfamily neighboring farm woman. They made trips to town together, shared nearly all of their work, and attended each other's separate church club meetings.

Farm women who were close neighbors might also coalesce around the social and political events connected with the numerous rural schools. Run by a board of (male) directors, a country school brought together people of all ages. In the absence of paid assistants for the teachers, directors' wives cleaned the schoolhouses each fall and tended to the nonroutine housekeeping matters. Students, parents and family members packed the schoolhouses for the parties, programs, and benefits, which were held at least monthly. The directors' wives and pupils' mothers worked together to provide food for these gatherings and to assist with the arrangements. The collective work and leisure put neighborhood women in contact with each other and provided a sense of common purpose. As mentioned, country schoolteachers, nearly always unmarried women, lived in farm homes, where they became friends with the farm women, as well as models for young girls.

A woman's social world of family and close friends blended into the ethnic communities. With people marrying within their ethnic groups (which were in turn geographically consolidated), neighbors, schoolmates, and members of the same church often came to be members of the same extended family. Each ethnic group had its own distinctive mode of interaction, including events such as Saturday night card parties in people's homes, picnics, ball games, community parties, dances, dinners, and work days on farms or in churches, which everyone from young to old attended.

For example, the Germans, who unlike most others, drank beer at their gatherings, had a dance hall where they gathered for Saturday night celebrations of weddings, anniversaries, and reunions or simply Saturday night community celebrations. Music was live. A German dance was not just for young adults: gatherings included refreshments and socializing for all. Women of all ages danced together. Older people and nondancers ate and talked. Young children who tired were put to sleep in a side room with beds and rocking chairs. Playground equipment stood outside the hall, and Germans returned to the hall for Sunday picnics and games.

In contrast to the Germans, the Norwegians neither drank nor danced. The Quaker contingent built a school in 1899, and this school served as a gathering place for the Norwegian community, both Quaker and Lutheran. A Literary Society was connected to the school. The community gathered one Sunday each month for a shared dinner followed by a "literary," which was a program in which both adults and children read poetry and prose. Singing and dancing was un-Quakerly, and perhaps because of this limitation they developed a tradition of hosting traveling speakers who addressed the entire community on religious topics or on such Quaker political concerns as pacifism. The Quaker school closed in 1923, but the building remained as a place where Quakers and their friends met.

Besides the Meeting for Worship on Sunday morning, Quakers also had a Midweek Meeting for Worship. Following these Meetings, people had a chance to exchange family news and to discuss farming practices and family matters. When no Sunday dinner event was held at the Meeting House, Sunday dinners in homes virtually always entailed visiting. In good weather, Sunday dinner was followed by a ball game.

The separate rural churches, most of them organized in the

1880s when the area was settled, supported family and ethnic ties both organizationally and ideologically. The church was a center for the retention of European cultural identity. The pastor conducted church services in the native language until this was forbidden during World War I; but even after changing to English, the church retained specific Christmas, Easter, and other holiday customs that connected life in Open Country to the nexus of meaning and value inherent in the symbols of the old country. Except for the Norwegians, who managed both Quaker and Lutheran contingents within families, membership in a church was by family; a person leaving a church was, for all practical purposes, leaving the circle of kin that recognized each other as family as well as leaving behind ethnic identity. Although based on common church membership, participation in the religious community went beyond church attendance. Even self-proclaimed nonbelievers joined in weddings and other ceremonies, which were for everyone regardless of sex or age. Membership in the ethnic/religious community entailed a general consensus on major moral principles. While some men were heretical enough to scorn religion, women did not.

Women were the mainstays of the church. A Methodist church outside of Center and the Friends Meeting also located in the country, gave explicit recognition to women as founders, and other religious groups would surely find key women to recognize if they desired. Although women could not be pastors or elders within the church hierarchy, they could be Sunday School teachers and choir directors, and, most significantly, they had their own separate woman's clubs within the church. Like the churches themselves, these clubs dated from the first years of settlement.

The larger churches had an assortment of woman's clubs. By the 1930s, the Farmtown Presbyterian Church had a Ladies' Aid Society, to help with the upkeep of church property, a Missionary Society to aid the missions of the church, a Westminster Club for young women with "a fun period following each lesson" (Farmtown Presbyterian Centennial Pagaent 1981), and a Guild for young mothers. Coral and her friends belonged to a Methodist club called WMB (We Mean Business), which met in the evening. Smaller churches, like the Friends Meeting, had only one woman's club, but the women were still active. Quaker women had weekly sewing bees that were well attended and that served a monthly dinner for all people of the Meeting.

Except for the Quaker woman's gatherings, the general format of a club meeting consisted of devotions, program, and lunch. Frequently the pastor was present to open a meeting with prayer and blessing, although he then left. The pastor's wife often had a major coordinating role in church women's club life.

The minutes of the Ladies Auxiliary of the Center Congregational Church date back to 1909 and document meetings held every two weeks with approximately 50 women. Their express purpose was to provide material support for the church property. To this end, they sponsored numerous events including ice cream socials, chicken pie suppers, bazaars, picnics, and dramatic presentations. When the church trustees were raising money for a new parsonage in 1913, the women held weekly ice cream and cake socials in the park during the summer months. They suspended these community social activities to sew for the Red Cross during World War I, but the sewing served a similar purpose in that it brought women together to work toward a common goal. In the 1920s, the Ladies Auxiliary donated approximately $800 annually to the church budget; in the 1930s they donated between $100 and $600 annually.

With a structure paralleling that of the family, churches had treasuries and business affairs which were formally controlled by the men, but the women's clubs made money, contributed as much as they deemed necessary to the general operation of the church, and exercised a fair amount of *de facto* control over church affairs. While the records studied do not indicate the precise impact of women's money in percentage of the total budget, the indication is that, just as in the home, their input was critical. In 1937, the Congregational Church Women recorded purchasing a stove for the church kitchen, paying to paint the parsonage, redecorating the pastor's study, buying new hymnals, and donating $330 to the trustees. In that year, they also had two work days during which they cleaned the church, thereby saving the cost of janitorial service.

What women donated to the church through their collective work was critical to the church's operation. With ministers being paid partially in farm produce and with much of the parsonage and church being built and maintained with donated services, cash budgets could be reduced to less than $1,000 annually, making women's organizations a pivotal factor in the overall financial picture. A 1921 minute of a Methodist church Board meeting read:

> . . . regarding the possibility of paying the balance of the parsonage debt this year. The representatives of the Ladies Aid Society present,

gave the Board the assurance of further help from their Society and it
was felt that possibly with this promised help, the balance could be
raised (Center M.E. Church Board Meeting minutes, March 9, 1921).

This suggests that although Board membership was restricted to
men, this Board was proceeding with, and only with, the approval of
the women. Formally, women had only advisory power within the
churches, but their collective work through auxiliaries, sewing bees,
and other clubs gave them a wider range of power than if they addressed the church governing bodies singly.

Quakers, without a paid clergy, had the most democratic form
of religious government, including decision making by consensus
of all members. Formally, Quaker women held equal rights within
the Meeting and separate Women's Meetings for worship and
business were structured to ensure that women were not overshadowed by men. With the separate business meeting, Quaker
women could, in theory, reach their own consensus, which they
presented in unity. Any differences between decisions of the men
and women then reverted to the separate meetings for further
discussion. Key components of the decision making process appear
to have occured outside the meetings, however. In addition, an informal understanding vested control of Meeting finances in the
Men's Meeting. Thus, the groups were not really parallel, and Ruth
said that the separate meetings were joined in 1936 because there
was not much business for the women to discuss anymore. The
money the Quaker women did control was not the official Meeting
treasury that the business meeting held. Rather, they controlled the
money in the treasury of their sewing bee. Because of the Quaker
testimony of simplicity and the absence of a paid clergy, the
Quakers had a relatively small cash flow, but the women's sewing
bee purchased its own sewing supplies, paid for coal and building
improvements, and donated money to the Meeting budget. Like the
women of other denominations, Quaker women exerted control, not
through formal equality, but through their separate organization
and their own treasury.

In addition to church clubs, secular clubs appeared by the early
1900s to bring women together across family and ethnic boundaries. Women who lived in town or had access to town could join a
plethora of clubs, such as the Friendship Club, the Lucky Thirteen
(Motto: "Culture, not affectation—Pleasure, not frivolity"), the
Music Club, the Study Club, and the Community Club. Club

meetings characteristically followed a familiar pattern of a religious/patriotic opening, a lesson, business meeting, and lunch, followed by conversation. The content of the lesson was a civic, literary, travel, artistic, or homemaking topic, depending on the theme of the club; but the most significant function of these clubs lay in the women's coming together.

Some women's clubs had restricted membership. The American Legion Auxiliary (founded after World War I), Daughters of the American Revolution, P.E.O. (an elite, secret organization), and a variety of lodge organizations had special conditions for membership. Clubs with restricted membership tended to have more status. Membership in the most prestigious woman's clubs was, for town women, an index of social standing as well as a source of self-esteem. The Progress Club, for example, limited its membership to twelve women from the richest, most established families of Center and, therefore, did not include any farm women. The Daughters of the American Revolution selected its members among those with male ancestors who fought in the Revolutionary War, thus excluding, among recent immigrants, the majority of farm women. Ruth Suckow (1934:49-50), in her novel *The Folks*, vividly described the feelings of a town woman who achieved membership in the Monday Club and was hosting her first club meeting:

> The ladies in the Monday Club were the ones she would have chosen beyond all others. But they were all in other churches as it was only this last year, since she had come into contact with Mrs. Bird at the Washington's Birthday bazaar, and had begun to get so neighborly with Mrs. Viele, that she had really felt as if she knew any of them. She had been delighted and surprised when they had taken her into membership. She felt as if this day marked the first real entrance into the social life of Belmond, and wanted everything to be up to the occasion. She wanted to *enjoy* it.

As the daughter of a small town pastor, Suckow had ample opportunity to feel the intensity surrounding women's club life in town.

Farm women had no such clubs of their own. What clubs they had frequently used work as the pretext for organizing. Around 1900, for example, the women in Emily's neighborhood established a club, The Cheerful Workers, whose members gathered to quilt and sew rags for rugs. The women held surprise parties for newcomers and work days for those who needed them. Although primarily for women, they sponsored an annual Halloween party and a summer picnic, both of which included all family members.

Local extension clubs and projects for Open Country women began in 1921, but not until 1933, when the first county home demonstration agent was hired, did the clubs and the extension service became a central part of Open Country life. Extension, a program of the USDA and Iowa State College, stated that its purpose was "to aid in diffusing among the people of the United States useful and practical information on subjects relating to agriculture and home economics, and to encourage application of the same" (Davidson et al. 1933:27). It was called *extension* because it was an extension of the expertise of the USDA through the land grant colleges and universities to county agents and through these agents to local township leaders who disseminated the information to all local farm families. The goal was to multiply those reached by branching out at all levels.

Extension operated through a locally based farm organization, which in Open Country, as nearly everywhere, was the Farm Bureau. With a small amount of local money and organization, local people received subsidies to hire county agricultural extension agents and home demonstration agents. A youth program associated with Farm Bureau/extension was called 4-H, representing head, heart, hands, and health. Four-H taught practical and social skills and brought new experiences to many farm children. Because extension was a federal and state government program, its agents were required to submit extensive reports of their activities. Therefore, extension clubs were more completely and accessibly documented than any other organizations of Open Country.

While the structure of extension work reflected the rural reality in its inclusion of women as an integral part of this farm program, it did not reflect the division of labor on most farms. From the time of the first federal extension program in 1914, the work was divided in a manner that reflected an urban middle class ideal rather than the farm reality. Men's extension was agricultural and directed by a male agricultural agent; women's extension was home economics and directed by a female home demonstration agent. The poultry program, for example, fell into the male side of the organization. While women could use the services, the program was explicitly aimed at promoting poultry raising as a male activity (ISES 1931).

Four-H was divided along lines similar to those of the adults' organizations: it included boys' clubs, directed by the agricultural agent and involving projects related to farm animals and crops, and girls' clubs, directed by the home demonstration agent and involving projects related to cooking, sewing, and home decorating. Open Country girls were allowed to join boys' clubs, but only if they also belonged to girls' clubs. No boys joined girls' clubs. As a government service, extension advice was available and free to anyone who requested it, but most of the early lessons were presented at meetings of the Farm Bureau, Farm Bureau Women, or 4-H.

Within the Farm Bureau, the Farm Bureau Women developed as a committee to direct and oversee the local home economics extension work. The system was planned to include a home economics project club in every township. These clubs depended on the local women leaders who received instruction from the home demonstration agent and then extended this to the township club members. Each year the women of the county, through their local leaders, who constituted the county extension committee, selected a major project in food, clothing, child care, or home management, and the home demonstration agent went to Iowa State College in Ames to get materials and training in this subject, which provided the focus for the year's work. In practice, the women chose projects from among the options privided by the extension service. Thus, while maintaining the flavor of local control, substantial central direction in the structure and the content of the program was levied.

For example, the 1939 clothing project entitled "Being Well-Dressed," involved demonstrations of correct posture and correct seating done with a book balanced on the head. The lessons instructed women on ways to counteract the problems of large hips, busts, or abdomens; flat busts; or round shoulders. According to the extension material:

> Lines . . . are used to create an illusion of correcting figure proportions which deviate from the one accepted as normal or ideal. In addition to incorporating a desirable figure correction care should also be exercised to also have a harmonious kind of design, one in keeping with facial expression, stature, posture and personal clothing (Open Country Extension 1939).

While the material did not state who accepted only one figure shape as normal or ideal, it was something for farm women to learn. The concern for one proper figure and the contrived harmony of design are urban concepts that had no history among Open Country farm women. Open Country women themselves selected this project from among available options, and it is impossible to determine how many women would have preferred a more practical help during the Depression years had they been offered a substantial program based on a critical analysis of their problems as farm women.

Extension, with its urban roots and bureaucratic framework, carried its own implicit agenda for farm women. In being modern and scientific, extension lessons promoted quantification and measurement in farming and homemaking. Following extension advice, many women started written household bookkeeping, cooking with recipes, and assessing children's growth by weighing and measuring them. One woman whose children were born in the 1930s said that she followed the advice of the extension service in establishing a feeding and sleeping schedule for her children based on the clock rather than on the babies' demands.

Because extension was a large, governmental program, the major accountability of the extension agents was in numbers. The extension record books show a myriad of statistics on hours worked, meetings held, and attendance at meetings. Extension agents had to demonstrate success through the compilation of statistics. For example, in 1939, one of the goals of the girls' 4-H program was for "[e]ach girl to improve posture by thinking tall, standing tall, sitting tall, and walking tall" (Open Country Extension 1939), which 90 percent of the girls did. In 1934, when child training was the major project, the home demonstration agent totalled up hours of sleep of each child, disaggregated these data by townships and town schools, and reported the exact number of children in each area who did and did not sleep the number of hours recommended by a White House Conference Committee (Open Country Extension 1934). On a state level, the 1930 Annual Report said that 243 children's emotional problems were solved and 315 parents secured better cooperation from their children (Iowa State Extension Service 1930:46).

Extension service constituted a popular modern replacement for the home remedies and expertise of women such as Ruth's Aunt Alis. Over 1,000 Open Country women participated in the 1939 program, "Being Well-Dressed." The clubs regularly brought farm women together and provided them with a glimpse of the world beyond. The 4-H program was also significant in its parallel introduction of farm youth into the scientific, quantified world they needed to understand as they left the farm.

Women's extension lessons were popular and well-attended.

Within the limitations of a program exclusively geared to home and family concerns, extension represented an energetic attempt to educate farm women and develop their leadership potential. The purposes, as presented in 1934 *Annual Report* of the Open Country Home Extension program, can be readily interpreted as empowering women:

1. To help strengthen the Farm Bureau organization.
2. To help secure worthwhile information and adult education.
3. To help develop higher ideals in child care.
4. To develop friendliness and community spirit.
5. To develop and secure leaders.
6. To raise the standards of living economically.
7. To strengthen the Home Made Happiness Program.
8. To develop hidden talents (Open Country Extension 1934).

Predictably, the first stated purpose of the women's organization was to support the men's organization; but beyond this there is evidence of concern with the women themselves. Extension gave women a range of activities that took them out and away from their rural neighborhoods. These included the preparation of cooking and sewing projects for display at the annual county fair in Center, a county women's chorus, a talent night, annual meetings and banquets in Center, and a drama contest. In addition, women could attend district meetings in nearby cities, state meetings in Ames or Des Moines, or an interstate conference of farm women. All of these activities represented avenues for the transmission of urban culture to farm women and farm women to urban culture. As in the church and the family economy, women could develop practical skills in planning and carrying out individual and community activities through extension.

Paradoxically, the extension home economists were unmarried career women who were role models of independent women. As women were being empowered to strengthen the family and the androcentric Farm Bureau organizational structure, they were also learning to know each other, to plan and carry out events, and to develop "hidden talents." Interviewed in 1982, women who had been involved in extension prior to World War II were unanimous in praising its role in developing women's leadership, bringing women together, and providing practical education for maintaining a farm household.

Conclusion

Starting with the premise that strong relationships among women are necessary in order to allow them to exercise power in a system that accords men formal control of the society, we see that pre-1940 Open Country women had this base from which to wield power. Farm women were by no means isolated from each other. Evidence is found that farm women valued their contacts with each other and sought to develop more extensive interaction, although they seem to have been somewhat isolated from the outside world. Moreover, their socializing occurred according to rhythms of season, work, and family responsibilities which were specific to farm life of that period. Later, when science addressed the problems of farm women, it did so in terms of an urban model. Urban life was the measure of progress and farm women were urged to improve their situation by adopting patterns of town life rather than by developing institutions to enhance the existing farm patterns. Better roads, automobiles, radios, and a changing economy, as well as the establishment of the extension service home economists, eased this transition. The minority of Open Country women who lived in town had different patterns of interaction with each other than did the farm women. With less work to do, town women had more leisure with which to hold elaborate luncheons and club meetings. Women like Coral went to dances and shared hobbies such as music. Notwithstanding the reality of this difference, the economic and social gap between the worlds of the town and farm women of Open Country narrowed somewhat in the 1930s.

The churches were central to the lives of Open Country people, and women, through church clubs, had material control over the priorities of the churches. Beyond the church, women's club life emerged as an increasingly salient factor of rural social organization. Clubs provided, first for the town women and later for the farm women, gatherings that were their own. Although the club programs often centered on home and family themes, they empowered women by bringing them together in new and larger groups and by developing a broad base of local leadership among women. Together with visiting and shared work, an array of clubs potentially provided something of what Sara Evans (1979:215) calls "free space" in which women together examined their shared situation and supported common goals. Thus, they contained within them a set of contradictions that promised continuing change and development.

Yet the process of development never worked through to a resolution. In the 1940s, World War II intruded into the hearts and minds of Open Country people, interrupting the Depression and dramatically changing all aspects of community life. The following chapter examines World War II as it affected the women of rural Iowa.

CHAPTER 5

World War II and Rural Women

Whoever you talk to, wherever you go, the talk is about the boys . . .
(Wherry 1945: 145).

Elizabeth Wherry, a rural Iowa woman with a son in the service during World War II, wrote this line in her "Country Air" column, a weekly feature of *Wallaces' Farmer*. From 1941 to 1945, news of the war appeared on virtually every page of this popular Iowa farm journal, in the form of editorials, letters from readers, articles, or advertisements. In Open Country, support for World War II and especially for the local "boys" in the service was a *sine qua non*; other issues became secondary concerns against this central goal. Just as with the rest of American society at this time, World War II permeated nearly all aspects of Open Country life. In addition to reading war news in *Wallaces' Farmer*, Open Country people read about the war in other magazines and newspapers and heard about it at extension lessons, on the radio, and in church.

Not only did Open Country people hear about the war, but they also had to change long-established routines because of it. Sugar, meat, coffee, and canned goods rationing affected daily shopping, cooking, and eating patterns. Building materials and farm machinery rationing meant that farm profits could not be reinvested automatically. Nearly every family was potentially affected by the draft. Seemingly insignificant actions assumed a real or imagined meaning from the war perspective. Loitering in the lobby of the post

103

office was forbidden. The owner of Center's telephone exchange reported that federal agents visited him during the war to ascertain whether there was spying or treason in the telephone conversations of Open Country people

World War II brought the outside world to the people of Open Country and gave them a sense of participation in a major global event. Henry A. Wallace, President Franklin Roosevelt's Secretary of Agriculture during the Depression, became Vice President in 1941. Being part of the Iowa family which published *Wallaces' Farmer*, his prominence enhanced the connection between Iowa and Washington. Indeed, the war made sense: it connected seemingly disparate events and gave coherence to disjointed elements of rural life. Even something as ordinary and familiar as an egg was suddenly connected to the war:

> An egg on an Iowa farm can be turned into a weapon of war when dried and shipped overseas to feed our army, allies, or civilians behind the lines who—in exchange for food—do work . . . (Food Wins Battles 1943:473).

In contrast to the sense of isolation from the rest of the world that farm people felt previously, war conditions made local events significant in the larger picture.

The war was not an unmitigated hardship. Farmers, plagued with surpluses and low prices in the 1930s, increased production and received higher prices for their products during the war years. Prosperity on the farm was good for rural Main Street, as town business grew in spite of rationing. Moreover, with the federal government's concern for wartime farm problems, Open Country people felt that the United States as a whole was on their side and wanted the same things they wanted. The enemy was outside the country, and rural people joined with city people in pursuit of a common goal.

On the farms as in the cities, the war effected a major recovery from the Depression, and this recovery occurred even before the United States was an official participant. Total Iowa farm income increased 12 percent from 1939 to 1940, attaining its highest level in 10 years. The Iowa State Department of Agriculture (ISDA 1940:10–11) made the following assessment in 1940:

> Exceptional and widespread expansion of business throughout the United States was recorded during 1940. The wars of the other

continents provided the impetus for the upswing of activities and from the beginning of the year the export demand for war materials was a major dynamic factor. Both government and industrial resources were marshalled toward a huge military defense program, which overshadowed all else in the business situation. . . .

The general position of agriculture improved materially in 1940. Increased acreage over that of 1939 and substantially improved yields during 1940 resulted in the best harvests since 1937, and livestock production attained a new record volume. With higher farm prices and larger marketings, the aggregate cash farm income rose nearly half a billion dollars despite smaller government payments than in 1939.

In the words of Willard Cochrane (1979:124), "The miracle for which farm people were waiting took the form of World War II." The war brought record production and the highest levels of income ever experienced on Iowa farms (ISDA 1946:17). By virtually any measure, Iowa farmers did well. The total value of Open Country farm produce increased from $7.1 million in 1939 to $15.5 million in 1944 to $22.8 million in 1949 (see Table 5.1). The value of the average Open Country farm increased from $19,358 in 1940 to $43,108 in 1950 (USDC 1942B:130, USDC 1952:43). The influx of money had a snowballing effect: increased income meant that the majority of farmers now gained access to hybrid seed corn and power machinery that was beyond their reach during the Depression. As new technology came within their grasp it in turn led to higher production and higher incomes.

Table 5.1
Value* of Open Country Farm Produce Sold or Traded
1939–1949

Year	All Produce	Live- stock	Poultry	Dairy	Crops
1939	$ 7.1	$ 3.6	$ .3	$ .5	$2.6
1944	15.5	10.1	1.2	1.1	3.0
1949	22.8	15.0	1.5	1.2	5.1

*Values expressed in millions of dollars.

Source: U.S. agricultural censuses.

Farm production was a specific and crucial part of the war machine. While urban industries were producing ships, tanks, and fighter aircraft, farms were producing food and other raw materials, also essential to the war effort. The USDA related most directly to the war effort on the farm, specifically through the extension network, where it had its separate channels and specific mode of relating to farm people. Thus, the war messages that reached the farms were different in substance and style from those given to the urban population. Parallels are found, however, in the gender specificity of these appeals. Just as in cities, women heard appeals to their patriotism, to their loyalty toward servicemen and to their spirit of self-sacrifice. Just as in urban industry, a good woman did her war work, not for wealth or status, but because it was the least she could do in the face of the supreme male investment in the war. So, on the farm as in the city, because men and women were different, their contributions were different, as were their incentives. Concomitantly, due to the different war experiences, men's claims to the fruits of victory were qualitatively different from women's claims.

Women in War Work

One Lucas County, Iowa, farm woman summarized the way she met the war demands:

> I have done chores, worked in fields, raised bigger gardens, canned more food and helped with Red Cross work ever since the war began (War Jobs at Home 1945:232).

Home economics extension, the government's voice in rural homes, covered a broad spectrum of topics during the war. In terms of their duties as housewives, women were responsible for producing healthy potential war workers and soldiers while consuming the fewest resources possible in the process. Women had to redouble their efforts to make do with less in order to free as much labor and produce as possible for the war.

Extension home economists taught women nutrition, which helped then prepare balanced meals so that only a minimal amount of food was diverted from the war effort. They pressed women to raise victory gardens, which enabled them to supply even more of their own vegetables. They taught women home safety and home nursing, which enabled them to care for their own households rather than use professional health workers who were needed in the military. They taught women how to manage household accounts, which in turn created a surplus that could be invested in war bonds. They taught women to care for clothing, thereby minimizing the need for production in the civilian sector.

Extension's Food for Freedom program enlisted special cooperators for every four square miles of rural area, through whom extension blanketed the country with a nationwide network, similar to a telephone tree, that relayed special appeals to all rural families. This program elicited a high degree of cooperation. In Floyd County, Iowa, for example, after a drive to encourage people to use enriched flour and bread, the local agent determined that seven out of eight families received the information and one-half of those families changed to enriched or whole wheat flour or bread within three weeks (Wilson 1942:6). As incentives, the extension service presented awards and certificates to the most effective neighborhood leaders.

The war ethos crept into every corner of extension work and turned all of its activities into avenues of support for the war. In 1942, the Open Country Home Demonstration Agent planned an Achievement Day with the theme, "Food will Win the War and Write the Peace." Township exhibits included "Carrots for Victory," "Vitamins for Victory," and "Whole Wheat for Vitamins and Victory." Rural newspapers across the state constantly reported on victory garden projects, and canning and nutrition classes focused on wartime food programs.

For an article entitled "How Farm Women Help," *Wallaces' Farmer* solicited replies to the question of what women were doing for the war effort, following the established pattern of using the work *help* to signify women's work. The journal received letters from women stating that they did more field work, less housework, canned more fruits and vegetables, and took care of older people in their own homes rather than having others do it. They adjusted time spent visiting and meeting in clubs so as not to interfere with farm work, and they sewed sheets and pillow cases from feed sacks (How Farm Women Help 1943:84). The war gave farm women a new reason to work hard, to take care of their own families, and to be thrifty.

Due to accelerated mechanization and the rural labor surplus during the Depression, the possibility of a labor shortage was not taken seriously at first. Draft boards selected farmers and hired men, and other men left of their own accord either to enlist in the service or to pursue better paying jobs offered in war industries. As the war continued, the combination of military demands on the heavy equipment industry with the increased demands for farm equipment brought rationing of farm machinery. Although a steady increase in the number of tractors and combines was seen during the war, this increase was not enough to meet the demands. Converging conditions of expanded production, machinery shortage, and the outflow of men all helped to change the farm operation drastically. In 1943, for the first time during the war, farm labor was in dangerously short supply. Hired workers' wages soared and these workers were hard to find at any price (Cherokee Times 1943).

In the face of the impending breakdown of the farm production system, the government sought ways to keep farm men on the farm, and private businesses helped their efforts with advertising. After 1943, local draft boards more frequently opted to give draft deferments to farmers and hired men, thereby keeping more farmers at home and underscoring the importance of farming as a war industry. As an incentive for men to stay on the farms, Food for Freedom awarded "Certificates for War Service" to 200,000 (male) Iowa farmers to help counter any derogatory remarks they received for not enlisting in the armed service (Des Moines Register 1943C; Cherokee Times 1943). One advertisment in *Wallaces' Farmer* (1943:177) appealed to the farmer as "A Soldier on the Food Production Front." An advertisement for coffee urged farm women to make Folger's coffee for their men to drink because, "They're on the job every day—sometimes eighteen or twenty hours. America appreciates their work" (Wallaces' Farmer 1945:232). The awards to and recognition of farm men encouraged them to think that their work was as valuable as that of soldiers, even if they never saw actual combat.

The forthcoming draft deferments and the varied forms of economic and moral encouragement for farm men to continue farming notwithstanding, farm labor remained in critically short supply. Planners began to seek other labor power elsewhere with farm women among the first to be considered a labor reserve. A survey by the extension service discovered that by 1943 80 percent of Iowa's farm women were doing daily farm chores as compared to

60 percent in 1941 (USDA 1942:4). In one of her 1943 "Country Air" columns, Elizabeth Wherry (1943A:19) estimated that the average Iowa farm had eight hours of work in simply maintaining a diversified livestock operation. Family members shared the work with a hired worker: two men fed the animals and cleaned the stalls, children helped milk and carry wood, and the woman tended the poultry and separated the cream (Wherry 1943A:19). A *Wallaces' Farmer* survey found that in addition to increased gardening and canning, 13 percent of the farm women drove trucks and tractors and 29 percent did "lots more" with livestock chores (War Jobs at Home 1945:232). More women were doing farm work and some women who had done farm work before the war were doing more during the war. This pattern was an intensification of the prewar work of farm women; it did not break any new ground. It was similar to that described generally in reports of women's farm work across the country (USDA 1942B:4; How Farm Women Help 1943:84).

In doing field work, operating machinery, and handling large livestock, farm women were indeed doing "men's work." They also increased their "women's work." In 1942, the government called for an increase of 200 million dozen eggs, or about 13 percent more than in 1941. Unlike the jobs women took over from men, poultry work had always been done by women and as such, the women were the recognized poultry experts—at least at the local level. The country now needed this poultry expertise for the war effort. *Wallaces' Farmer* joined the government in disseminating extension service poultry management advice, including labor-saving techniques, plans for feed efficiency, and instructions for makeshift chicken houses. As before, the *Wallaces' Farmer* poultry material was written as if the primary poultry producers were women, although they urged the women to persuade their husbands to help if extra hands were needed (Thompson 1942:61). Advertisements and pictures accompanying articles about poultry showed women. A section of the weekly poultry column called "Sarah Jane Says" was written by an anonymous woman who gave a cheerful, optimistic, and amusing, but educational, running account of the practical problems she encountered with her egg operation during the war years (see for example, the Farm Flock 1942:442). This was women's work and the model for coping was a woman.

Chicken and cream enterprises had long been managed by women, but even increased wartime tasks did not qualify them for general farm management. A newspaper story illustrating women's farm work told of a farmer whose son was in the service and who had his work done by his daughter, who was married to a serviceman:

> "Her mother and I would have been in a spot without her," Mr. Martsching declares. "I left all the driving of the tractor to John—I didn't even drive the family car. I worked only on the jobs where horses could be used."
>
> Marie . . . has disked for oats, disked corn stalks, plowed for corn and beans. In addition she is raising 1,000 chickens, a garden and is now milking eight of the 18 cows night and morning.
>
> All winter she drove the farm truck, hauling grain to the elevator and coal and other necessities to the farm (Des Moines Register 1943B).

Here was a woman doing many of the men's and women's tasks that were required on a farm, while her father was not able even to drive a tractor. Yet the father remained the farm manager and the one who served as spokesman to the reporter. The extension service in Iowa developed a program to give women instructions in farm business management so they could run the farms without men (USDA 1942:6), but I found no record of any woman who actually took over management of a farm as a result of the war.

With intensified work both outside and inside the house, farm women naturally felt considerable stress. In 1943, Elizabeth Wherry (1943:86) wrote in *Country Air*:

> Apparently, it takes each group a long time to appreciate its own sacrifice and responsibility. It isn't that I can't see farm women doing the work that lies before them. The thing that alarms me is whether they can keep their health and add one single more chore to their full days. The big problem is whether there can be recruited from the towns enough woman-power to take over some of their work.

Yet the planners, slow to consider women as real workers, were also slow to acknowledge that women who worked made real sacrifices and that there was nothing trivial about that work. A 1943 *Wallaces' Farmer* poultry article stated, "The main problem in raising more chickens is not labor—the women and children say they'll supply that—but housing" (More Chicks This Year 1943:118). Only women's and children's labor was taken for granted. Implicit herein was the assumption that men's labor was scarce and valuable but that other sources of labor were plentiful and waiting to be tapped.

In spite of Elizabeth Wherry's warning of exhaustion among farm women, women's labor seems to have been treated as a separate, unquantifiable resource. As before the war, neither men nor women really saw men's and women's work in the same way. A farm woman who picked corn said,

> I'm never fully accepted at corn picking. It is "man work." Remarks such as "the All-American Drawback" or "Handicap" reach my ears (Noll 1945:860).

In spite of the conceptual separation of women's farm work, their increased farm earnings were real. With rising demand, egg prices increased by 140 percent from 1940 to 1943 (USDA 1965:130). Income from livestock, dairy, and crops all showed increases, but Open Country's five fold increase in gross income from poultry production from 1939 to 1944 was the most pronounced (see Table 5.1). This increased poultry income went almost entirely to farm women. For the first time, women began to keep written records of egg and cream income. Rose, a farm woman, left an extensive record of her income from poultry and cream sales, coupled with detailed notes about her expenditures during the war years. Not only was she able to purchase the necessary food and other items consumed in her household, but her record also showed a substantial surplus. The following sample month's income and expenditures for October 1943 illustrates a typical wartime farm household economy. Rose's purchases included:

Oct.	2	hired help	$ 5.00
Oct.	2	pills	1.80
Oct.	2	groceries	5.60
Oct.	2	miscellaneous	2.00
Oct.	2	rug and picture	12.00
Oct.	9	telephone	7.94
Oct.	9	groceries	8.00
Oct.	16	groceries	4.50
Oct.	23	groceries, miscellaneous	4.75
Oct.	25	daughter, birthday	10.00
Oct.	30	groceries	10.50
Oct.	30	son, Christmas present	5.00
Total			$77.09

Her receipts for this month totalled $126.87, from which she paid for her own hired help and any other expenses for her poultry operation that arose. Shopping on Saturdays, she purchased such things as food, medicine, and household furnishings. Throughout the war years she frequently bought things such as furniture and wallpaper for her home; she paid for a daughter's wedding; and she paid for her chicken feed, chicks, fencing, and equipment. She was also paying the telephone bill and buying presents for her children. Her purchases seem to have been aimed at enhancing her social status and in cementing ties with her children, both of which might have represented an investment in her long-term security, but no indication is found that she was seeking to accumulate her own farm capital.

In 1943, she earned $1,541.17 and spent $963.54. Her $577.63 surplus was not unusual during the war, and it represented a modest sum which was entirely hers to spend or invest. She bought her children a total of $663.75 in government bonds over the war years. Even with these extras, she still had a surplus of several hundred dollars and her record does not indicate what she did with this money. A woman featured in *Wallaces' Farmer* as having an exceptional egg operation made $1,119 from eggs alone in 1942 (They'll Get More Eggs Now 1943:219). This amount afforded her a surplus beyond what she used in the farm home. Such surpluses, if they continued, might have put farm women in a position to make real choices about what they wanted for themselves and their children.

Even though women put a great deal of effort into wartime farm production and, in some cases, reaped modest profits from this effort, the reality was that women and children could not stretch themselves indefinitely. Wartime farm production demanded increasing labor input from outside the farm population. Food for Victory (a program sponsored by the U.S. Employment Service, the Iowa Farm Bureau Federation, and the USDA's War Board) worked to recruit this labor. The program established county farm labor advisory boards, and each local board was responsible for assessing labor needs, advising on labor efficiency, canvassing schools and townspeople for farm labor, and placing workers. The Open Country board publicized appeals, canvassed and eventually secured several hundred additional farm workers. In 1943, it recruited 143 men and 38 women farm workers (Open Country Extension 1943).

Much farm work could not, however, be done by any willing worker and some farmers were unhappy with the inexperienced recruits, particularly women, who wanted to work for them. Yet women's labor was needed and some women did find farm employment doing what previously had been men's work. As a speaker at a state meeting of the Iowa Federation of Women's Clubs said, "Women offering to go on the farms do face lack of co-operation from the farmers, but I believe that when the need really arises they will be glad to have part-time workers" (Des Moines Register 1943A). The exceptions notwithstanding, men remained the preferred workers; the county boards recruited men first and most vigorously.

Still, women could perform some tasks better than the resident male workers. Detasseling seed corn was one. Producing hybrid seed corn requires a short period each summer of hot, uncomfortable, and boring work removing tassels from corn so it will not pollinate itself. In 1943, the seed companies needed 8000 workers for detasseling and no regular male workers were available. Across Iowa, war prisoners, Menomini Indians, Mexicans, Japanese-Americans, Haitians, and conscientious objectors were formed into detasseling crews. Women also did detasseling. One newspaper said:

> All a woman needs to do the job . . . is a desire to perform a patriotic service and the willingness to work for good pay (from $4 to $5 a day for a period of two weeks to a month) (Toledo Chronicle 1943).

In Open Country, 160 boys and girls earned 50 cents per hour plus a bonus for detasseling in 1943 (Open Country Extension 1943).

Jobs as field hands, which most rural people saw as slightly stigmatizing for women before the war, became more fashionable as a war service. Women found general affirmation and support for this work when it was done in the context of patriotism and sacrifice. The USDA modeled a Women's Land Army, consisting mainly of nonfarm women, after a similar body established in England. Universities offered special short courses to teach women farming skills. Not only were nonfarm women willing to do farm work, city women who became farm workers were portrayed as spunky and attractive as they lent their energy to wartime farming. Far from threatening women's feminity, farm work could be healthy, invigorating, and beautifying so that even glamorous women wanted to do it. Emergency women workers received a special insignia and a "highly practical, and at the same time becoming [outfit of] well-fitting dark blue denim overalls" (Hall 1943:216). Camp Fire Girls, Girl Scouts, YWCA, and numerous smaller urban organizations similarly recruited women and girls for farm work.

Women also did more "men's work" in town. In spite of shortages and rationing, the farm recovery brought money and jobs to rural towns. The first resource for handling the extra volume of commerce was the labor of women within the family. Elizabeth Wherry (1945:233), whose husband had taken a town job and moved the family to town for a period, reported on town women's war efforts in *Country Air*:

> Mostly, the small-town woman has contributed thru being a two-sided person. In the first place, there is practically no by-the-day help any more, few handy men to be hired for odd jobs, and not enough reliable high school boys for the after-school jobs.
>
> On top of that, most women with husbands in business are busy keeping books and taking orders coming in over the counter. They go home to prepare an occasional meal or go to the restaurant, often coming back downtown at night to unpack goods or restock shelves—if there's any stock.
>
> In our town, the undertaker's wife is on call at all times. The barber's wife runs his beauty parlor. The wife of the druggist and the wives of both hardware merchants are practically full-time clerks and bookkeepers. Both coal yards have housewives in their offices. Two feed-store wives keep books or keep store. The post-master's wife pinch-hits during the busy half of the day.

Women's small-scale home industries continued. As in the 1930's, town women did laundry, cared for children and the elderly, kept boarders, and styled hair in their homes to earn small incomes. In addition to writing about the commercial activities of town women, Wherry casually mentioned that two nights a week, and occasionally on Sunday, four teachers boarded at her home, in addition to a regular full-time boarder.

Besides helping their husbands and working at home, town women found that the war brought a number of new and reclaimed paying jobs for them. Married women teachers, dismissed during the Depression, found that with the shortage of men they had a chance to regain their lost jobs. Although their return to teaching was partially thwarted by the ongoing consolidation of rural schools, once again married women became a significant percentage of the teaching force. A small number of war-related jobs were available to women through the local political patronage system. Ardith, who lost her job as principal of Center High School at the outbreak of the Depression, was tapped to work in the rationing office. Another woman was named to a job with the Iowa Board of Control where she placed orphans in northwest Iowa counties. Open Country extension service hired two women to run the office which placed farm workers.

The majority of nonfarm women did volunteer work through a variety of organizations, all of which oriented their agendas toward addressing war conditions. Many women voluntarily sacrificed to meet needs of men who were in positions of hardship because of the war. Women's church groups, which previously focused on such projects as church upkeep, visiting invalids, and mission work, cancelled church suppers because of rationing and focused their attention on the war. The Farmtown Presbyterian Women's Guild replaced its annual Christmas party and gift exchange with an offering taken for a "War Service Fund." Church women packaged boxes of books, cookies, and personal articles for the servicemen of their congregations. The Red Cross distributed wool yarn to women who agreed to knit sweaters and mufflers for soldiers (Open Country Bulletin 1942C).

The most important result of this volunteer work was in the broadened and diffused sense of purpose it bestowed on the women workers rather than in the practical benefits rendered to servicemen. D'Ann Campbell (1984:69) described the busywork developed by the Red Cross to involve women in its programs:

> The most spectacular waste of volunteer time was the Production Corps, which attracted 4 or 5 million women. Their job was to hand-knit millions of garments for soldiers and to roll billions of surgical dressings. The Red Cross vehemently denied that machines could do the job—arguing first that not enough factories could make dressings, then that the Army had specifically asked for their help, and finally that, though the machinery existed, a labor shortage prevented its utilization.

Regardless of whether the women's work was a real necessity, wartime service organizations became a way to extract surplus value from women's unpaid work. Because of many women's general patriotism and concern for U.S. soldiers, they supported agencies that concentrated their resources for uses which they themselves only vaguely comprehended.

Beyond material work contribution, voices from all sides told women to strengthen home and community life so that the population would be mentally ready to dedicate itself to the war. As the Secretary of Agriculture Claude R. Wickard, said in a speech, "Another thing that's up to the women is the matter of morale; holding the family together and keeping everyone cheerful in spite of difficulties" (quoted in USDA 1942A:10). Women frequently heard and read instructions on personal behavior that told them not to display the stereotypically female faults. According to an extension lesson, women needed to be calm, to contain fears rather than passing them on, to learn to accept sacrifices and losses without worry, self-pity and bitterness, to invest their increased war income into war bonds, and to be "facing changes without surprise and fear, to build up a sense of humor to meet trivial difficulties" (Open Country Bulletin 1942D). The League of Women Voters material submitted to the local newspaper asked each woman to vow to "curb my tongue, . . . not spread foolish stories, not criticize allies and not jump to hasty conclusions" (Open Country Bulletin 1942B).

The model woman was a mother or wife who gave moral and material support to her son or husband who was doing the real work of the war. A *Wallaces' Farmer* (1943B:118) story told of a woman who raised poultry, but not for her own profit:

> [She] has doubled her poultry production this year. She has a special reason for this increase. Her son Hilmar is in the army and may some-day eat these eggs in powdered form.

Another woman who did farm work while her husband and brother were in the service disclaimed any credit for her contribution:

> Work, she says, helps to keep her from thinking of the danger her husband, an officer on a flagship in the Pacific area, faces daily. "I can't do enough to equal his service. I'm just trying to take my brother's place on the farm where I know I am needed." (Des Moines Register 1943B).

When a 58-year-old woman helped detassel corn, the newspaper story related this to her role as a mother as it presented her as a model for other women:

[She] has five sons in service, four of them in the army and one in the navy. . . . She never detasseled corn before in her life, and altho she is 58 years of age, she said that this year was a good time to start. It is another way of doing her part to help win the war (Grundy Center Register 1943).

The ideal wartime woman worked without expecting any return other than the satisfaction of knowing that she was supporting her men. Although she accepted the money that came to her, she did not question the amount. She did not seek rewards for herself; rather, she sought new ways that she could help.

The gender specificity in acceptable wartime goals becomes apparent when the configuration of appeals made to women is compared to those made to men. Enlisting in the military, besides being a patriotic duty, took a man around the world and showed him places and things he had never seen before; it was an opportunity. An Open Country school superintendent, commissioned as a naval officer, found that his training included radar instruction at Princeton University and further training at Massachusetts Institute of Technology. Affirming the superintendent's good fortune, the local newspaper editor wrote:

[He] said he was thrilled over his appointment and that it seemed like a dream too good to be true—getting to attend Princeton and M.I.T. both. His training in radar will be invaluable to him after the war (Open County Bulletin 1943).

A man did not risk public scorn for seeking his fortune in the war. He became a hero to local people, who followed his letters and news in weekly newspapers' special columns. Acceptable women were supportive and helpful; they did not seek personal gain or public recognition.

Some women left Open Country for jobs in industry or to join the military, but even those who left were encouraged to think in terms of sacrifice, not personal gain. A local notice of training opportunitites with stipends and living allowances for women learning aircraft construction ended with the statement, "No single and unattached trainees will be given subsistence" (Open Country Bulletin 1942A), the implication being that a proper woman war worker was married and stable and that single women should not view the war as a chance to establish their independence or to seek adventures.

Open Country women who responded to the pleas of the

government for wartime service were entering a system that viewed men's activities, both on the battlefield and on the homefront, to be inherently more worthy. Contrary to the attitude toward men, the government valued women according to their usefulness, not as people who had intrinsic value and rights to work or to have their needs considered. While the wartime crisis happened differently in Open Country than in the cities, it must be considered in the context of a national and local spirit glorifying the male as warrior and subordinating the personhood of women.

Effects of the War

One way of assessing the cumulative effects of World War II is to compare the situation in 1950 with that in 1940. The 1940s saw a significant movement of women from the farms, a movement not solely the result of the decline in the number of farms. In 1950, Open Country had 25 fewer farms than in 1940, but Table 5.2 indicates a decline of 472 adult women on farms. In spite of the encouragement for women to be more interested in others' needs than in their own, some of the women were ready and willing to leave the area in search of better prospects elsewhere. In fact, women who did hard, grimy work on farms before the war fit in well with the "nontraditional" work found in urban war industries. Karen Beck Skold (1980:65) cited an Idaho farm woman who felt that her wartime job in a Portland shipyard was less grueling than the hard work and cold weather she endured on the farm. The number of farm women in Open Country decreased 16 percent from 1940 to 1950, and part of this decline can be attributed to those who left for more promising careers and did not return after the war. About one-half of this migrating farm population can be accounted for in the increased number of women in Open Country towns.

Table 5.2
Number of Open Country Women Older Than
Age 14, 1940–1950

Year	Farm	Nonfarm	Total
1940	2,899	2,698	5,597
1950	2,427	2,869	5,296

Source: U.S. population censuses.

The Open Country farm population decreased slightly in the 1930s, and this trend was intensified in the 1940s and later. As shown in Table 5.3, Iowa population statistics show a net decline in the farm population and an increase in both the urban and rural nonfarm populations, thereby indicating an overall urbanization process which the war intensified.

Table 5.3
Rural and Urban Population of Iowa*
1930–1950

Residence	1930	1940	1950
Urban	979	1084	1251
Rural	1515	1454	1370
Nonfarm	527	537	587
Farm	985	917	783

*Figures expressed in thousands.

Source: U.S. population censuses.

The war increased the mobility of the U.S. population. Further, it expanded the populations of coastal cities and major midwestern industrial cities such as Detroit and Chicago, while it drained the rural areas of Iowa. The Depression slowed the process of urbanization in Iowa, both because adults and children were needed for the survival of farms and because of the lack of opportunity elsewhere (Cochrane 179:123). However, many farm youths were ready to leave as soon as they could. Curtis Harnack (1981:187) wrote of his mother's determination that her children not remain on the farm: "Almost mystically, she had a sense of launching us into the mainstream of future American life, for we would die if we remained where we were born." Harnack, his siblings, and all but one cousin left in the war years and after. The future of American life did not lie in the backwaters of rural Iowa, and the war meant that many rural youths such as Harnack did not have to go home—and they did not.

The net decline of farm population is only a partial description of the demographic change. While many people were leaving the area, people were also moving into Open Country, particularly in the years immediately after the war. Martha, for example, was raised in a city in Ohio and met Henry, a young man from an Open Country farm, when they were both in school. Henry was drafted, but he kept in touch with Martha and saw her whenever his service schedule allowed. After Martha received her B.A. in biology, she and Henry were married while he was still in the service. Martha accepted a secretarial position in Philadelphia so that she could work and be near Henry. When Henry left the service, they moved to Ames, Iowa, where Henry finished college and Martha continued to work as a secretary. In 1949, they moved to Open Country, where Henry took over his parents' farm. His three sisters, who also grew up on the farm, had already left Open Country, married, and settled with their husbands in other states. Thus, while Henry returned to his farming roots, his three sisters moved. Martha, as a new wife, had none of the Open Country enculturation that her sisters-in-law had.

There were numerous similar cases of farmer-soldiers returning with wives who had no experience in farming. Farm women like Martha came from the world outside of Open Country. Conversely, one-time farm girls, like Henry's sisters, often left to study, work, marry, and settle outside of Open Country. This pattern, which came to prevail in postwar years, represented a major discontinuity in the kinship relations and in the practical and emotional attachment of farm women to farming. In fact, in 1950 the extension service listed the scarcity of local marriageable women in rural areas as a particular postwar farm problem (ISES 1950:A10). Men had to seek wives outside their home communities. Whether as soldiers, students, workers, or travellers, men as well as women were reaching outside the community for marriage partners. In 1950, approximately 7 percent of the Open Country population had lived outside the county the previous year (USDC 1953:103). While determining the number of returning natives and the number of newcomers is impossible, if this degree of mobility held constant for 10 years, approximately 70 percent of the people would have lived outside the county, and this would almost certainly include a substantial number on non-natives. A man who married outside the community and brought his wife home was the partner with the stronger community and family ties, while his wife usually came as a stranger to the community, with her only link being through her husband.

European and American history shows a patrilineal tendency in farm land inheritance (Ankarloo 1979; Sachs 1983). After World War II, however, with farm daughters leaving in greater numbers, patrilineal inheritance produced a distinct "patrilocal" type of residence pattern, in which the husband was living close to his kin and the wife was often far removed from her kin. Both the nature of

military service and the GI Bill, which gave veterans support for college educations after the war, in addition to the land inheritance
system, reinforced the patriarchal custom by which married couples
planned their lives according to the career development contingencies and the family imperatives of the men. The "imported" wife was
a stranger in her husband's community, inexperienced in farming,
and had scant extended kin ties within the community.

The degree of their involvement with the farm varied among
the transplanted farm women. Martha, the city woman who came to
Open Country as a wife in 1949, spent much of her time at Henry's
side learning to be a farmer. One of the first tasks, in the coldest
period of the winter they arrived, was to remove the dead trees from
their shelterbelt. Martha, the only help that Henry had, was needed,
and she *wanted* to be part of the farm operation. She read extension
brochures and farm journals and relied heavily on the friendship
and help of an older, more experienced farm woman, as well as a
close circle of four transplanted wives who came to the community
at the same time she did. She started her own poultry enterprise and
did substantial work with other livestock. Other such women had
less interest in doing farm work, but they were all called upon to run
errands, drive tractors, help sort cattle, or help with other work
when an extra pair of hands was needed. Indeed, Henry said that
Martha had the advantage of not having the "bad habits" of some
women who had grown up on the farm—she did not refuse to do any
particular tasks because women in her family had never done them.
Farm women continued to fill the void left by hired farm laborers
and children who never returned after the war. Few of these women
had jobs off the farm.

Among the Open Country women living on farms, the number
working in nonfarm jobs dropped from 171 to 85 between 1940 and
1950 (USDC 1943B:925; USDC 1952A:137). Table 5.4 indicates
that professional and domestic services experienced the greatest
decreases. Part of the decrease can be attributed to escape. Working daughters who were forced by economic necessity to live at
home during the Depression accumulated enough resources to
leave during the war, and their families were no longer dependent
on their incomes. The ongoing consolidation of rural schools
decreased the need for rural teachers, who constituted the majority
of the professional women living on farms before World War II. The
most drastic decline, however, was in the number of domestic service workers living on farms, again reflecting the increasing non-

farm job opportunities for those women who were mobile. Some of the new Open Country women were, like Martha, busy learning farming and helping their husbands establish farm operations, and they are not counted as workers in any of the government's labor force statistics. These factors notwithstanding, the 50 percent decline in farm women in nonfarm employment is significant, particularly in light of the continuing improvement of highways and automotive transportation and the increasing number of farm women with nonfarm backgrounds. The conclusion that farm women were more universally identifying as wives and subsuming their work lives under that of their husbands is justified.

Table 5.4
Change in Number of Open Country Farm and Nonfarm Women with Nonfarm Employment, 1940–1950

Occupation	Farm	Nonfarm
Professional	-27	-3
Managerial	-3	+9
Clerical, sales	+2	+82
Operatives	-5	+34
Domestic service	-72	-38
Other service	+1	+42
Other, unreported	+18	-1
Total	-86	+125
Percent change	-50%	+24%

Sources: U.S. population censuses.

Compared to the prewar period, an increasing percentage of postwar farm women were married. Statistics regarding the marital status of Iowa farm women are not available for all of the census periods, but federal census figures indicate that 25 percent of Iowa farm women over age 15 had never been married in 1930, but the corresponding number was 15 percent in 1960 (USDC 1963:343; USDC 1932:774). Considering only those women older than age 20, 5 percent of Iowa's farm women, compared to 11 percent of its nonfarm women, had never been married in 1960 (USDC 1963:342,343).

For farm women, even more than for other women, the postwar family came to mean the nuclear family of husband, wife, and children. Their own parents and siblings lived elsewhere. In contrast to the prewar situation in which the nucleus of a farm woman's social circle was her extended kin network, the postwar farm woman's link to local society was through her husband and her in-laws. Thus, the husband found himself assuming not only a more central role in teaching his wife the farming trade, but he was also assuming some of the intimate emotional and social functions that had previously been in the domain of a woman's extended kin. More than ever, a wife expected her husband to be her best friend as well as a compatible business partner and companion. Those farm women who did not marry left for the towns and cities.

As illustrated in Table 5.4, Open Country town women increased their participation in nonfarm employment during the 1940s. As mentioned, part of this increase can be interpreted as the movement of employed women from the farm to town. The number of professional women, mainly teachers, living in town decreased, again a product of school consolidation and the general rural-to-urban population shift. Throughout the country, the number of domestic workers decreased drastically in response to the newly available industrial jobs. The number of women managers increased slightly and the number of women working in factories doubled. The increase in jobs for women in retail businesses is directly related to the thriving rural economy that the war brought in the form of the strengthened market for farm products.

The most striking trend was a concentration of women in clerical, sales, and other nonprofessional services, and it is consistent with the findings of Karen Anderson (1981) and Susan Hartmann (1982), who described the postwar restructuring of the gender division in which women were concentrated in the service sector of the postwar labor force. While the overall number of women in the recognized labor force rose, the status of women as workers in the prestigious managerial and professional fields did not.

The total number of Open Country farm and nonfarm women working off the farm rose by only 39 between 1940 and 1950. Adding one farm woman per farm to approximate the number of actual working women results in a substantially higher estimate of working women throughout the decade of the 1940s: 2,675 in 1940 and 2,689 in 1950, representing approximately 50 percent of the total number of working aged women. The major change was not that many women moved into the workforce, but rather that they shifted from self-employed farm work and professional jobs to service work.

The postwar extension service highlighted and elaborated its material on women's housekeeping. Rather than the wartime housekeeping advice on whole wheat flour and canning, the 1946 Open Country women's food and nutrition program featured a unit called "Gracious Family Living" that instructed women in how to plan a meal with "English Family Service," including appropriate table decor and etiquette. In the same year, the local women's program planning committee selected units on the better groomed homemaker, the home water supply, maintaining a standard of living, child development, care of equipment, salads, and preservation for the following year's work (Open Country Extension 1946). The Iowa State Home Economics circular series begun in 1948 had topics dealing with home decoration, cooking, sewing, entertaining, child rearing, grooming, dieting, consumer information, and laundry hints. Typical of the postwar focus on elaborate housekeeping was a 1950 circular entitled "Let's Do Dishes," which gave a detailed description of the proper way to wash dishes (Kagerice 1950).

None of these postwar extension themes reflected conditions specific to farm women. They seemed, instead, to constitute a denial that farm women did farm work and that their role in a family economy was in any way different from that of the majority of non-farm women. Accordingly, in the years after World War II, home economics extension ceased to address only rural women and directed increasing resources toward reaching urban women (Gordy and Gallup 1952:1). As one extension circular maintained, home economics extension logically reached out to urban women because making a division between farm and city women's lives was no longer possible (USDA 1950). Extension clearly envisioned women spending most of their time and energy in the home and leaving the major part of the farm work to their husbands. This change of focus in women's extension promoted the removal from farming of even the diminished number of women who remained in residence on farms.

While women took care of the home after the war, men were in charge of the farming. Anderson (1981) and Hartmann (1982), in separate analyses of the nontraditional work done by women in manufacturing industry during World War II, found that the majority of these women lost their jobs after the war. Rather than retreating from the labor force, however, women moved into an already over-crowded, poorly paid female sector of the labor market. Rather than welding and riveting, women were typing and clerking and doing other work that soon came to be associated with women. Not only did a similar process occur in Open Country towns, a parallel development occurred among Open Country farm women. The women who stayed on the farms expanded and intensified their work as farmers during the war, but this ended with the war. While no valid statistics are available comparing farm women's work with that of women working in nonfarm jobs, indications are found that farm women also gave up some of their work after the war and retreated into stereotypically female roles, including the role as helper to the husband rather than independent producer.

For example, women, who had been the major poultry producers, lost ground after the war. The cash economy that prevailed during wartime effectively did away with the barter system, which was the most common way of marketing eggs even as late as 1940. The wartime poultry boom was, however, short-lived. Even given the heightened wartime demand, as early as 1944 there was a surplus of eggs and production diminished by 10 percent (ISES 1944). After the war, egg production was adjusted further, and this presented the opportunity for the restructuring and modernizing of the egg market, a development that the extension service had envisioned before the war. Extension articles encouraged farmers either to produce eggs solely for their own households or to have large poultry enterprises. As discussed in the following chapter, the enlarged enterprises were to be run by men.

All of the Open Country extension farm planning program committees were limited to men. After the intense physical and emotional energy needed to meet wartime crises, women's farm production saw a pronounced deflation toward the end. The Depression preceding the war was not a viable model for postwar normalcy and even if it had been, return to prewar patterns would not have been easy. The war made lasting social and economic changes, not only in what people did, but also in the way they viewed themselves in relation to the rest of the world, the way they organized their lives, and where they looked for direction.

The role of the government in the lives of rural people changed qualitatively during the 1940s. Once remote to the people of Open Country, government now entered into many aspects of local life. Even during the war, the extension service, which established the rural information system to change the habits of rural people, saw in this network a wider potential for reaching them readily—and permanently—for postwar educational programs (Wilson 1942:11). After the war, production expanded, people were richer, and more people had seen the world outside of Open Country. They had the government (and the war) to thank for freedom and prosperity, and most were ready to receive further direction from the same source.

Americans exalted Americanism and demanded the same strong, unified expression of patriotism in peace that they had during the war. But the tide of postwar patriotism took the form of a standard ideology rather than the overt action of the war period. The Farm Bureau, which before the war had restricted itself to largely nonpolitical administration of the extension service, became the rural voice of the political right (see Berger 1971). Departing from the original aim of teaching practical skills, its popular 4-H program, for example, initiated programs to instill religion and patriotism by means of special ceremonies involving prayer, candles, ritual drama, speeches, songs, pledges, and display of flags (USDA 1945A). Prayer and the Pledge of Allegiance became standard at all Farm Bureau–Extension meetings. Another example of the new patriotism was the pervasive isolation and prejudice against the Open Country Friends Meeting, which had not supported the war. While some Quakers were conscientious objectors during World War I, they and others had been prominent Farm Bureau leaders in the period between World War I and World War II. Quakers never again assumed these central positions even though they were stable, respectable, and prosperous farmers, and most retained their membership.

The Quakers were forced into greater awareness of a phenomenon that touched on other Open Country people in more subtle ways: the focus on "the boys" was nearly as pervasive after the war as during the war. The social perceptions of gender underwent an emotional and cognitive shift, and the Quaker men had not done their duty in being men. Many of the women who came to Open Country after the war had varying war experiences and those who stayed at home certainly did their share to win the war, but no one could match the honor and prestige of a returning soldier. The small rural community fully extended itself in offering a fitting hero's welcome and in offering him the job or opportunity he needed. As Wherry (1945C:811) wrote in her "Country Air" column:

> It will be important when they (the soldiers) return for the boys to find an interest at once, to be busy. That is, after that eon of sleep has

been caught up on. That's why there must be jobs and little businesses that they can get into.

Throughout the United States, returning soldiers were greeted first with celebrations and later with preferential access to jobs, housing, and education. Of the farm machinery that appeared on the market after the war rationing ended, 20 percent was earmarked for returning veterans. Farmtown Presbyterian women gave the returning servicemen red carnations in a ceremony of appreciation.

War distinguished a young man in a qualitatively different way than anything else could. When a rural woman wrote to the *Wallaces' Farmer* editor about her son's problems adjusting to civilian life, she received this advice:

> Better not tell him about the "hardships" civilians had to endure. Service men look at these things differently. And civilians who keep talking about the minor difficulties of war-time life at home simply make a veteran sure that civilians don't know anything about war, can't understand what he has been thru, and aren't worthy of his confidence. . . .
>
> You can help him a lot by your patience, your affection, and your willingness to let him alone (When Frank Gets Back 1945:611).

Or, as the "Country Air" column apologized to the returning heroes:

> [W]e'll be dumb—so dreadfully dumb! We just won't have the background to understand. . . . We'll try, fellows, but we'll miss the boat a lot of times. Be as patient with us as you can (Wherry 1945C:811).

Just as during the war, Open Country women received frequent and persuasive messages about their proper roles, but the emphasis shifted from making sacrifices for the war to making the necessary adjustments for the returning servicemen and structuring the postwar society. Women found many new situations to face after the war, most of which centered around home and family. Articles in *Wallaces' Farmer* in postwar years showed an unmistakeable shift in tone. War messages had celebrated the almost infinite resilience and adaptability of the Iowa farm woman: she could rise to virtually any challenge, she adjusted to wartime shortages, and she helped maintain the morale of both her family and her community. Even if these were not always seen as natural female traits, for the most part, women did what they were called upon to do. After the war, the message was more complicated and ambivalent.

Beginning in 1945, *Wallaces' Farmer* had a steady run of pictures and short news items on farm women who were buying new kitchen equipment. As one woman wrote:

> During the depression years, farm women didn't have the money to improve their homes. When things began to get better, it seemed every extra dollar on the farm was needed to buy new stock, repair machinery or build new fences.
>
> To farm women, it has seemed it has just been year after year of hard work with not much coming our way, but now at last we feel free to make some of those home improvements for which we've waited so long. . . .
>
> Am I dreaming? If I am, don't wake me up! (York 1945:846).

The lead story of the November 3, 1945 issue discussed what women would buy with their Victory Bond money. Farm women reported plans to buy the following equipment: 34 percent would buy refrigerators; 27 percent, stoves; 26 percent, vacuum sweepers; 21 percent, new water systems; 20 percent, washing machines; 19 percent, linoleum; 16 percent, wallpaper; 14 percent, carpets; 18 percent, pressure cookers; 14 percent, bathroom fixtures; 19 percent, radios; 15 percent, electric irons; 10 percent, furnaces (What'll You Buy? 1945:785). Other articles gave instruction in remodeling farm homes, buying home freezers, and using the new food mixes that made cooking easier and faster (Murphy 1948:28; Wherry 1948:83). In the 1940s, many farm homes installed electricity, running water, and other conveniences, which greatly eased women's housework. By 1950, only 151 farm homes in Open Country were without electricity, as compared to 802 homes in 1940 (USDC 1943:495; USDC 1953:184).

In the face of the outmigration of so many farm women and the consequent necessity of attracting nonfarm women as wives, modernizing farm homes could not have been easily sidestepped. Henry said that his parents first installed an indoor water system so that Martha, who they hoped would be their daughter-in-law, would not be discouraged by the thought of farm life. They need not, however, have worried: Martha's attraction was to Henry. In the prevailing norms of the postwar period, woman's role as wife superseded concerns for physical comfort, as well as career plans and relations with other women, whether they were sisters, mothers, or friends.

The pervasiveness of male-female sexual ties has, since World War II, come to be so commonplace that it passes almost without comment. One early manifestation of this pervasiveness was the theme of sex appeal in advertisements for household products which had no obvious or direct connection to sex. While advertisements in *Wallaces' Farmer* were still directing women to buy poultry feed and equipment, some of the new advertisements showed thin and glamorous women in ecstasy over household products. A young woman was shown on a full page hugging a box of Tide detergent (Wallaces' Farmer 1948:250). Another full page advertisement showed a woman floating in space, ecstatic over Breeze dishwashing detergent, which was "MILDER than the MILDEST Beauty Soaps!" (Wallaces' Farmer 1948:211). The point of wanting dishwashing detergent to be like mild beauty soap was obviously to please a man.

The silliness of these advertisements and the selfishness implied in the consumer mentality was not lost on anyone. Alongside this image of luxury and ease was a new and overt expression of scorn for the pampered woman. A hired man wrote a bitterly humorous letter complaining about the scatterbrained farm woman who would not prepare the quality of food he deserved. She had a brand new stove, but this did no good, because she was always running off to town and never stayed home to cook carefully. Although she bought prepared foods, she managed to ruin them. As soon as she put something on her new stove, she would talk on the telephone or read women's magazines until it burned. The hired man reported that he had seeded a fine vegetable garden that she could not be bothered to cultivate or harvest (Country Cooking? I Eat It! 1948:281). The inept woman who could not handle her housekeeping was the butt of derisive jokes. In a *Wallaces' Farmer* (1948:297) cartoon, an obviously bored man was sitting at the table saying to his frowning mate, "Just like mother used to make—and oh, boy, was she a lousy cook!" These are just two examples that represent the rural manifestation of the postwar misogyny which was more generally displayed in the work of Philip Wylie (1955), who coined the word "momism" to described the disdain felt for the roles of women.

The women remodelling houses and keeping everyone happy and the men farming might have constituted a system in which parallel spheres of equal value existed for women and men, but this was not the case. While some attempt was made to portray the housewife's role as an extremely important one for society, there were material indications that men's work was more highly valued. On the farm new machinery, chemicals and hybrids changed the nature of farming and the skills required. Men needed training and development to do their work. A *Wallaces' Farmer* article on education for farmers discussed the increasing complexity and "scientific" nature of farming and found that successful farmers felt the need for two years of agricultural training in college (What Education Do Farmers Need? 1948:134). No mention was made that women received any formal education. Iowa State College had a substantial home economics program, but few claimed that this training was essential for a successful farm women. While a good wife was an asset on the farm (farming was, after all, becoming a complicated and intricate operation), she was strictly an assistant. An article entitled "Farm Records are Important" (1948:185) told of the careful records one farmer kept:

> He calls on his wife to look over the final figures on his record. Sure enough, he had forgotten all about the chickens; [he] has to start over.

The article did not broach the possibility that the wife herself might have been in a better position to account for the chickens.

A sense of deflation in farm women's lives was most poignant in the "Sarah Jane Says" column, the on-going tale of Sarah Jane's poultry enterprise and a good-natured encouragement for other women in dealing with their poultry flocks. Still writing in 1948, Sarah Jane said

> I have felt for some time that I have hardly enough to say to warrant writing a letter. But I will try to write once more, anyhow (The Farm Flock 1948:360).

Rose, who kept the detailed records of her wartime cream and egg accounts, made fewer and less reliable entries after the war, and her last entry was in 1946. Although she kept a laying flock for many years afterwards, she never again kept written records.

For men, the intensity of feeling associated with the war lasted long after the immediate postwar years: men's war stories are still told and retold. In 1982, a conversation involving a local farmer and a Farmtown businessman turned rather naturally to a favorite subject—World War II experiences. When asked about the centrality of the war, both said they found themselves thinking about the war years much more than their duration suggested. Both said that their lives were greatly enriched by the travel and informal education received during their service. Although neither had actually been in combat, they recounted in detail where they were stationed and what they did. Also in 1982, a World War II veteran who led the parade and gave the Farmtown Centennial celebration opening speech chastised the Centennial Steering Committee for not orienting the yearlong festivities around veterans, stating that Farmtown would not exist if the veterans had not served their country. Many of the World War II servicemen maintained continuing close ties with their former comrades. One reported a continuing "round-robin" letter among a group of 20 former servicemen; another said that he and his war buddies got together for a three- to four-day annual reunion; another who rarely got as far from home as Minneapolis or Des Moines took a vacation to New York to visit with an old army friend. Few women maintained these kinds of close ties with those they had known during the war, unless the women happened to be married to men who had maintained those ties.

When asked about their wartime activities, servicemen's wives invariably responded with further details about what the men had done. This is partially understandable in light of the realities of military life. Having no control over his orders, a man by necessity was the independent variable in a couple's plans. The date of marriage, the place of residence, and the amount of time spent together depended on the contingencies of a serviceman's life rather than on the needs of the woman. The GI Bill, passed after the war to finance college educations for veterans, was the first impetus for many veterans to attend college. Of the veterans eligible for the benefits, 97 percent were male. Since a large number of veterans married and the GI Bill did not provide sufficient money to support a family, veterans' wives found themselves working at supplementary jobs. As Anderson (1981:174–75) wrote of wives of World War II veterans

> [T]he essential challenge was to reconcile the autonomy and competence they had demonstrated while on their own with the needs and wishes of their returning husbands. In order to promote domestic harmony they were told to subordinate their interests and needs to those of their husbands.

As with military service, the man's education also meant that the place of residence, the length of time spent in the college city, and the amount of time spent together also depended on the husband's needs. Those Open Country farmers who returned after serving in the military and (occasionally) receiving college educations were coming home to farms, a residence again determined by their occupations and foreign to the experiences of many of their wives.

The extension service gave rural women advice with regard to adjusting to returning soldiers after the women themselves were accustomed to coping independently. One extension circular told the story of Mrs. Green and her preparations to relinquish her own authority, to ease her four children into accepting the father in the home again, and to help Mr. Green adjust. While everyone had to change, the responsibility for orchestrating and monitoring the process clearly rested with Mrs. Green, not Mr. Green. To keep her family happy, Mrs. Green had to be watchful and willing to change her approach:

> I must plan for signs of irritability in both children and father. I must immediately notice signs of fatigue. I must notice whether the children are avoiding their father or are spending most of their free time away from home. For, if I'm not getting results I must change my plan (USDA 1945B:8).

While this may be read as a statement that a woman was capable and emotionally stable, it also may be read as a statement that a woman's place was in the home, making her husband's job as the breadwinner as easy as possible. Thus, her capability was used to make herself dependent on the returning serviceman.

Experts in family focussed on the nuclear family in the postwar period. A study done at Iowa State College on Iowa families' adjustments to wartime separations and reunions began by reducing the question of family adjustment to marital adjustment:

> The literature on dismemberment is scanty as far as reference to family adjustment *as families* is concerned. Most or our hypotheses will, therefore, be drawn from the studies of marriage adjustment and the crises of demoralization and change of status. . . .
>
> Certainly a good marriage adjustment between man and wife is the foundation of family adjustment (Hill and Boulding 1949:16).

Moreover, the study found that a woman's independence or

close associations with extended family were negatively correlated with a good reunion adjustment with her husband. A woman's happiness in childhood and adolescence and a "low neurotic score" were associated with a good adjustment to separation, but not to reunion with her husband (Hill and Boulding 1949:154). The report established as a model the woman who sacrificed her personal goals for those of her mate and denigrated the woman who "wanted to be boss" (Hill and Boulding 1949:179). Women were needed for the war effort, but they were not supposed to take advantage of the national crisis by being bossy; they were not supposed to assume that because they had men's jobs and temporary independence they now had the same prerogatives as men.

The record from rural Iowa is consistent with what happened nationally in women's recruitment into the war effort. Although women, as typified by the Rosie the Riveter figure, did enter traditional male jobs, they did not enter as equals of men. As Doris Herrick Cochrane of the Business and Professional Women's Federation warned during the war, "Equality for the woman worker during the war is essential if we are to have equality in the postwar world" (Cochrane 1943:216). In the nation as a whole, women were recruited into heavy industry only when manpower was clearly insufficient, and they lost their "men's" jobs after the war when confronted with a re-entrenched gender division (Anderson 1981; Hartmann 1982).

The national government itself was a model for the ambiguous position of women in wartime and the ensuing re-entrenchment. Eleanor Straub, who studied women's equity issues in the intragovernmental political process during World War II, found that the Women's Bureau of the Department of Labor was largely ignored and without real power. In articulating women's interests, the women in the government found themselves shunted to the side. The Women's Advisory Committee (WAC), established to represent women's interests in the War Manpower Commission (WMC), never achieved an effective voice, in spite of straightforward resolutions passed requesting that women be part of the WMC process. In effect, the WAC functioned solely for publicity and propaganda. Thus, while women were needed for the war effort, the government allowed no powerful advocate for women's interests either during or after the war.

Straub attributed the women's weakness in setting policy to the diffuseness of their plans, the lack of an organized constituency, and the continual care to deny that they wanted anything for women in their own right. In other words, the pains they took to distance themselves from feminism guaranteed that women would not emerge in powerful positions. Straub (1973:254) concluded:

> No evidence indicates that a more avowedly feminist stance would have improved the WAC's record, but in hewing a middle course, the committee undoubtedly made it easier for the WMC to ignore its presence.

A parallel conclusion emerges from the experiences of Open Country women: No evidence indicates that a more avowedly feminist stance would have enhanced the position of Open Country women, but in failing to articulate their position as women, they undoubtedly made it easier for everyone to assume that they existed first and foremost to solve the problems of their husbands.

Conclusion

World War II made vast changes in the lives of rural Iowa women. Many left the area as outside opportunities arose, but those who stayed intensified their work, whether on the farm or in town. They made more money than before, which eventually translated into material improvements in their living standards. In spite of these gains and a small increase in the number of women in the workforce, they achieved no lasting political or economic power from their war experience. Instead, the war brought a renewed emphasis on men and the value of male experiences. Open Country women learned a new and more intense lesson that their value lay primarily in supporting and enabling men to do the critical work of protecting and leading society.

This chapter has provided an overview of the war experience, including the economic, demographic, and social disruptions of the 1940s. The following chapter takes a longer range look at one thread of this change—the egg industry and the shift from the dispersed, small scale enterprises of farm women to the concentrated, large scale egg factories run by men.

CHAPTER 6

Eggs: A Case in Point

Practically all the eggs produced in Iowa come from farm flocks. The farm flock is cared for and managed by farm women. The poultry industry of Iowa is a farm woman's enterprise. The farm woman is not only interested in eggs as food for her family, but also as a salable surplus product. With the money received from the sale of poultry products, she buys food and clothing, educates her children, and buys other essentials and meets debts.

—Iowa State Extension Pamphlet, "A Project of Marketing and Nutrition Relating to Eggs," 1929.

Representative Joseph Vigorito: "The days when the housewife took care of the strawberry patch and the egg money, I guess, are gone, right?"

John Wallace, President of the United Egg Producers: "Those are pretty well gone."

—Egg Price Situation Hearing, U.S. House of Representatives, April 10, 1974.

In the 45 years between 1929 and 1974, egg production in the United States shifted from being women's work to men's work. Once a dispersed, labor-intensive industry, it became concentrated and capital-intensive (See Table 6.1). Herein lies an account of the change and the subsequent resistance to that change as it occurred in Open Country.

Table 6.1
Concentration of Egg Production in Open Country
1925–1982

Year	Average Hens per Flock	Percentage of Farms with Hens	Number of Hens*
1925	146	95	254
1930	169	98	325
1935	164	95	312
1940	154	94	288
1945	202	94	371
1950	186	88	321
1954	235	85	389
1959	280	75	378
1964	257	51	210
1969	388	24	139
1974	1,007	11	153
1978	595	6	47
1982	na	4	na

*Values expressed in thousands.
Source: U.S. agricultural censuses.

Although stating that no men ever did any poultry work is inaccurate, work with poultry belonged in the women's sphere of the pre-1940 farm economy. Being associated with women, poultry carried a certain stigma for men. The current slang association of the word *chicken* with cowardice conveys some of the disdain men felt toward poultry. The male sphere of farming, which included work with cattle and horses, was tied to the symbolism of the cowboy and the bravery and strength of conquering a frontier. An exchange at an 1894 Open Country Farm Institute illustrates the low status of poultry as farm production. The Institute speakers, who were farm experts, were men. They spoke seriously and at length on such topics as dairying, hogs, and grains; but poultry was a joke. A man who reluctantly consented to speak on the poultry topic proceeded to humorously distance himself from it:

> They could not have made a worse selection [than me, as speaker] for this subject; it is one that I am not at all interested in: I have not read up on the subject at all; not even read the poultry department to the agricultural papers that I take. . . . (Open Country Bulletin 1894).

Another expert used the humor of poultry to express his power of control over his farm and household:

> I presume you would not think a cattle man would have anything to do with ducks, [but] my wife got it into her head one time that she would like to keep a few ducks. I finally consented and she got her ducks. The result was the ducks began to raise Cain and I began to raise Cain and my wife being of a kind disposition sold the ducks (Open Country Bulletin 1894).

One participant protested that, in spite of this, poultry could mean real money on the farm:

> A friend at Rock Rapids said to me the other day that two men came to him to straighten up their money matters, one came to borrow one hundred and sixty dollars. What for? To pay his store bill. The same day the other man came to him and paid a note of one hundred sixty dollars, *men in about the same circumstances.* One paid his note, the other borrowed the one hundred and sixty dollars he paid in. Now then, he asked the question, "How did you get this $160.00? Didn't you have any store bills to pay?" "No, we paid our store bills with poultry. We keep some chickens, ducks, etc. and we keep our store bills paid up." The other man didn't keep any poultry, consequently his bill was standing and he had to borrow money to pay his store bill. This is a good practical lesson for the farmer. Statistics show that the poultry and poultry products are worth pretty near double what corn or cattle or any of these products are worth, so that while they are little things, they could amount to a great deal and should not be overlooked (Open Country Bulletin 1894; emphasis added).

Noteworthy in this story is that the characters are men. Although the poultry enterprise would have been run by the one farmer's wife, in this context, with the proceeds being quantified as a factor in the overall financial health of the farm family, men were doing the computations.

Further, that the speaker said that two men were in *about the same circumstances* even though one had $160 to invest and one was borrowing $160 is remarkable. What he undoubtedly meant was that the farmers had approximately the same size farm and approximately the same number of cattle and hogs. In the male farming system, poultry was not normally something that contributed to a man's worth and it did not matter that one farm had poultry and the other did not. Poultry was woman's thing and as such, was qualitatively different from man's things, which established the wealth of the farm. So separate was woman's poultry operation that the customary procedure on a tenant farm was to exempt poultry products from the tenancy contract. The common practice was for the farm owner to receive a specified share of what was produced on the farm, but poultry products were not included with other farm commodities. A farm owner permitted the tenant woman to keep poultry, to feed them from the farm supply of grain, and to retain the poultry products and income for the household. Poultry did not figure into the cash farming enterprise. Being in woman's sphere, it was separate and men were surprised when they found it had any monetary significance at all.

The ascribed triviality of poultry notwithstanding, farm experts began to contest women's management of Iowa's poultry. In 1908, Iowa State College established a poultry department; in 1914, the new agricultural extension service started poultry improvement work. Poultry being a woman's enterprise, women were the first to seek help from the extension service. However, extension assigned poultry to the male sphere and extension personnel sought to upgrade Iowa poultry production by shifting it to the commodity farm system of the men. The goal of the poultry experts was to transform poultry from what they called a "sideline" to an integral part of the farm economy. Women were a hindrance to this transformation.

An historical account of the poultry industry summarized the difficulties in transforming it into a real *agribusiness*:

> The farm experts reckoned you could not compete with a system in which labor was free, feed was free, and the farm wife was counting on this whole thing for her spending money (Sawyer 1971:36).

Feed was considered to be free because much of it would have been wasted if the hens had not eaten it. George Stewart (1946:157), an Iowa State College poultry expert, estimated that 100 chickens could make efficient use of what they could scavenge in a farmyard. In addition to household scraps, they ate grass (farm homes did not have lawns to mow), weeds, insects, waste from butchering, excess garden produce, and spilled grain. Labor was considered free because farm analysts did not accord women's labor a monetary value in the farm economy. With "free" labor and feed, egg production remained outside the usual male farm accounting system.

Interviewed in 1982, Hans described his wife Sharon's poultry enterprise, an enterprise which supported their household during their first years of marriage:

> We got married in 1922, and we started with chickens right then. . . . She [Sharon] did everything in raising them as far as that goes. I kept the buildings clean and got the feed ground. I put the feed in the bin, but she got it out of there and put it in the feeders.

While chickens could scratch for themselves during good weather, obtaining good year-round egg production necessitated feeding them. Hans remembered adopting the feeding program recommended by the extension service in Ames:

> I was one of the first ones to mix mash. We couldn't buy no concentrate for them at that time. We had to buy meat scraps and ground up corn and oats and oyster shells and middlings. We always put mids in. That's a by-product of wheat. . . . Then the veterinarian said, "You guys raise a lot of chickens. You should feed them better, too. I've got the Ames formula." So he wrote down the Ames formula and I went and mixed it myself. I didn't have a grinder then, but we got a grinder to come and grind some oats and corn and we even put some alfalfa in.

Also recommended by the extension service was careful culling of the flock. Stewart (1946:161) wrote that in 1920 the poultry extension workers from Ames held 6,000 poultry culling demonstrations, with a total attendance of 56,815. A snapshot of a culling demonstration held in Open Country in 1926 showed only women in attendance. Hans told of culling one-third of the laying flock each year:

> We soon raised 500 chicks. But half of them would be roosters. [We'd have] 250 pullets [hens less than one year old]. We kept the best pullets out of those and we'd have 500 hens because we'd cull them out. Some of them you'd keep for three years.

Marketing the eggs was as simple as transporting them to town where a retailer/egg handler sold them or shipped them to points east. Like most other women, Sharon took them to a general store where she traded for groceries and other household items:

> You'd bring the eggs to the grocery store and you'd get one cent more for them than you would get at the produce store. They did that

to get the trade. . . . They knew they were going to get paid for their groceries.

Although Sharon had adopted the recommendations for feeding and culling her laying flock, her marketing and accounting procedures were not quantified. A major component of the poultry professionals' campaign was the move to quantify the factors of production. As part of the household economy, eggs had use value. They were food for the family, but their trade also meant that the women could purchase the flour, shoes, cloth, and school tablets that their families used. Often, as with Sharon's enterprise, the egg accounts were kept by the merchants, as farm women avoided quantifying the value of poultry products themselves. When I asked Ruth, born in 1892, if women ever kept records of their poultry enterprise, she replied,

> Oh yes, they kept their own money. They didn't keep books. . . .
> When they got some butter or egg money they used it for any-
> thing—household money, groceries or anything.

For Ruth, the significant thing about women's money was not the precise quantity (they did not keep books), rather the value lay in what they were able to buy. Ruth referred to the *use* of money, not the quantity. Money was, for women, something to use rather than to count.

This type of low-capital, nonquantified egg production was in direct contrast to the image of the mechanized and efficient poultry business advocated in a 1928 Iowa State College thesis. Attempting to redirect the dominant mode of thinking about poultry, the thesis proposed that each Iowa farm was a business; and within this business there were several departments. In the poultry department, the hen was the machine, the feed was the raw material, and the eggs were the output (Termohlen 1928:82). Rejecting the informal character of production and marketing, the thesis built a case against the marketing of eggs in small stores that did not maintain proper records (Termohlen 1928:52). With more efficient selling and grading of eggs, Iowa producers would have incentive to produce more top quality eggs, thereby causing the price of eggs to rise.

To promote more quantified recording of poultry enterprises, extension initiated the poultry record flock project. Approximately 50 poultry producers from across the state were selected as leaders and model farmers who would diffuse improved poultry raising practices, including that of quantifying the expenses and output. Managers of the poultry record flocks received printed postcards with blanks for the numbers describing each laying operation—the number of hens, number of eggs, prices, costs, death loss, and number of chicks purchased. For sending in these cards each month, the flock owner received an annual analysis of her (or his) operation and individual suggestions for improvement.

Some of these record flocks were in men's names and some were in women's names. In 1932, for example, 24 of the 50 Iowa record flocks were in recognizably feminine names (ISES 1932). Extension saw this as a problem. If poultry could be considered part of the farm commodity economy rather than being an adjunct to the household economy, it would warrant greater capital outlays and more systematic labor inputs. A cover of the 1930 Poultry Record Report of the extension service was a split-frame cartoon. On the left side was a modern truck heading toward a bank. A panel on the side of the truck read, "New Era Poultry Farm. B. Bright, Owner"; the caption read, "Farm Man and Wife Operating a Good Poultry Unit." On the right side of the cartoon was a dilapidated car going to a building labelled "Mortgages, Loans." Painted on the car was "Sideline Poultry Farm, J. Gloom, Owner"; the caption read, "A Little Help from the Husband Needed Here." The extension service clearly saw improvements in terms of male involvement.

The efforts of the extension service notwithstanding, poultry remained largely a woman's enterprise. Even some of those record flocks that were in men's names were actually managed by women. One of the 1937 monthly reports submitted in a male name had a written apology for being late: "Illness, building construction and many men to feed prevented getting report on time."[1] The fact that "many men to feed" delayed the report indicates that a woman was actually reporting. Moreover, the man did not submit the report when his wife was unable to do it; it waited until she had time to do it.

Even with the casual, unquantified production procedures of women, Iowa became the leading state in egg production (Mason 1946:109). This production was dispersed over a large number of small flocks. Writing in 1946, Stewart (1946:166) stated that, from the beginning, farm flocks could be classified in four groups:

[1] *Backyard flocks* of 10 to 50 hens to produce eggs and meat for the farm table;

[2] *Pin-money flocks* of 50 to 100 hens to supply spending money for the family in addition to eggs and meat for the table;

[3] *Grocery-bill flocks* of 100 to 200 hens to provide enough income to cover most of the grocery bills; [and]

[4] *Semi-commercial flocks* of 200 hens or more to supply a fairly large portion of the total farm income and place the poultry enterprise on a level with that of dairy cattle, hogs, etc.

Leaving aside the possible arguments to the contention that a flock of 200 hens was "on a level" with major livestock, assessing Open Country laying flocks in these categories reveals that the largest number were "grocery-bill flocks" in 1940. That year, Open Country farms had 137 backyard flocks, 316 pin-money flocks, 814 grocery-bill flocks, and 603 semicommercial flocks (USDC 1942A:239–40).

Often women's egg money saved their farms during the Depression. With no money realized from men's commodity production, egg income, although small, was crucial. A 1934 extension circular stated that poultry was a leading source of farm income in Iowa (Henderson and Vernon 1934:4). Extension record flocks, unlike other farm production enterprises, showed consistent net profits.[2] Not only did egg money pay household expenses, as mentioned in Chapter 3 egg trade was also used for a veterinarian's bill, farm machinery, and land purchase.

Costs of raising and marketing eggs increased with state involvement and regulation. The Iowa Legislature passed the first law relating to eggs in 1924. This law established the mandatory licensing of egg handlers, with the exception of farmers who sold directly from their farm. All of the eggs offered for sale by an egg dealer had to be candled, that is, they were held up to a light and checked for cracked shells, blood spots, meat spots, movement of the yolks or enlarged air cells inside the shells. In 1933, a new hatchery code was instituted to upgrade the quality of eggs and poultry and to do away with informal accounting procedures. By this code, hatcheries were barred from giving away chicks or selling them for less than the cost of production. Further, production costs were controlled by establishing a minimum wage for all hatchery workers. To maintain the quality of chicks, eggs smaller than 23 ounces per dozen could not be incubated and no chicks could be substituted on an order (Open Country Bulletin 1933). These standardization laws helped promote higher production standards. The producer who adhered to these standards did not have to contend with competition from the shoestring operations that did not weigh and measure their production factors. Some of these shoestring operations were run by farm women from their homes, and they lost these businesses. For the farm women who had been using low-priced hatching services, the new code meant higher production costs. With these higher costs, their profits depended on a correspondingly higher market price for eggs.

Increased production costs were detrimental to Iowa women who marketed eggs, because their profits depended, to a large extent, on low production costs. The average Iowa producer price of eggs was 41.1 cents per dozen in 1920, but egg prices fell rapidly after World War I and did not reach World War I levels again until the 1970s (See Table 6.2). The 1930 price was less than one-half that of 1920. In addition to the major fluctuations, the prices shifted

Table 6.2
Average Iowa Producer Price
Per Dozen Eggs, 1909–1982

Year	Price	Year	Price
1909	18.9¢	1943	34.7¢
1915	18.2	1944	29.8
1917	30.8	1945	33.1
1919	39.3	1950	29.2
1920	41.1	1955	31.9
1921	26.2	1960	28.0
1929	26.8	1963	26.4
1930	19.7	1964	25.3
1932	11.8	1967	30.8
1934	14.3	1971	30.3
1936	18.8	1974	46.3
1938	17.0	1978	38.8
1940	14.4	1980	47.0
1942	27.8	1982	46.6

Sources: USDA, 1965, Prices Received by Farmers for Chickens, Turkeys, and Eggs, p. 130; Statistical Yearbooks, 1964–1983.

according to the season and the local market. While the average Iowa price of eggs decreased to 11.1 cents per dozen in 1933, many Open Country farm women reported local prices as low as six cents per dozen and one farm woman mentioned selling eggs for as little as two cents per dozen. Egg prices were not dependable, and women minimized their production costs by making do with the available facilities and substituting labor for capital when they could.

Most of Iowa's poultry enterprises were still run by women with relatively low cash-flow levels through the 1940s. Sally, born in 1934, was one of many reporting similar situations:

> She [Mother] had 500 chickens. . . . Saturday afternoon you took the eggs to town and sold them and you bought groceries. . . . She always made sure the egg money bought the groceries. If there was any money left over we could get something else, but the egg money pretty well was grocery money. . . . Everybody had chickens then.

In 1942, *Wallaces' Farmer* conducted a survey in which the editors posed the following problem: Mary earns $4 per week working for John, a farmer. They marry. Should Mary still be paid $4 each week? Of the women surveyed, 50 percent thought Mary should get an allowance as compared to only 36 percent of the men. Younger people were more in favor of an allowance than were older people. But many said that Mary would get egg money and this was better than an allowance. One reply was, "The egg and cream money belongs to the wife. Her husband doesn't have to give it to her." (Should Egg Money be Mary's Share? 1942:140).[3]

Farm advisers continued to chip away at this pattern through the 1940s. Articles in *Wallaces' Farmer* tried to interest men in poultry. One wartime article, addressed to women, urged them to enlist the help of their husbands and then provided a hint on a way this could be done:

> In Greene County, a young wife told me she turned the trick by showing her husband the cost accounts of her laying flock. They looked pretty good alongside his ups-and-downs in cattle feeding (Thompson 1942:61).

The appeal to men was in terms of money and the assumption was that the farmer might then consider it as the same kind of enterprise as his cattle operation. The modern "young wife" raising poultry had quantified her proceeds and could demonstrate her effectiveness in terms a man could understand. Supposedly, through his input, the laying flock would be upgraded to be an integral part of the farm commodity economy—forseeably, an attractive alternative to cattle feeding. If he could understand that money could be made, a man would then want to raise poultry, the "young wife" would have more leisure, and the poultry enterprise would flourish. Getting the man to take charge was progressive.

This 1942 story of favorable cost accounts as incentive for more male investment in egg production was part of a major turn in the egg industry as a result of the increased profits that the war brought to egg producers. In the 1920s farm women like Sharon combined the production of eggs and the production of chickens into one enterprise. By the 1930s, geneticists were developing new leghorn varieties which were especially suited for egg laying and unsuited for meat production. This, together with Japanese-Americans' discovery of how to determine the sex of newly hatched chicks, made it technically possible to purchase only female chicks for egg producing flocks and to completely avoid handling male chicks or poultry meat. During World War II, such enterprises became economically feasible as well. A 1943 report stated that, with wartime demand, for the first time entrepreneurs could make profits by building "egg and broiler factories":

> A decade ago the broiler factory was just a crazy idea of a few poultrymen. Today egg and broiler factories are classified essential war industries. . . . No housekeeper, no matter how neat, worries as much about cleanliness as the factory-broiler growers (quoted in Sawyer 1971:80–1).

By putting laying hens in separate wire cages, more birds could be housed in a given space, the feed input and egg output for each bird could be efficiently monitored, the operation could be mechanized and sanitized to a greater degree than before, and the labor input per bird could be decreased. Although establishing an egg factory necessitated a considerable outlay of capital, such an investment could be profitable if the demand for eggs was sufficient, which it was during the war.

The leaders in the new egg industry were on the Atlantic coast and major facilities were soon established in California. The *1945 Iowa Year Book of Agriculture* states:

Historically it is probably true that Iowa has not been a leader in promoting the type of results that are associated with specialization in the chicken business. The commercial producers of the Eastern Seaboard with their high-producing costs are the specialists who have led the field in promoting pure bred strains, culling, and methods of intensive feeding and care. As a result their rates of lay have been and still are the nation's best (Hampton 1946:39).

But Iowa women's egg production also increased substantially during World War II: Iowa produced 214 million dozen eggs in 1940 and 370 million dozen in 1945. Gross egg income went from $31 million to $121 million in the same period (Mason 1946:114). Iowa record flocks showed major gains both in total net income and in net income per bird (see Table 6.3). Farm women accomplished these increases with their dispersed, small-scale enterprises; they did not have access to the capital necessary to build "egg factories." Adopting "egg factory" production depended on men, both on the farm and in the financial institutions, being willing to invest.

The increased volume of eggs mandated different methods of marketing and handling. New processing techniques were developed to handle the increased volume of wartime egg production and to make it suitable for military purposes. Major food companies built egg processing plants. By 1945, 48 egg breaking plants, which reduced eggs to liquid form, and 14 egg drying plants were in operation in Iowa (Mason 1946:113,115).[4] Furthermore, the practice of trading eggs for groceries nearly disappeared.

Remembering the sudden drop in farm commodity prices after World War I, farm people were understandably concerned about what would happen to the farm economy after World War II. Eggs were already in surplus by 1944 and Iowa production had wavered slightly in response, but the government kept prices relatively stable by buying surplus eggs and storing them in dried form. In 1945, *Wallaces' Farmer* surveyed Iowa farm people about what they believed the government should do to regulate the price of eggs if the market price dropped below 20 cents per dozen. Only 14 percent favored letting the market set the price with no government support; 13 percent were undecided. Others favored distribution of surplus eggs through food stamps, continued government purchase and storage of the surplus, or cash subsidies. The report of the poll concluded:

Table 6.3
Proceeds From Iowa Extension
Record Laying Flocks
1930–1957

Year	Gross	Net	Profit per Hen
1930	$ 876.54	$ 384.14	$1.86
1931	596.22	233.54	1.14
1932	444.45	178.56	.60
1933	500.26	176.12	.72
1934	569.46	160.72	.64
1935	1174.15	469.30	1.55
1936	828.20	272.05	.98
1937	884.78	296.23	.99
1938	818.55	444.39	1.59
1939	662.73	297.30	1.01
1940	937.35	456.48	1.36
1941	1169.62	678.85	2.29
1942	1970.87	1091.42	2.42
1943	2021.47	1153.27	3.56
1944	1678.93	752.04	2.40
1945	1763.69	942.95	3.58
1946	1262.71	390.60	1.43
1947	1485.19	431.17	1.93
1948	1830.90	594.12	2.40
1949	1419.04	392.58	1.67
1950	1135.94	153.62	.53
1951	2164.23	591.75	1.56
1952	1537.86	−71.95	−.09
1953	2019.21	525.23	1.42
1954	1320.91	−213.21	−.52
1955	1911.77	520.25	1.15
1956	1937.67	364.40	.75
1957	1686.93	313.28	.70

Source: Iowa State Extension Service, yearly reports of record flock project.

Undecided votes were scarce on this question. Most folks had ideas on what ought to be done. Only 13 percent declined to express opinions. And there were fewer undecided women than men.

That shows who raises the chickens in Iowa. And who worries more about egg prices (What Price for Eggs? 1945:282).

Women *were* concerned about the egg business and were not prepared to relinquish their part in it.

Farm prices rose during the war, and the U.S. government had nominally supported egg prices, eggs being one of the fourteen "Steagall Commodities" (Cochrane 1979:143–44). These supports extended to 1948, but since that time egg prices have been determined in the market. As expressed in a 1978 report, "The egg subsector, with other poultry subsectors, has been a leader in nonprice coordination arrangements" (Schrader et al. 1978:75). The "nonprice coordination" held egg prices fairly constant in the 20 years following the war (see Table 6.2). The 1963 average Iowa egg price of 26.4 cents per dozen matched the low prices of the 1920s. The only way egg producers could survive with this price situation was to decrease the unit costs of production. To the extension service, this meant increased scale of production and capital expenditures—which men controlled.

More and more men entered the egg business following the expanded egg economy of World War II, a move that the extension service promoted. Before and during World War II, approximately one-half of the state record flocks were entered in women's names. Beginning in 1945, however, only one recognizably female name was among the list of 55 record flock keepers in Iowa (ISES 1945). In the 1950 Plan of Work for the state extension service one criterion for selection of the farm cooperators for the record flock project was male involvement. Besides youth, previous practice of keeping poultry records, and community leadership the extension service required that "both man and wife [be] interested in improving the income from poultry sufficiently to make changes . . . (ISES 1950:41)."

While apparently quasi-parallel in requiring both "man and wife" to participate, the effect was to disallow egg enterprises run by women alone. The point of this criterion could only have been to make sure that men were involved and that the time and resources of extension personnel would not be taken up in dealing with women, who had no real power to effect the kinds of changes promoted by extension.

Women, however, were still claiming the egg money and they resisted losing it. A 1948 *Wallaces' Farmer* survey asked farm households to respond to the question of who did most of the work with poultry. Fifty-one percent of those responding said the wife; 30 percent the husband; 15 percent both; and 4 percent hired help and

children (Chickens?—That's Woman's Job 1948:805). A picture of a
young, pretty woman carrying a basket of eggs accompanied a
1949 extension article on farm flocks. The caption underneath read,
"She's the power behind the 'farm flock' on most midwest farms"
(Bodensteiner 1949:11). Unlike the advice that tried to lure men
into poultry production, this article stated that the poultry flock
should not be so large that it would require the men's time:

> [N]o chickens at all or a very few chickens failed to use the farm wife's
> time and skill to best advantage. Keeping a large flock, on the other
> hand, took the man's time and skill away from other farm enter-
> prises. And on a typical Corn Belt farm it seldom pays to raise fewer
> hogs in order to raise more chickens (Bodensteiner 1949:11).

The article stated that, although chickens yielded the greatest profit
for the amount of feed they consumed, the labor required could be
invested in hog production more profitably.

The contradictory pulls took some men into major investments
in poultry, but left most of the low-capital enterprises in the
women's domain in the years immediately following the war.
Stories of women's egg money reached into the 1950s. Dorothy,
born in 1932, was supported by her parents until she completed two
years of college and received a teaching certificate in 1952. She
remembered her mother's egg enterprise of approximately 200
hens providing for special purchases more often than it did for basic
things such as groceries:

> Her [egg] money went for us for special things. . . . Like when I was in
> college, I'm sure the five bucks that came in my letters were from egg
> money. . . . She bought a set of dishes she wanted and she liked
> clothes and lipstick and things like that. . . . Through the 1940s up to
> 1952, that's the time I really remember as getting money from the
> egg money.

A 1956 Wisconsin extension analysis of midwestern trends in the
poultry industry stated that the major obstacle to eliminating small
flocks and rationalizing the industry was that "on many farms the income from the farm flock goes to the housewife," and she insisted
on maintaining her enterprise (Wisconsin State Extension Service
1956:46). The farm experts were, indeed, contending with a practice
ensconced in tradition. Chapter 3 described the importance of
women's egg income in pre-World War II Open Country household

economy; quantitative and qualitative changes in egg economics came in the years following.

The laying flocks in the Iowa extension service's record flock project were farm flocks of several hundred hens. These enterprises were never modelled on the large-scale production systems that had arisen during the war, but they did receive the most up-to-date advice available from the poultry department at Iowa State College. Following the advice of the poultry experts, the managers of these flocks did increase the scale of operation. Between 1950 and 1957 flocks increased from an average of 289 hens to 449 hens, but farm flocks still fell far short of the scale of the model egg production facilities built on the coasts during the war. Profits declined on even the well-advised model Iowa farms, a signal that such intermediate-scale modernization was not viable: it brought higher production costs without higher prices. The post-World War II drop in profitability from egg enterprises was more pronounced than can be explained by the decline in prices (see Tables 6.2 and 6.3). The average net egg income went from $942.95 in 1945 to $390.60 in 1946. By 1954, there was an average loss of $213.21 or 52 cents per bird. As the 1955 demonstration flock report stated, "The so-called bad years of the early thirties were good years when compared with 1954" (ISES 1955).

The number of Open Country farms with laying flocks declined slightly after the war, while the total number of laying hens climbed to a record high in 1954 (see Table 6.1). At the same time, average annual egg production per bird went from 134 eggs in 1932 to 216 eggs in 1957 (ISES 1932, 1957). Increased wartime sales volume had substantially decreased the extent of bartering eggs for groceries, but the new, favorable marketing situation had not survived the war years. Overproduction and the free market economy wreaked havoc on the post-war egg income.

Besides the overall downward turn in egg profits, the wide and unpredictable swings in the egg economy were disconcerting. During the Depression, women's egg income was low, but they counted on it, nevertheless. In the 1950s, the profits were lower still and some years even saw a net loss. Furthermore, the poultry record flock data show a rise in flock size and a corresponding rise in production expenses. Such expenditures were difficult to justify, indeed, when no reasonable assurance of profit was evidenced.

The extension's 1954–1955 Plan of Work stated, "Many operators will need to be urged to discontinue in favor of enterprises more suitable to their particular situation" (ISES 1954–55:B–53). The declining number of egg enterprises in Open Country indicated that most of the egg producers, whether by looking at their own finances or by listening to extension advice, were coming to the same conclusion.

In 1955, a controversy arose which directly pitted the larger, more technologically sophisticated egg producers against those with smaller volumes. A new egg candling law came before the Iowa Legislature. Under this law, candling of eggs for resale would have to be done by a stricter, more time-consuming and expensive method than previously required. Critics of the measure maintained that the law would make small laying flocks unprofitable, increase the price of eggs, and eliminate the last of the small grocery store egg markets who could not afford the new candling equipment. On the other hand, a grocery chain representative claimed that the proposed law required nothing his chain could not handle (Des Moines Register 1955A). With support from the extension service and the Iowa Farm Bureau Federation (fast becoming the voice of the large-scale farm producer), the measure passed and was upheld in court (Des Moines Register 1955B, 1955C).

Majorie and her husband, Abe, moved to Center in 1951 to operate a general store that sold groceries, dry goods, and appliances. She remembered the early days of their business when people brought in eggs to trade on Saturdays:

> When we first came to town, people used to come in [on Saturday nights] at six o'clock and park the car so they'd have a place. They used to bring eggs in. There was a law that changed that. They had to be candled. . . . There was a law that said that just certain places could do that kind of candling. I guess it was a matter of sanitation. . . . Anyhow, when we no longer took in eggs they went to the feed and seed companies like Frank's Farm Store. They took in all the eggs, in addition to which they would go out in the country and pick up those eggs. That made a tremendous difference.

That tremendous difference affected Marjorie and Abe's business, as well as that of the small-scale egg producers. Egg pickup trucks went only to farms with moderate-sized units of production.

As a result, small producers, the majority of whom were women, felt increasing pressure to discontinue their operations. The trend was toward much larger units and the inevitable losers were the majority of producers without access to the capital needed for "egg factory" production. The extension's 1954–1955 Plan of Work recognized this trend by stating that many small producers would have to be urged to discontinue egg production. Yet this was not the message that reached the producers. The 1954 report of the poultry demonstration project shifted the analysis from the structure of the egg industry to alleged deficiencies of egg producers:

> Your success with chickens both now and in the future depends largely upon your attitude. If you like chickens and enjoy working with them you have the first essential to success. One of the weaknesses of Iowa farm producers is the attitude that chickens are not a satisfactory source of income. . . . Another factor underlies success. It's called integrity. Integrity of a person is his honesty to himself and to his fellows. The lack of integrity among farm producers or others within the poultry industry produces a lack of confidence in the industry (ISES 1954:1).

Perhaps because they had good attitudes and integrity, Open Country egg producers responded slowly to the realities of the market. An attempt was made to adapt some of the new technology to farms. A story headlined "Iowa Egg Business Gets New Lease on Life" appeared in the December 18, 1966 Home and Family section of the *Des Moines Sunday Register and Tribune.* A poultry company was selling prefabricated caged-layer facilities for 5,040-unit flocks of hens. According to the article, bankers were beginning to lose their "traditional fear of feathers." Continuing, the article stated,

> As a result of the new attitude, egg production in Iowa is slowly, but surely, moving from a pin-money enterprise for the farm wife to an important part of the farm economy (Des Moines Register 1966).

The story projected that the "wife and children" would still do much of the egg handling, but the man would do the feeding and watering, both of which would be done mechanically. Usually financed through a local Production Credit Association, the cost of the new facility was $3–4 per bird, depending on how elaborate the structure was and how many optional features were included. The dealer recommended that a farm have three or four such units. The cost of starting such an operation was, therefore, between $50,000 and $100,000—considerably more than women previously invested in their egg enterprises. Negotiating the loans was the man's responsibility, as he was the one most closely involved with the farm finances and the one who usually dealt with financial specialists. Women entered the enlarged operations as wives, not as principle operators. A spokesman for the manufacturer said, "We take a good look at the wife because she will probably be involved to a large extent in the operation" (Des Moines Register 1966). A wife was a factor of production only available to a man. Furthermore, a requirement for financing was land ownership, which secured the loan, and most of the farms were in men's names.

One of the dealers for these facilities was located near Open Country, and at least one Open Country farm family purchased one of these laying facilities. But the 5,000-layer facility was short-lived; it cost a great deal of time and money and did not produce a profit. By the 1960s, a 5,000-layer flock was a small operation that was not an inexpensive enterprise that a woman could maintain with her own resources, nor was it the size of the current commercial flocks. A 1979 USDA account of egg and poultry production stated:

> The definition of "large" has persistently changed, increasing along with the expanding share of output such units produced (Rogers 1979:152).

When Maurice Pickler of the United Egg Producers testified before a U.S. Senate Subcommittee in 1972 he called himself a medium-sized producer with 100,000 hens (U.S. Senate 1972:25). In 1946, a flock of 200 hens was a "semicommercial" enterprise that supplied a sizable share of the farm income (Stewart 1946:166). By the 1970s, these were considered very small enterprises, the vestige of women's egg enterprises.

Women's laying flocks, which persisted largely outside of the change of production scale, were losing money in competition with the large enterprises. Sally, whose mother raised poultry throughout the 1940s and 1950s, described the demise of her mother's production in the early 1960s:

> I can remember when we finally got Mom talked into getting rid of her chickens. It just wasn't paying. She was paying more for feed than what she got for eggs and chickens and everything combined. . .
>
> We just kept laughing, saying, "Mom, it's a losing proposition."
>
> But she always said, "What am I going to have for spending?"

Of course by this time it wasn't buying the groceries anymore. It was just a matter of some spending money for her.

She said, "Where am I going to get my money from if I don't have my eggs?"

And we said, "Well, Mom, this is so funny because it's a losing proposition. It's coming out of the farm income. You're going in the hole. You're not making any money."

A two-tier pricing system was established in 1962 for Iowa eggs. Grade A large eggs produced under "quality and volume incentive programs" brought one price; Grade A large eggs labelled "other production" brought a lower price independently of any differences in the eggs. The difference between the two prices was only 3.2 cents per dozen in 1962, but had increased to 11.8 cents by 1975, a factor of approximately 30 percent (Schrader et al. 1978:71).

Of the 1,368 farms in Open Country in 1978, only 79 had laying hens (see Table 6.1). The average number of birds per flock was 595, but this average included a wide variation in the size of the flock. Sixty-five of the 79 laying flocks had less than 400 layers (USDC 1981:161). Women and retired men kept these flocks, which supplied eggs not only to their households, but also to those of their friends and neighbors. While three flocks were larger than 1,600 hens, none had more than 50,000 (USDC 1981:161). By 1982, the number of laying flocks was reduced to 51, with only one enterprise in the category of 10,000 to 19,999 layers (USDC 1984:3). This enterprise did packing and local delivery to retailers and restaurants, but was not large enough to be regarded as a moderate-sized commercial operation. The smaller egg producers met local needs and most of the eggs raised by the large producers were funnelled into commercial egg markets outside of the county.

Iowa lost its position as the nation's leading producer of eggs in 1959; and since that time its position further declined so that by the 1980s Iowa was no longer a leading producer of eggs. Egg production has been concentrated closer to the nation's population centers, with the major producers located in California and the southeastern states. Because chickens are small and have a relatively short lifespan, production is subject to much greater control than is possible when time and money are tied up in longer, natural growing and ripening processes and when many miles are needed for large-scale production. As a poultry expert explained,

> Eggs are essentially a continuous flow commodity, like milk. . . . Dif-
> ferences from other products occur because of the shortness of the
> reproductive cycle for poultry, because hatching is a year-round
> activity, and because the numbers of birds are large in relation to
> poundage. Thus, all of the activities related to poultry, whether basic
> breeding programs or production volume, can be accelerated or
> decelerated at a much more rapid rate than for other livestock
> species. Poultry also are readily adaptable to confinement in large
> units and assembly-line methods, given adequate technology
> (Rogers 1979:150–51).

Starting in the 1950s, the national trend was toward *vertical integration*: a single corporation owned the hatchery, feed plant, packing stations, and trucking systems needed for large-scale production and distribution of eggs. Often these corporations contracted
with farmers to maintain laying facilities with feed and chicks supplied by the company. While this preserved a vestige of the independence and free enterprise so highly valued in the United
States, in actuality, the large corporations maintained control of the
production process. Proximity to these companies' facilities is
critical for those farm people wanting to produce and market eggs
through commercial channels. A 1960 discussion of major problems in Iowa egg production mentioned the need for increased coordination in production:

> Isolated flocks, regardless of size, may prove uneconomical since
> they will not have the advantage of services and market outlets which
> are available in more concentrated areas (ISES 1960:B–44).

Of all the segments of egg production—from feed and equipment manufacture and breeding to retail distribution—the riskiest
and most subject to loss is the laying segment, which involves large
numbers of birds kept in close quarters. Disease (such as the avian
influenza of the early 1980s) or accident (such as the loss of electricity) can destroy an entire laying flock. Therefore, companies
realized that not owning the laying facilities was advantageous, in
that it provided more flexibility and control over the total production process:

> In a region where expansion occurs with contract production having a
> major role, the need for contract growers often draws in many new
> participants. Terms are relatively favorable in the beginning. But in-

tegrators soon become more selective with respect to contract growers as cost differences based on size and performance appear. The demand for new entrants may even slacken. And a sorting-out process begins as integrators make performance standards and housing requirements progressively more stringent. Contract payment rates also can begin to lag behind rising grower costs, particularly where local monopsony exists or there emerges an "oversupply" of contract growers. . . . Growers who could not or did not attempt to meet new requirements have been paid less or dropped (Rogers 1979:169).

If contract payments lagged behind rising costs, the contract growers—not the company—absorbed these costs. If the return for their labor fell to less than the minimum industrial wage, the company surely would not want to acquire these facilities and be forced to pay minimum wages. Rogers (1979:169) further noted that income tax incentives were given for enlarged production.

With vertical integration well underway, the next logical step was toward horizontal integration, whereby a single producer owned several vertically integrated systems:

As much of the poultry and egg industries came under the influence of vertical integration, horizontal integration became more common. Currently, integrated firms (some public) may operate in more than one area, state, or region, owning several input-supplying and/or processing units. With each, there may be an associated growing complex or a set of contract growers. Area differences in type and quality of production may exist, along with different growing specifications and terms, but many decisions which affect the production segment are influenced by broad company policies (Rogers 1979:156).

The largest producers were closely associated, and they coordinated their interests and lobbying efforts. The small producers were, for the most part, independent of each other and had the least collective control over the egg market.

But size and integration did not solve all of the problms of the egg economy. At a 1983 U.S. Senate hearing, representatives of the egg industry sought protection, explaining their situation and presenting a case for establishing egg marketing orders.[5] When H. H. Adams of Piedmont, Alabama, testified, he expressed the opinion that large-scale producers deserved help from the government. In his view, 20 or 30 years in the past, egg producers' losses were correctly attributed to inefficiency and obsolescence. Now those in trouble usually maintained flocks of 15,000 to one million hens. In addition, they were vertically integrated operations with their own hatcheries and feed mills and even they, the best of all producers, were at the point of bankruptcy. Protection had not been forthcoming for the many small producers like Sally's mother who had lost their enterprises, but Congress passed legislation allowing egg marketing orders in 1983, at which time society began to assume responsibility for economic dislocations caused by the free market in eggs.

By 1985, approximately 450 commercial egg enterprises remained in Iowa, most of which were still situated on farms, and whose operations were run by household members located on the same tract of land as the poultry enterprise. The workers in egg enterprises lived and farmed in the rural community before acquiring their laying flock and they considered egg production as a farming alternative.

Depending on the location, egg producers usually had a choice of six egg markets, with two or three being decidedly better choices. An average-sized family farm egg enterprise had 50,000 laying hens, more than any of the Open Country producers had. Starting an egg enterprise of this magnitude required an investment of approximately $9 per laying hen, or $450,000.[6] While such an investment was not large by standards of U.S. corporate capitalism, it was a considerable investment to most of the people of rural Iowa. Nevertheless, the majority of commercial egg enterprises in Iowa in 1985 were still household enterprises. Women worked in them as family members, but they no longer exerted the extensive control they had with the earlier egg enterprises. The nominal head of one of these enterprises was usually a farm man, who was, in turn, under a substantial degree of control from financial institutions. In 1985, Iowa had only one large, vertically integrated egg enterprise that looked like a factory and operated with hired workers.[7]

The majority of Open Country producers in 1982 were still marketing in some semblance of the traditional system. In every neighborhood, at least one farm produced eggs, and neighbors bought eggs from this farm. Several of those who had laying flocks were grandparents who enjoyed having them for the pleasure of visiting grandchildren. They gave or sold eggs to family members and friends. Regardless of whether they broke even with egg enterprises, they did not expect that this income would cover any major expenses.

Conclusion

Egg production, once a broad-based industry, is now a highly concentrated industry. Egg money was central to the household economy of Iowa farms during the first half of this century, and women controlled this money. Since poultry, as women's work, was conceptually separate from the cash-oriented farm operation managed by men, egg income was considered *pin-money* derived from *free labor.* Egg production won the support of the government only after it became capital intensive; when oriented to meeting human needs, egg production was clearly outside the interests of the government.

The structural changes in egg production were not inevitable. Although the technology for large-scale egg production was available as early as the 1930s, it was not used; rather the circumstances of World War II set this production system in motion, with massive government egg purchases providing the infusion of capital that led to the changes.

The state-supported extension service furthered the shift in egg production by selective inclusion of participants in its record flock program, by repeated counsel to increase the size of production units and by research designed to improve the efficiency of large-scale, vertically integrated production systems. As one federal report stated:

> Much Federal-State research during the mid-1950's to mid-1960's focused on documentation of the potential economies of scale which existed in production, processing and packing, hatchery operation, and feed milling. . . . Additional work beginning in the 1960's focused on the assembly and distribution functions, and the combination of these with processing and input production (Rogers 1979:164).

When the economies of scale failed and large-scale producers faced bankruptcy, Congress intervened by providing regulation of the market in the interests of the large producers. In lobbying for this regulation, an industry representative stressed that he did not intend for the benefits to go to small-scale producers.

The values implicit in the state-supported program were efficiency, free market, and profit, all related to the male side of farming—the commercial operation. Using egg money for family needs (as women did) diverted resources from farm capital investment, which according to the State, was not progressive. *Progress* mandated rational, male involvement. While unwilling to support the inefficiencies of women's production, the government *was* willing to aid large producers.

In the years following World War II, farm women lost control of their egg enterprises. The overwhelming majority discontinued production when they realized that they were no longer making a profit. Some retained a vestige of the former production system, and a few (but none in Open Country) became factors of production in commercial egg production.

Far from liberating women, progress in the egg industry forced most women out of business and marginalized the rest. While individual women, such as Sally's mother, suffered in isolation from displacement, society as a whole did not view the loss of women's work as a social problem. Indeed, increased profits earned from their husbands' specialized work in hogs, beef, or grain production more than compensated for the loss of pin money. Although some farm people were leaving the land, many Open Country women prospered in the 25 years after World War II, and Americans did not look seriously at the structural changes in agriculture until the 1980s.

CHAPTER 7

Women's Work After World War II

I think rather than do chicken chores, if the woman is going to earn some extra income she'll take a job. A lot of farm women do that. I would say that if a farm wife is going to earn extra income, she'll take a job. Because, you know, the chickens are gone and as far as feeding the hogs or cattle, the men do that. . . . [In my case,] as far as earning more money, I felt I could save us more money by working for my husband than I could if I went out and got a job.
— Sally, Open Country farm woman, age 48,
interviewed in 1982

Farm women lost their chickens after world War II. They could get outside jobs to earn a little "extra income," but it was so little extra that Sally did not see much point in it. The dual economy, which characterized Open Country farms from the time of European settlement, collapsed into a single base in commodity production. Without her traditional role providing produce and cash for the farm household, a farm woman working on the farm became her husband's helper; the woman as a full partner on a family farm was rarely, if ever, a reality. Farming itself was less stable than ever, and increasing numbers of rural people were working in nonfarm occupations. The search for nonfarm work enmeshed women in a larger structure of dependency; women's income was low and their position in nonfarm employment was tenuous. The change was the natural development of the technological, economic, and social forces emerging from the restructuring of agriculture accelerated by World War II.

The Farms

The movement of people off the farm gained momentum after World War II. After 1940, the Open Country farm population decreased by more than one-half and the nonfarm population increased, with the most drastic decline in farm population occurring after 1960 (see Table 7.1). But even by 1960, although Open Country was completely rural, less than one-half of its population were living on farms. During World War II, farms produced at record levels with fewer workers than before. After the war, ever fewer workers produced at ever greater levels. World War II military research in heavy equipment and chemicals brought new farm technology, allowing bold and expansive farmers to survive the continuing outflow of workers.

Table 7.1
Change in Farm and Nonfarm Population
of Open Country, 1940–1980

Year	Nonfarm	Nonfarm Change	Farm	Farm Change
1940	6,642	+12.0%	8,883	-3.0%
1950	7,215	+8.6%	7,754	-12.7%
1960	7,503	+4.0%	7,086	-8.6%
1970	7,466	-0.5%	5,466	-23.3%
1980	7,673	+2.8%	4,311	-21.1%

Source: U.S. population censuses.

Expensive machinery, once purchased, led to increasing specialization: having a combine to harvest 40 acres of oats was not economical. Using a combine substituted capital for labor, and farmers could not too easily adjust their production inputs once this machinery was purchased; to get a return on the investment, the machinery had to be used. Iowa farming, with its fertile, rolling land, developed specialized corn and soybean production. In 1982, 93 percent of the harvested Open Country cropland was planted in corn or soybeans (USDC 1983B:1, 3). Furthermore, because most livestock production moved into more marginal cropping regions of the northern and western plains, fewer farms raised livestock (see Table 7.2).

Table 7.2
Percentages of Open Country Farms with Livestock
1940–1982

Year	Dairy	Hogs	Hens
1940	94	90	94
1945	92	86	92
1950	84	87	88
1959	52	78	75
1964	39	72	51
1969	22	61	24
1974	13	47	11
1978	7	53	6
1982	6	43	4

Source: U.S. agricultural censuses.

Hogs, still remembered as the *mortgage burners*, remained on slightly fewer than one-half of Open Country farms in 1982. Milking and poultry nearly vanished. In 1982, 32 percent of Open Country farms had beef cattle and a few farms had sheep (USDC 1983B:2–3). A typical Open Country farmer planted corn and soybean crops and kept either hogs or cattle as livestock. However, the diversified farm, with a variety of grain and hay crops, milk cows, beef cattle, hogs, and chickens had all but disappeared by 1982. The many small jobs on the farm became a few large jobs, and large jobs were men's specialty.

The new technology, particularly the hybrid seeds, fertilizers, and pesticides, increased production dramatically. In Iowa, corn went from an average yield of 46.5 bushels per acre in 1945 to 121.0 bushels in 1982; soybeans, from 18.0 bushels per acre to 37.5 bushels (ISDA 1946:8; ICLRS 1983:21, 31). Given the law of supply and demand in the free market economy, the result was lower producer prices; consequently, the grain companies—not the farmers—benefitted from the production increases. Farmers responded by intensifying their production. Farmers who had big-ger machinery covered more acres; those with more acres lived with a smaller net return per acre. Both of these factors encouraged ex-pansion in the scale of farming. The early farms were approximately 180 acres in size, but 1980 farm economists projected that a begin-ning Iowa farmer needed a minimum of 240–320 acres depending on the type of operation (Drabenstott and Heady 1980:21). Since 1940, the average Open County farm size has increased by more than 50 percent; the number of farms has declined by approximate-ly 33 percent (see Table 7.3).[1] By 1982, some of the empty farm-steads had been dismantled and the entire area plowed under. Other farm buildings stood empty and falling. A few of the houses on the dismantled farms had tenants who commuted to jobs in town or to other farms where they were hired workers.

Table 7.3
Increasing Scale of Open Country
Farming, 1940–1982

Year	Number of Farms	Average Acreage
1940	1986	181
1945	1948	184
1950	1961	182
1954	1948	182
1959	1796	197
1964	1604	224
1969	1514	243
1974	1357	264
1978	1368	276
1982	1337	271

Source: U.S. censuses.

Farm structure change presented itself in different concrete situations. For the elders in Curtis Harnack's account of growing up on a northwest Iowa farm in the 1930s, success was leaving the farm:

> Our triumphs glowed beyond the rim of this region, and our elders' pleasure in having us successfully out of the nest kept us pushed out (Harnack 1981:177).

For them, empty farm buildings were signs that things were getting better, that the past was giving way to a better future.

Successful farmers defined progress as increased productivity with less labor input, and they welcomed the time when they could share some of the personal options that postwar technology brought to middle-class Americans. The situation of wealthy farm women blended with that of wealthy women in town; few of them depended on their own income to set their living standards. Calvin Jones and Rachel Rosenfeld (1984:6, 9), who conducted a national survey of farm women in 1980, found that women on larger farms tended to do a smaller range of farm tasks and were less likely to be employed off the farms than were women living on smaller farms. Dennis Poole (1981:344) found that women on larger farms were more removed from the farm operation and functioned less as business partners than did women living on smaller farms. Although some of the newly acquired wealth dissolved with the ever-deepening valleys of recurring farm depressions in the post war period, other enterprising people steeled themselves and continued to grow.

Some farmers adapted to the change without looking forward to creating a large, competitive operation. Alma, married in 1939, began with a diversified farm where she did chores and worked in the field. Their diversified operation lasted until the 1950s, as they wanted to pay their daughter Marilyn's state university expenses with profits from their hard work. In 1956, Alma's husband fell and broke his shoulder. While his brother was able to help out with some of the fieldwork, the milking and other chores fell to Alma. With the onset of this labor crisis, they decided to simplify the operation, thereby reducing the required labor. By 1958, the cows were sold, and they no longer had to do the milking chores. Alma described their change to specialized corn and soybean crops:

> My husband had always said, "As soon as Marilyn is through college I'm going to quit milking." That was our biggest source of income for those years. The cows tie you down. That's how we quit milking. Then the next year we quit the chickens. Then we raised hogs. I think we quit raising hogs six years later.

The income from their corn and soybean production provided a comfortable living, but they did not forsee passing the farm operation to Marilyn who, in 1982, had an urban career.

Carla attempted without success to preserve the traditional farming pattern on the 160-acre farm of her family. Born on an Open Country farm in 1930, she left to enroll in a nursing program. She eventually married a military man and subsequently lived in military bases across the United States. When her husband retired from the Air Force in 1966, they and their four children returned to her family farm. With Carla's income from her nursing in the Open Country hospital and her husband's military pension checks, they hoped to support themselves by running a diversified, subsistence-oriented farm. Both Carla and her husband were familiar with farming and understood the realities of farm life and farm work. In fact, Carla's husband was raised on a small West Virginia farm and he was eager to return to the farming he had learned as a youth.

In the beginning they kept 100 hens; they kept a cow for milk, cream, and butter; they raised the cow's calves for beef; they ground their own wheat flour; and they raised plums, raspberries, and vegetables, which they preserved. For farm income, they raised and marketed hogs and sheep. With time they discovered that not only were they making no money on the farm, but their nonfarm income was not enough to cover the production expenses. First, Carla discovered she could buy eggs and chickens for less than it cost her to raise them, and she got rid of the chickens. Next, the cow was sold and with this they lost both the milk and the calves they had raised for beef. Then they realized that their hogs were costing them all the money they made on their sheep and they sold the hogs. Gradually their diversified operation evolved into a corn, soybean, and sheep operation. Although both Carla and her husband were raised on farms, they were not able to meet their expenses on a 160-acre operation. Even after they specialized, the farm was not enough to support them. Carla said,

> If we didn't have our Air Force retirement pay we couldn't make a living. Not raise a family and educate them and keep the buildings up. There's no way we can see.

Others, like Carla and her husband, were nostalgic for the old days of small-scale, diversified farming, but no one was able to make a living from such a farm in the 1980s. Sally and Frank maintained a B John Deere tractor, an early, small machine used on many farms in the 1940s. Reflecting on former farming methods, Sally attributed their passing to a generic *they*:

Really, they kind of force you into getting bigger, because you can't just walk in and buy a little B John Deere anymore—and you can't get parts. . . . They're considered antiques now. . . . They force you into bigger things. I think it's after 10 years they consider it obsolete and they don't stock parts anymore. . . . This little B John Deere is just a toy. We really don't have the machinery small enough to use it.

As the farm commodity production expanded, women's sphere of the family economy diminished. Production for consumption and egg money, which women contributed to the household subsistence before 1945, were being eliminated from modern farms. This, together with remodelling of farm homes, made life easier. When Joan married an Open Country farmer and moved from a city to his family farm in the early 1950s, she found one indoor kitchen tap and a toilet in her farmhouse, and she immediately began to remodel and modernize her surroundings. Throughout the 1950s, every issue of *Wallaces' Farmer* had pictures and articles about plumbing and appliances in farm homes, and modernization was a major concern of Iowa farm women at this time, particularly the younger ones and those who, like Joan, had not grown up on farms.

Sally, who lived on a rented farm without running water for a year after her marriage in 1957, was one of the last to have to contend with this inconvenience. Although unusually charitable toward most people, she was critical of the landlord:

I always said to Frank, "I don't need an inside bathroom. I'm well and healthy and can run outside and I can wash these diapers and carry them outside and there's nothing wrong with me. But if the day ever comes that we own a piece of land or a house we rented out I hope I can be kind enough to let the renter have things as convenient as what I have." I always thought this was being a little hard-hearted or dense, whichever it was.

That she was resentful of the landlord's stinginess suggests that such amenities were beginning to be thought of as basic necessities rather than mere conveniences.

Farm women gradually diminished the time they spent preparing food. Freezers and electric stoves made preserving meat and garden produce faster and easier. The amount of food necessary to fuel a farm workforce decreased as the number of farm workers declined. Buying bread regularly at five loaves for $1 was a welcome saving of farm women's labor. "Isn't it nice that we can buy bread?" said one woman.

In 1982, while some women took pride in their own baking and cooking, many others used the cake mixes, fluffy white bread, instant potatoes, and frozen foods that were popular throughout the United States. Ironically, the one thing that is not readily available in Open Contry is fresh fruits and vegetables. By 1982 many farm homes had microwave ovens, which made preparing and reheating meals quicker, while freeing farm women from rigorous meal schedules: most farm men could learn to microwave prepared food for their meals. Automatic dishwashers also saved women work in the kitchen.

With these technological changes, women's production for consumption on the farm diminished to gardening, canning, and freezing. By the 1980s, however, it was not significantly more than that done by many urban and suburban women.

Modern technology also diminished the time necessary to do laundry and housecleaning. Alice, born in 1931, said that her mother used to have a hired girl do laundry, but Alice had a washer and dryer and they were her servants. Vacuum cleaners and no-wax floors also saved housecleaning time, but farm women still contended with mud and dust. A young woman who was new to the farm said, "If you don't fight back every day, the mud takes over." Some women fought back more than others, but only the women fought the dirt, cleaned, and laundered. As before, it was very unusual for a farm man to do this work.

Improved roads and automobile transportation made shopping for food in town easier for farm women. In addition, restaurants became a option for feeding workers. Both Farmtown and Center have restaurants catering to the farm trade with inexpensive daily meat-and-potatoes noon specials. In 1982, a crew of 12 corn shellers went into a Farmtown restaurant, sat down at two large tables, and ate heartily. Their $35 bill was tax deductible for their employer. With food prices at 1982 levels, a farm woman did not make significant economic contributions to the farm by buying food and preparing meals for work crews.

The number of people per household diminished after World War II.[2] Hired farm hands no longer looked to the day when they would own their own land; most of those who had board and room in farm homes left for urban employment where the wages were better. In addition, fewer children were born, and the decrease in the number of small children in the home further eased women's work.[3] Although farm workers were still hearty eaters and some women cooked occasional meals for hungry work crews filling silos or shelling corn, the number of people they cooked for each day has lessened. The decline in the number of farm workers and future farm workers diminished the work required in the reproduction of the farm labor force.

Even on the intermediate-sized farms, many of the women were less likely to be involved with the farm work directly. The Jones and Rosenfeld (1981:18) survey revealed that a majority of U.S. farm women regularly gardened, but otherwise did only indoor work such as bookkeeping and housework. Of the women surveyed, 47 percent did farm errands. Other women reported that they occasionally operated farm machinery and worked with the livestock. However, more than 50 percent of the farm women responding reported that they never plowed, disked, cultivated, planted, applied chemicals, worked in the fields without machinery, made major farm equipment purchases, marketed produce, or supervised hired laborers.

The minority of women who did farm work were not maintaining their own production enterprises. As Kate Young (1980:7) found, even when women owned land, they often lacked the means to recruit labor and find capital to work the land. While male farm managers have access to women's and children's labor, women in modern nuclear families are rarely able to use men's labor for their farm enterprises. Men, as the primary farm managers, coordinated the labor and disposed of the products even when women legally owned the land. As in previous decades, women working on the farm usually maintained that they were helping their husbands.

Sally grew up on a farm and saw her mother maintain an egg enterprise that provided grocery money for their household. After she married, Sally had four children and did the farm's livestock chores. Her husband, Frank, hired young men from a neighbor farm to help with farm chores, but in the 1960s they were drafted for the Vietnam War, and Frank was unable to hire workers at the wages he could afford. He turned to Sally for help. Her description of learning to drive a tractor made it clear that the farm operation was his—he was the manager and she filled the role of hired hand:

> Frank got two tractor cabs—one for Mom and one for Pop. I just about died, because I had helped with chores at home, but I had never driven a tractor. We decided that was the only way we could make ends meet and make a go of this thing. You know you can do it if you have to. . . .

So Frank showed me how to drive a tractor. He had the patience of a saint putting up with me. There's just an awful lot to learn, you know. But he was real patient. He would take one of the little ones and I would take one. I enjoyed it out there. Once I got past that first year I could relax a bit. He laughed at me because I said, "Frank, I pray all the way across the field. I got to think about what I'm going to do when I get to the end."

When you're first starting and especially if you've got a little one in the tractor to keep your mind on, you go across there and you think, "Boy, if I just don't put this through the fence." You've really got to keep using your head and thinking what you're going to do when you get there.

Sally and Frank had a "Mom and Pop" farm, often called a family farm, and Sally combined her productive and reproductive roles as she drove a tractor with a child in the cab. But this farm was different from the family farms of earlier days where men and women had interlocking, interdependent spheres of production. Sally clearly stated in this and other contexts that she helped her husband or that she worked for him.

Martha, raised in a city, came to Open Country to her husband Henry's farm in 1949. Since she had never worked on a farm before, Henry taught her much about farming, and her understanding of the way a farm operated was through his instruction. Martha entered into farming with a spirit of adventure, loved working with Henry, and took considerable pleasure in performing her work well. With delight and humor she told of many things that had happened with the animals and of many good experiences their two children had on the farm. She laughed about one hectic day when Henry went to a meeting in Des Moines:

I used to help him. . . . We were farrowing like crazy out there and he told John [a neighbor] to help. . . . I went out and looked and we had two litters. So I called John and he stayed with me all day. We farrowed 14 sows that day. It was so funny because every time I'd go out there there were more pigs and we had to catch them and trim their teeth and spray their navels with iodine and do all those preparatory things. We blew fuses. I went to town a couple or three times to get things we needed. Henry came home that night and we had all these heat lamps going and all these sweet little pigs and he couldn't believe that we had that many. We got one of them in that broke out. It was the most hectic day I've ever had on the farm. That was in 1967.

Martha expressed pride in her work on the farm, and she and Henry were unusually successful and prosperous as farmers. Starting small, they expanded to a much larger operation, employing a full-time, year-round hired man. As often happened with successful farmers, they were able to rent a substantial farm from a neighbor who was retiring and who wanted a responsible farm family with good machinery to work his land. In 1967, they purchased an additional 160-acre farm in Martha's name. Since that time, they also purchased cattle in Martha's name, and Martha, therefore, was increasingly drawn into legal partnership in the farm operation.

Martha and Henry were typical of many of those on modern family farms who shared the tasks involved with operating a farm. In their case, a strong marriage of two hard-working individuals was the basis of a strong family economy. Qualitative differences were, however, apparent with regard to the way they approached the farm. As was true with Sally, Martha came to the farm and learned farming through her husband, who instructed her. When Henry left for the day he—not Martha—arranged for someone to help her if she needed it. Martha, like Sally and most other farm women, said that she "helped" when she did traditional male work. Henry clearly relied heavily on Martha and he respected her intelligence in all matters, but just as clearly he was the person who knew the most about the technical and economic matters of the farm. When buying cattle, he assessed and selected the animals; he decided when animals should be taken to the veterinarian; he negotiated with cattle dealers. When they bought the 160-acre farm in Martha's name they seem to have entered the land market with different views. Martha said,

> That's been an interesting addition because we've gotten more and more into debt. I have tended to be one who's more conservative about that kind of thing. Did we really need that land?

Henry negotiated the purchase. When he explained his strategy in acting decisively and quickly when buying this land, he did not mention Martha's input, although Martha's account of the purchase indicated that they did discuss the matter.

Like many farm women, Martha sought identity in a farming operation which was closely and emotionally tied to her marriage. She had become a self-conscious feminist by the 1980s, and was clear about wanting to be called a farmer rather than a farm wife. Yet as early as the 1970s, when their operation was still expanding, Martha was becoming less involved with farm work as she became increasingly involved in activist movements within and outside of Open Country. The lessening of daily involvement in farming and the broadened base of interests typified most farm women whose family operations were as prosperous as Martha and Henry's farm.

Martha called herself a farmer: she lived on the farm; she worked on the farm; she loved the farm. As true as this was, material and historical factors made her a farmer's *helper* rather than a *farmer* in the sense that most English speakers use the word. Although she raised poultry in ther first years in Open Country, she lost this source of grocery and household money. The very success of the operation she helped to build, including the possibility of hiring a full-time, year-round farm hand, meant that she was not needed to help as much as before.

Some farm women did an inordinate share of work for the farm commodity operation without any formal recognition or control. Ellie was one such woman. Born in 1956, she grew up on a farm and went to Iowa State University to study veterinary medicine. While a student, she met Si, a young man from an Open Country farm. In 1976 Ellie quit school, married Si, and went with him to his family farm. Children were born in 1977, 1980, and 1982, and Ellie did almost all of the childcare as well as much of the livestock production work. Ellie described her work in managing the cattle herd, which included their cattle and her father-in-law's:

> We own all our own cattle. Almost all the cows are ours. We're trying to build his dad's herd back up. When I came, there were a lot of old cows and a lot of mean ones. We've slowly gotten rid of those and we're starting to keep replacing them so that we can get his herd built back up. . . .

> Out in the kitchen I have a calendar I write calves down on. During April a lot of the days we'll have five or six calves in one day and it wouldn't fit on any other kind of calendar so I made one up. . . . I've been used to this ever since I can remember. It was just natural for me to start doing that. Si's dad wasn't that involved with it and they'd let their cows calf and check them once in a while, but that's not the way I was raised. We'd check them more often. It made me so upset when I was younger to lose a calf. . . . When we worked cattle, I was always out there keeping track of everybody or helping move cattle through. It was something we just kept up. I do the same thing here now. Main-

ly keeping track, writing down all the cows' numbers and when we worked the calves, writing which ones got dehorned or implanted or whatever, so we could keep track and know when it came time for billing. Sometimes I'd give shots. I enjoy it because I like getting outside. I'm not a housewife. . . .

Through the summer we fix fence almost constantly and check the cows to make sure there's no sick calves or cows and we do fly control and treat calves for pinkeye if they get it. We have to make sure the neighbor's bull does not get our cows. In the past we've had a lot of trouble with that.

When we move them in the spring when they're out in the pasture I take the horse. It's easier to get up and down the hills. If there's a cow that's a little bit touchy, she won't usually try to take you if you've got the horse versus if you're walking.

Ellie's experience with cattle stemmed from her girlhood on a farm. She was more knowledgeable and more meticulous with the cattle than were either her husband or father-in-law:

As a girl, one of the things I used to do was help Dad take care of sick calves. I tagged calves and registered them. Si really never was involved that much in raising calves. In fact, he'd never seen a calf pulled until the one year we had Herefords. He first bought some cows just before we were married. I don't know if that was to impress me or to get something started. We kids had a registered herd of Angus at home that Dad started for us. Then when we got married I brought eight cows with me that were part of my herd. . . .

Having three children did not prevent Ellie from caring for her cattle. She juggled babysitters and sometimes got Si to watch the children.

When we're calving in the spring, we check the Herefords every four hours even during the night. . . . It used to be [that] our babysitter lived in town and I could get her to come out for a few hours every day while I went up and did most of it. Or if Si didn't have that much to do I'd run up and he'd take care of the kids.

The only time Ellie was unable to take care of her cattle was when she was in the hospital giving birth. During this time, however, the men did not fill in for her and they lost cattle:

When Billy was born [1980] it was right in the middle of calving and it got cold and rainy and they lost a lot of calves. I was in the hospital and Si was with me. His dad won't take them in the barn and dry them off like I would and feed them or milk the cow out. Even Si doesn't like to do that. He doesn't like messing with baby calves. He doesn't have the patience. I suppose you learn the patience from taking care of kids or I learned patience with the kids from taking care of calves. A little baby calf needs a lot of patience. If you take care of them it's not that much trouble.

Even though Ellie put more time and effort into the on-the-ground cattle operation than either Si or his father, the cattle checks were issued to the men who had formal ownership of the cattle enterprise, including the issue from Ellie's cows that she brought with her when she married Si. As Ellie evidenced, there was no limit to the amount of initiative that a woman could show; but as in the early years of farming in Open Country women's initiative was properly directed toward enhancing her family and not herself. Whether or not Ellie will chafe under this restriction in the future, she expressed no dissatisfaction when interviewed in 1982.

Some husbands were more concerned about their wives' work situations than others. While Martha was fortunate to have a husband who praised and rewarded her input, other farm women were isolated with tyrannical husbands who took their work for granted, restricted their freedom, and felt that all farm income belonged to them. In these instances, women without their own sphere of farm production had little recourse. Achieving even limited parity on the farm depended on her husband's willingness to share more than on the woman's willingness to work.

Whether men had anything to share, however, depended on the state of the farm commodity market. Thus, women were inclined to see their economic interests in terms of enhancing their husbands' farm economies rather than in enhancing their own sphere of production. Where women once had an integral part in supporting the family farm operation, farm women of Martha's generation became, in general, structurally subordinate to their husbands. This was reflected in the Jones and Rosenfeld survey. In contrast to the 1915 survey of farm women taken in connection with the beginning of the extension service (USDA 1915A,B) in which women wrote eloquently and at length about their interests on the farm, the 1980 researchers found farm women unable to articulate what they wanted for themselves as farm women:

Our original intention was to finish each woman's interview with a single open-ended question asking her opinion about what policy action by USDA would be most beneficial to farm women. We expected women to answer using a clearly female perspective, though not necessarily from a feminist or "women's lib" point of view. . . .

Somewhat to our surprise, we found that no matter how much the question wording emphasized our interest in the specific problems and views of farm *women*, most pre-test respondents chose to answer the question from the broader viewpoint of the agricultural producer, eschewing a more particularistic reference to their own gender. To these respondents, the "farm women's agenda" was simply the farm agenda articulated by a woman. When interviewers probed for a second response, reemphasizing the focus on federal policy toward farm women as a group, many respondents could give no answer, explaining that they had never before considered farm policy issues in gender terms (Jones and Rosenfeld 1981:215–16).

A woman's sphere of farm work existed at one point, but by 1980 only commodity production was left. If the husband was doing well, he had the means to provide for his family; whether he actually shared the money was a personal matter and certainly not something the government could address.

Although Open Country had no independent women commodity farmers, I heard references to married couples who were equal partners in the farm operation. Such cases, however, were easier to find in magazines and newspapers than among Open Country farm women. Alice, a farm woman who seemed to me to be as fully involved with the farm operation as any, was most aware of the loss of women's place on the farm and the contradictions of her own position. Born on an Open Country farm in 1931, she told of her mother, Sharon, supporting the family with her egg money in the 1920s. In 1982 Alice, a farmer's wife, did a large share of the work on their farm. She did not refer to any of her farm work as *helping* her husband; she *worked*.

Alice raised sheep in partnership with her youngest son, who was away at college, and they divided the work and the profits. (Alice might, however, have done more than half of the work, with her son away for nine months of the year, and she might have used "her" profits for his tuition.) She had charge of a large farrowing operaton, and she transferred these pigs to her husband, who fed them for market. The farm had two combines, one for Alice and one for her husband; they did similar amounts of fieldwork. To clarify her role on the farm, Alice explained that she had done farm work, including driving a tractor, since she was a young girl. Before the advent of power steering, she was driving tractors through the field; before hydraulic lifts were used to pull up the plow at the end of each row, Alice tripped the plow with a chain. She learned new technological advances as they appeared, and she was as capable of controlling farm machinery as anyone. Yet she observed that, unlike her mother who raised hens and her daughter-in-law who worked in town, she did not have her own income. She expressed her frustration:

> Now, Jean, my daughter-in-law, works at the Medical Center, and Ray [Alice's son, a farmer] says her paycheck buys the groceries, this kind of stuff. What the farm makes goes right back into the farm—improvements, the machinery, the buildings. You know, like her chickens, my mom's chickens, they paid the groceries the same. Now Jean brings home a paycheck which they spend for clothing and so forth. I don't bring a paycheck home and my work goes right into the farm operation, too.
>
> I can't even say, well, like Mom could say, "The eggs are mine." I can't even pick out one thing. I work in the field. I do the pigs only as far as the nursery and then they're part of the farm.

Later she pondered the irony of her farm work:

> Well, I'm probably an odd one. A farm wife who really works that much with the pigs and the field. I think the younger ones, like Ray's wife, they'll go to town and work. . . . I think I probably put in more hours, but I don't bring a paycheck home.

Alice, who really was like a farm partner to her husband, understood that she was not an economic equal, that she was not a farm partner.

In Alice's family, as in many farm families, the oldest son stayed in Open Country to farm with his parents; Alice had five more children who went away to college and dispersed themselves across the country. The emerging family farm has frequently been an intergenerational operation with the father and son (or sons) as principal partners. A marked deficit in the number of young women between ages 18 and 25 in the Open Country farm population has arisen. Most young people who graduated from high school in the 1960s and 1970s left after graduation. The young men going into farming either left for some years of agricultural training and the opportunity to meet wives, or they remained on the farm and sought their wives at home or in the surrounding area.

Alice and her husband farmed 160 acres when they were first married in the 1950s. In 1973, they had a chance to buy another 160 acres in geographic proximity. Knowing that Ray wanted to farm, they bought the farm, thereby making the combined operation more viable than the smaller one had been. They assumed that Ray would gradually take over the enlarged farm. Acquiring extra land became a common practice as the postwar farm baby boys reached maturity. The inclination for farmers to buy more land was strengthened by the optimism brought on by the massive grain sales to the Soviet Union in the early 1970s. The difficulties of the farm commodity economy seemed to have passed, and Malthus' theory that population tends to increase at a faster rate than its means of subsistence gave farmers hope that they would one day be rich. Indeed, buying fertile Iowa farm land seemed a wise move, and this inflated the land market.

Between 1971 and 1981 the average price of Open Country land went from $531 per acre to $2,863 per acre, an increase of more than 400 percent (Muhm 1982A). In 1981, one hog farmer with two sons entering farming paid in excess of $4,000 per acre for Open Country land. Land purchased at $3,000 per acre required approximately $300 per acre annually in interest. If the land was used for corn, the farmer would incur approximately $100 in production expenses, excluding the costs of labor, taxes, insurance, and constant capital.[4] Thus, the farmer had to make $400 per acre before any profit could be realized or any payment of principle could be made. By the 1980s, however, the price of corn declined to a low level. The average price of corn in 1982 was $2.25 per bushel, and the average yield was 115 bushels per acre (ICLRS 1983:89). Hence, the gross income from one acre of corn would be $258.75, resulting in a net loss of more than $141.25 per acre. One hundred acres of corn raised on these terms would lose $14,125, before considering the costs of machinery, insurance, and taxes. The only farmers who could manage such a loss were those with other sources of income, often from substantial farms purchased at cheaper prices. A farmer who bought land for his son explained: "You have to be crazy to buy this land—and the craziest ones are those with sons who want to farm."

The land boom drew farmers deeply into debt. As Alice explained,

We didn't have any debt when we first got married. I don't remember when we started. I suppose to buy this farm. We borrowed some to make the downpayment. Nine years ago [in 1973] we bought this farm. We sold the other one to Ray. He was just out of high school and he didn't have no money, so we didn't get no downpayment from them, but we did have to have $30,000 to make a downpayment on this farm, so that's what we borrowed. But now most farmers operate on borrowed money.

Bankers eagerly lent money on the expanding land market. Interest was tax decuctible, and this was an incentive for some farmers to increase their borrowing. With their money tied up in land, farmers negotiated operating loans to plant crops each spring. *Leveraging*, investing in land to use as collateral on the next loan, became a common practice in the rapidly inflating land market. One farmer explained that debt was not a bad thing if the interest payments were manageable. Buying land was high drama in Open Country in 1982. Land auctions drew crowds of anxious and attentive people, and confidential negotiations were done with a great deal of finesse.

As indicated in Table 7.1, the majority of the farm people left the farm, with the heaviest out-migration occurring after 1960 with the accelerated specialization, demands for capital, and low profits. The ones who stayed were a minority. Some were able to stay on the land by cutting back on their farming activities and resorting to nonfarm sources for a larger part of their income. Those who thrived as farmers were hard-working survivors who managed to expand at the right time. The expanding land market masked the fact that the commodity farming of the post-war period was not economically viable. Farmers obtained annual operating loans collateralized by their land's equity, but farm debt mushroomed. Iowa farm commodity production had not been independently viable for long periods before 1940, but during those periods it was subsidized by women's egg production and the significant degree of production for consumption.

After World War II, the federal government replaced farm women as the major subsidizers of farming. Government payments to Iowa farmers increased sharply, with the only major dip in the increase being the brief boom of the early 1970s sales to the Soviets, which coincided with the general economic chaos of the first oil crisis. Iowa farmers, who received .7 percent of their money income from the federal government in 1949, received 43 percent in 1982 (see Table 7.4).

Table 7.4
Money Income and Production Expense on Iowa Farms*,
1949–1982

Year	Money Income**	Govt. Payments	Production Expenses	Net Money Income	Net/ Govt.
1949	$ 2,041.4	$ 5.3	$ 1,259.2	$ 787.5	0.7%
1952	2,247.1	13.0	1,605.5	654.6	2.0%
1955	2,158.1	7.4	1,537.8	627.6	1.2%
1958	2,547.8	59.4	1,849.4	757.8	7.8%
1961	2,462.6	129.6	2,003.9	588.3	22.0%
1964	2,758.4	226.3	2,214.2	770.5	29.4%
1967	3,405.5	142.8	2,678.1	870.2	16.4%
1970	4,129.0	235.8	3,120.6	1,244.2	18.9%
1973	6,949.8	186.8	5,030.2	2,105.8	8.8%
1976	7,154.7	26.8	6,544.7	636.8	4.2%
1979	9,247.0	69.2	9,043.6	272.6	25.4%
1982	10,343.3	215.9	10,057.1	502.1	43.0%

**Values expressed in millions of dollars.
*Income from sales of crops and livestock.
Source: Iowa Agricultural Statistics 1984 (ICLRS 1984:85); Farm Income State Estimates 1959–72 (USDA 1973:16); State Estimates of Farm Income 1949–59 (USDA 1960:16).

The bottom fell out of the land market in 1982 (Muhm 1982B). A combination of low producer prices, high production costs, and high interest dampened the land purchasers' enthusiasm. As land prices fell from a high point in 1981, farmers who borrowed extensively found their bankers scrutinizing shrinking farm assets more closely. When farmers began to consolidate their operations by selling some of their land, land prices plunged further. In 1984 alone the average value of Iowa farm land fell 20 percent (Muhm 1984). From a high of $2,863 per acre in 1981, Open Country land averaged $1,599 per acre in 1984. People throughout the United States talked about the "farm crisis." A farm crisis organizer stated that 21 percent of Iowa's farmers would probably face bankruptcy in 1985, and a farm journal survey suggested that 42 percent would be insolvent within two or three years (Moberg 1985:8). Rural banks, which had made extensive loans to farmers, were also in trouble. In 1985, just before it would have closed, the bank in Farmtown sold to out-of-state investors who assumed the collectable loans. Some farms were forced to sell out; others were forced to sell their land at low prices. Although the Reagan administration did not cause the farm crisis, its *laissez-faire* economic policy sharpened the downhill slide when it did not come to the farmers' rescue by increasing spending on farm programs. The farm crisis of the 1980s was the predictable explosion of a volatile system that had inflated far beyond its reasonable boundaries.

Rather than being a sudden phenomenon of the 1980s, the erosion of the self-contained family farm structure was gradual and could be observed in a number of indicators over the years. People had been leaving farming steadily for 50 years, a movement which accelerated after 1960 with the increasing mechanization. Another indicator was the increase in the number of farmers seeking employment off the farm. In the 1970s the average off-farm income was greater than the farm income on U.S. farms (Drabenstott and Heady 1980:8). The 1980 federal census revealed that, in 1979, 30 percent of the Open Country farm households realized less than one-half of their income from farming (USDC 1983A:472). In 1982, 16 percent of the farmers listed their principal occupation as being other than farming (USDC 1983B:2). Furthermore, 23 percent of the farmers (mostly men) worked off the farm more than 100 days (compared to only 4 percent in 1959), and nearly twice that many had done some work off the farm (see Table 7.5).[5] Although the farmers working off the farm steadily increased, the steepest increase was in the 1970s, coinciding with the land boom. Some farmers were easing themselves out of farming; others were seeking capital for their farms.

Table 7.5
Open Country Farmers Working Outside
Their Own Farms 1959–1982

Year	Any Work	More Than 100 Days	
		Actual	Percent
1959	383	75	4.4%
1964	406	106	6.6%
1969	534	192	12.7%
1978	460	196	16.4%
1982	494	256	22.8%

Source: U.S. agricultural censuses.

Table 7.6
Open Country Farm Women Engaged In
Nonfarm Work, 1950–1980

Occupation	1950	1960	1970	1980
Managerial, professional	24	38	97	125
Technical, sales, clerical	20	54	106	93
Service	16	63	112	79
Operatives, blue collar	3	22	37	47
Other	15	4	—	13
Total	78	181	352	357

Source: U.S. censuses.

Farm women also left the farm for nonfarm employment. Census figures show that the number of farm women employed off the farm has increased since 1950, although not as markedly as the number of men working off the farm. The prewar employment level of farm women was again reached in 1960, and the percentage continued to inch upward through the 1980 census (see Table 7.6). The 24 percent of Open Country farm women employed in nonfarm work in 1980 was still substantially less than the percentage of town and urban women who were employed. As Sally explained in this chapter's opening quote, a farm woman could go out and get a job, but sometimes her labor was worth more on the farm than outside the farm.

Nonfarm job prospects for women were often discouraging. A woman could not earn enough to save a farm, but some farm women wanted to work to gain some control over even a small amount of resources—to pay the telephone bill, to take children to dance lessons, or to paint the kitchen. Women's nonfarm work depended on their need to work (for social or economic reasons) and on the availability of suitable employment.

Open Country Women in Nonfarm Work

Rural towns were already stagnating by 1980. Although factories were built in surrounding areas to utilize Open Country's labor after 1950, farming remained the major source of revenue entering Open Country. With fewer farmers and an unstable economy, Farmtown and Center served fewer and poorer customers. Discount department stores and supermarkets were built in nearby cities in the postwar years, and most people were willing to drive 25 miles once or twice each month to stock up on groceries, housewares, and clothing at these businesses with larger selections and lower prices than those offered by hometown merchants. Both Farmtown and Center lost railroad service in 1980. Farmtown alone experienced a 16 percent drop in retail business between 1980 and 1981 (Sheldon Mail 1982). In 1982, the editor of the *Open Country Bulletin* complained that businesses were not buying advertising and the newspaper was losing money. Farmtown, which had eight grocery stores in 1940, had a supermarket, one family-owned grocery store and one convenience gas/grocery store in 1982, but the family-owned store failed and was sold in 1983. The usual explanations for the economic malaise were the deteriorating farm economy and the high interest rates (Cochran 1982). All of this impinged directly on both the necessity of women to seek employment and their employment prospects.

As elsewhere in the United States, the majority of employed women found work in the areas of clerical, sales, or other services (see Table 7.7). Many women worked as grocery store cashiers, waitresses, school cafeteria help, and office workers. Other women were teachers or nurses. A few had their own businesses. The 34 percent of Open Country women who were listed as employed in 1980 was significantly less than the 43 percent of rural women employed across the state of Iowa (USDC 1983A:465). This smaller incidence of recorded employment undoubtedly stemmed from Open Country's isolation from Iowa's industrial centers.

Getting Jobs in Town

While census figures provide a broad outline of some of the work of Open Country women, they do not reveal the dynamics of Open Country women and the job market. Open Country women did most of the work in the reproductive sphere. Outside home they tended to work in the margins, to work for employers unable to pay standard wages, to work during short-term periods of expansion,and to move in and out of the job market. The image of a working person having a single, secure job is inappropriate for Open Country women; they adapted to a system that was not

Table 7.7
Occupations of Open Country Women
(Farm and Nonfarm), 1950–1980

Occupation	1950	1960	1970	1980
Managerial, professional	220	251	307	300
Technical, sales, clerical	298	278	390	558
Service	273	317	503	482
Operatives, blue collar	115	89	155	192
Other	45	102	32	99
Total	951	1037	1387	1631

Source: U.S. censuses.

organized for their needs. The men who employed workers developed the rules of employment outside the home and women adhered to those rules with some discomfort and personal sacrifice.

As in the time when Coral was negotiating a job in a grocery store before World War II, job hunting remained a matter of luck, personal ingratiation, and informal connections. Far from being an assurance of employment, formal qualifications have in some cases intimidated employers. Paula, who farrowed hogs in an enterprise operated jointly by several Open Country farmers, described the personal connections that led her to her job:

> Well, like me finding what I found was just through a lot of good friends I know who had hog confinements. They had just asked if I'd be willing to work only part-time to help out. They were just starting to get on their feet. Then I just ended up full-time. My job has been through mutual friends. I know all the board members real well.

Women were often asked to work by men who knew them and knew that they might want to work. As with Coral's employment, Paula was "tried out" before she was hired full-time.

Getting and keeping a job could be treacherous. Betty, who worked for the local government, compared job-hunting notes with her supervisor's wife, who was informally looking for work. They concluded that Betty, making $5.50 per hour for office work, had one of the best of the women's jobs in the county. Later that year (1982) Betty lost her job and the supervisor's wife was hired.

Teaching was an attractive job possibility for rural women who had college degrees. In the 1950s women with teaching credentials usually found jobs in Open Country. The consolidation of schools and the declining student population since that time, however, meant fewer teaching jobs. Concurrently, farmers began to marry college-educated women more frequently, and many of these women came to Open Country with teaching certificates, seeking work in the public school system. Most were disappointed.

Susan and Dale married in 1972 when both were students at Iowa State University. Dale was studying agriculture, and after graduation they returned to Open Country to take over part of Dale's family farm. Susan received a teaching certificate and unsuccessfully applied for positions in all of the towns within driving distance of the farm. One school informed her that it would not hire someone who did not live in the town. While this type of informal discrimination was not part of a publicly stated policy, it was not unusual. Because Susan moved to Open Country to live on her husband's farm and had no wish to relocate, she soon gave up her hopes of teaching.

Laura, who also married an Open Country farmer, lived on the outskirts of Center. She had a master's degree in education and several years of teaching experience. She desperately wanted to teach in Center, but she was overqualified as an elementary school teacher and the salary she would command was too high for the budget priorities of the Center school system. As an alternative, Laura organized a children's reading program at the public library and taught Sunday School, both done as volunteer services.

The local understanding was that Susan and Laura, as married women, did not need jobs. Farmers should support their families, and farm women wanting to work outside the farm could only have frivolous reasons. Therefore, women's employment applications did not warrant the serious consideration that was due their male counterparts. Men who wanted to be teachers usually moved specifically for the jobs. Hence men were less likely to be local people seeking local jobs, and school superintendents thereby had less personal information to consider when evaluating the applications.

Open Country schools took advantage of the availability of qualified women who did not have "real" jobs. When Farmtown could not hire an elementary art teacher, they recruited a local married woman to teach without remuneration. Such women added breadth and flexibility to the program. The treatment of Carole is another example of this type of exploitation. In 1979 she accepted a teaching position in Farmtown. In 1981 she married an Open Country farmer, and in 1982 her position was officially reduced to part-time. Although she still spent full days at school teaching classes and sponsoring extracurricular activities, she now cost the school district less money than she had as a full-time teacher.

School systems had the advantage of being almost the only employers in Open Country that hired people on the basis of their college degrees. Other positions that required formal qualifications in urban areas were filled more informally in local areas. Jane, the Open Country welfare director for many years, was hired through a personal connection and had no formal qualifications. Although some criticism was voiced when she was appointed, the growing consensus was that she was doing a good job. Similarly, the hospital administrator was a woman hired with no formal qualifications and no previous experience. Like the welfare director, she proved her worth by operating the small hospital efficiently.

Women got the few available jobs through personal connections and by maintaining the norms of Open Country life. Seldom, if ever, was a woman hired locally by answering an employment advertisement and convincing the employer that she was the best qualified person. Political office holders hired their courthouse office staff informally. With Republicans invariably winning all local elections, all of the courthouse office employees were Republicans.

When a Center church needed a secretary, the pastor (who for practical purposes made the decision) was aware that many of the women of his parish wanted the job. Women did not actually apply for this position; they were selected. The pastor knew that inevitably he would be criticized by some segment of the congregation for any selection he made. He decided to hire a young woman who was getting married and transferring to another church, thereby avoiding jealousy and resentment among his parishioners. While women were serious about wanting jobs, the qualities required for getting jobs did not permit passionate job searches or openly expressed frustrations.

Hiring women to work in the retail businesses was similarly personalized. When asked how she hired workers for the store she and her husband operated in Center, Marjorie said,

> You get to know the people who live in the vicinity and when you are looking for somebody you say to yourself or to your husband, "Don't you think so and so would make a very good employee?" When the

consensus is that yes, they would, you approach them and ask if they would like a job. In fact, I think . . . a great number of women who work in a store of our type are asked if they would like to work.

In a rural community, where everyone knew each other, idiosyncracies could squash women's job prospects. In 1982 when Joanne, a young woman, was being considered for a job at a local cooperative outlet, the board was skeptical. Although they un-doubtedly preferred an experienced man, Joanne had experience dealing with farm products and was clearly well-qualified. But she was a woman, she was unmarried, and she had previously lived with a man. By 1982, her past indiscretion in itself was not enough to totally disqualify her. What troubled the cooperative board was that her live-in friend had not been a stereotypic man; not only was he a writer, but he had not supported Joanne. Although the chairman of the board, a farmer, came to her defense and she was hired, the prin-ciple that it was proper for a local employer to oversee a worker's personal life was not questioned.

The one exception to the difficulty of finding local jobs was nursing. A registered nurse could easily find a position at the hospital or in one of several nursing homes. Nurses did ex-press—although rather poorly—dissatisfaction with their pay and working conditions. Carla, who returned with her husband to her family farm in 1966, was a registered nurse, and she worked briefly at the local hospital when she first returned. The only reason she gave for leaving the hospital was that she had a strong difference of opinion with her supervisor. It was not because she did not need the money—she took a job as a waitress. Other nurses quit their hospital jobs to work in nursing homes or to commute to larger hospitals. Nurses who remained in the hospital were responsible for covering the available shifts and were forced to work longer hours than they would have chosen.

Women were constantly juggling and rearranging part-time jobs. Alice, for example, in addition to her farm work, taught eve-ning classes in upholstery. Norma, a hired farm worker's wife, worked one day a week in a beauty shop. Lucy, a single mother of three, was a clerk at the hospital, and she worked part-time in a retail business. Lynn, a nurse, worked during the evenings at a bar. Marjorie, who hired workers for the store she and her husband operated, expressed her general preference for part-time employees:

We've found part-time help is a great deal preferable to full-time help. We would much rather have been able to have somebody that we could call on anytime to come in and cover for us when we were at a market, [somebody] that wouldn't normally be working that many hours or [somebody we could call on] at Christmas time who would come in and work a whole week, or [somebody we could call on to do] inventory. Our type of store is not liable for the minimum wage law.

The county health nurse, probably the only male nurse in the county, was budgeted to employ two full-time staff members. He chose to divide these positions among four women, citing significant savings in benefits and greater flexibility in hiring part-time people.

Sometimes, getting hired was a gradual process rather than a discrete event. Many, like Paula, started working part-time and gradually became full-time employees. When Pam was in high school in 1966 she became friends with a young woman who was working as a printer. She gradually started doing small tasks around the print shop while visiting her friend. Sometimes the manager surprised her by giving her $20 for her input. Eventually, Pam found a work niche in the print shop and has worked there for nearly twenty years. Not all of Pam's forays were as successful, however. In 1980 she casually suggested to the owner of a bar that he could increase his drink trade if he let her sell tacos in the bar one night a week. After several weeks of planning, purchasing supplies, making tacos, and selling them she made the mistake of telling the owner how much she made. He took over the concession.

Low Pay, Working in the Margins

The conditions under which women worked were maintained in part by their extremely low pay. As Marjorie mentioned when describing the convenience of hiring casual workers, their store was not required to pay minimum wages. Businesses doing less than $362,500 in total annual sales were not required to pay minimum wages. Newspapers and restaurants were further exceptions to the minimum wage law. Thus, many women working in drugstores, cafes, and variety stores worked for less than minimum wage. In 1982, one woman made less than $2 per hour as a salesperson.

The low pay scale was not limited to retail establishments. I arranged to teach an evening course in anthropology at a nearby technical college for $18 per two-hour class. Considering that, for each two hours of time spent teaching the class, an average minimum of four hours was needed to plan and develop a syllabus, read and prepare for the class period, evaluate student work, and be available to talk with the students, the salary was actually close to $3 per hour, which was less than the minimum wage. (Although I agreed to teach the class, it was cancelled for lack of sufficient enrollment.)

Table 7.8
Average Income of White Iowans With Income, 1979

Residence	Men	Women	Women % of Men's Income
Urban	$13,104	$5,089	39%
Rural	12,055	4,336	36%
Farm	11,494	3,926	34%

Source: U.S. census.

Table 7.8 indicates the gender inequality in Iowans' incomes in 1979. This table illustrates that the most pronounced gender disparity in reported income was among the farm population: white farm women earned only 34 cents for every dollar that white farm men earned, and white women of rural Iowa in general earned 36 cents for every $1 earned by white men.[6] This table, which includes all those with income in 1979, shows a starker inequality than would be apparent if only year-round, full-time workers were included. Working full-time for pay was a privilege that few women shared, and Table 7.8 shows the results of unequal access to full-time, paying jobs as well as low pay for women's jobs.

Betty, married in 1966, lived on a farm with her husband and five children. Her husband was a hired farm worker and with his limited income she felt forced to seek whatever work she could find within driving distance. For a time she worked as a helper in a nursing home, but this income was insufficient: when she quit in 1975, she was making $1.65 per hour.[7] She then held a variety of babysitting jobs, and she weeded soybeans in the summer for $4 per hour. In 1977, after an informal job search, she heard about a position in a local government office. She got the job at $4.50 per hour. Before losing her job in 1982, she was receiving $5.50 per hour, which she supplemented by cleaning the office for $4.50 per hour. Betty had one of the highest paying jobs available for women without formal education.

Employers were aware of how hard it was for women to get jobs. They knew that women worked harder for less money because finding jobs was difficult and employers found ways to exploit womens' situations. Pam, a part-time bartender in 1981, was repeatedly asked to wait on tables, which was a hard and unfair request: even in desperation few women were willing to venture out among the tables of drinking men to serve drinks. Pam complained to the owner's wife, who explained that the reason they hired her—and not a man—for the job as second bartender was that they thought she would be willing to wait on tables during busy hours. In this case, they miscalculated and Pam quit, stating that she did not need the money that desperately. Obviously, her employer thought she needed the job so much that she would work beyond the agreed limits.

The Open Country area has been saturated with women maintaining home dealerships in items such as cosmetics, plastic dishes and containers, vitamins, cleaning products, jewelry, and home decorations. The companies supplying these products promote dealerships by emphasizing that women can earn money at home. They prohibit advertising. Often the products are sold at home parties at which the dealer entertains the guests with games promoting the products, and the guests, in turn, make purchases. Women who gave parties for the dealers received bonus gifts.

Some women have other small enterprises in their homes. Norma sews; Karen bakes and decorates cakes, sews, and keeps a boarder; Paula, who works in the farrowing enterprise, breeds and sells dogs at home; Karla, among others, gives music lessons. Most of the local newspaper copy is prepared by women who telephone neighbors for social news which they write at home. Other women report on meetings and other events.

One step larger than most of the home enterprises are the small Main Street businesses which are now owned by women. From 1982 to 1985 different Center women operated a clothing store, a second-hand store, a gift shop, a variety store, two beauty shops, a bar, and a newspaper. In Farmtown, women operated dress shops, beauty shops, and a restaurant, and another managed a branch office of a savings and loan company. All of these businesses suffered severely with the recent poor economic conditions and few provided total household support. Two of the women's businesses failed and others are barely profitable, even with the low cost of conducting an Open Country business. With the growing number of empty storefronts in Center and Farmtown, building rent has declined correspondingly. This, combined with the low cost of rural labor, means that only a small investment is required for many businesses. Typically, women's businesses employ only a manager and a part-time worker to relieve her when necessary. Such businesses are not viable in a competitive urban setting.

Open Country still has some husband-wife businesses, the majority being restaurants and retail stores, which are continuations of the older family economies of prewar days. However, a general decline in the number of local merchants has included family businesses; and there are correspondingly fewer women with access to this employment.

Some women manage several jobs continually. Indeed, typical Open Country women of the 1980s are more likely to work intermittently at a variety of jobs or be seeking employment. The published government statistics, which show each person either working or not working at one job, make the situation seem simpler than it really is. Currently, many Open Country women work at several poorly paying, exploitative jobs whenever they are "lucky" enough to find them.

For example, Jerri, a single mother with three children, had a full-time job managing a branch office of a savings and loan company in Farmtown. From April through November the office closed at 4:30 in the afternoon, and she went to work until 10:30 at a drive-in restaurant. On Thursday nights, her night off from the restaurant, she worked at the bowling alley. Although her children were old enough so that they did not physically require child care, Jerri's time with them was necessarily shorter than she would have liked.

Yet Jerri, having had her jobs since the mid-1970s, was lucky. At that time, the manager of the restaurant was having trouble finding enough workers. These types of small jobs were easy to find, and the restaurant manager even resorted to employing high school students. By 1982, the manager employed only one or two of the most popular students, who brought in high school customers. Many responsible adult women were now willing to work at the drive-in. Jerri held onto her jobs, realizing that she would have a difficult time finding other part-time evening jobs.

Factories and the "Right to Work"

A few of the Open Country women worked in factories, which ranged in size from very small local plants to those in surrounding areas employing several hundred workers. A lamb slaughtering plant opened in Farmtown in 1981. Of the hundreds of applicants, only 40 workers were hired, most of whom were men. Conversely, a small poultry slaughtering operation south of Farmtown employed approximately nine workers, almost exclusively women. Poultry processing, unlike pork, beef and lamb meat packing, was traditionally done by local women.

In this case, a local farmer who specialized in broilers built a small custom poultry dressing enterprise for his use and for that of the surrounding poultry raisers. The enterprise operates from mid-May until December 31. The workers butcher, clean, cut, and pack chickens through the summer and early fall and then switch to turkeys, ducks, and geese for the holiday season. Growers bring in anywhere from a few birds to truckloads of poultry for processing at the plant. With the exception of an electric chicken plucker, the women clean the chickens by hand, usually dressing 85 to 90 broilers each hour.

Ellen, who came to Open Country in 1955 when she married a farmer, was working at this poultry plant in 1982. She and her husband rented farms for several years before they inherited his family farm in 1967. In 1966, Ellen began to supplement the family income by working for the poultry packer and has worked there since that time. When the plant's bookkeeper was killed in a automobile accident Ellen, the longest-tenured worker, assumed the duties of answering the telephone and planning the work flow, in addition to her regular job on the poultry line. When asked how workers were hired, Ellen said,

> Usually by word of mouth. He never advertises for help. . . . If someone wants a part-time job or something to just get a little spending money they usually call and ask him if he has an opening. He takes their name.

During the slaughtering season, Ellen worked from early in the morning until about 4:30 in the afternoon. She did not state what her wages were, but she did say that she made more than the women who worked in town. In spite of the overpowering stench and the hands-on work with chicken entrails, these were sought-after positions.

Ellen was extremely positive about her work:

> It's just amazing. You have to see it to believe it. We talk to each other while we work. We have some pretty wild days sometimes, talking about the things going on.

Furthermore, Ellen was always eager to start work in May:

> It gets kind of lonesome at home I guess. [Processing poultry] is something you get used to after that many years. . . . It's kind of nice to have a little job like that where you can just put in a few hours every day. It helps in the bank account a little bit.

For Ellen the pay, along with the intimacy and informality of the work and her friendships with her coworkers, made poultry processing at this small plant a good job. A growing number of women worked at impersonal factories where the easy banter that made Ellen's work fun was not permitted (see Table 7.7).

A few women worked in the lamb slaughtering plant in Farmtown. Others drove 25 or 40 miles to two meat packing plants outside of Open Country, but most of the packing plant workers—other than poultry workers—were men. The major sources of factory employment for Open Country women were three apparel factories located within a 20-minute drive of Open Country. These factories were specifically planned to tap the labor of rural women. As one manager confided, the factory's location was chosen because the owners understood that rural women needed jobs and they were unlikely to question the structure of authority imposed by the factory owner.

One of these factories, opened in 1955, employed approximately 100 workers, 90 percent of whom were women. When I visited the plant in 1982 I observed a workroom about the size of a large high school gymnasium. The manager (a man) had a glassed-in office above the work floor, so he could observe the entire sewing assembly operation, from the cutters on one end to the packers on the other. Most of the floor was occupied by women sitting at sewing stations. Cutters loaded unassembled garments in lots on carts that the women pushed from one assembly step to the next.

The manager did not permit workers to talk with each other; some wore radio headphones and seemed to be moving to the rhythm of music as they worked. They worked an eight-hour day, with a 15-minute coffee break in the morning, a 30-minute lunch, and a 10-minute coffee break in the afternoon. A woman was allowed 120 days for maternity leave if she had a signed statement from her doctor stating that she needed a leave of absence. The normal maternity leave was four to six weeks. One woman, who had six children, had to take a year off for maternity leave; she was forced to give up her job, although she was rehired when she was able to return.

Being hired at this factory entailed applying and passing a manual dexterity test. After an initial training period, each woman was expected to attain a speed in which a given number of garments passed through her station each hour. Women who sewed faster received bonuses, and the manager put signs on their stations praising them and announcing the amount by which they exceeded their quotas.

At another factory I was allowed a tour of the floor, as well as conversation and interaction with the workers. This factory was similar to the previous one but it employed about four times as many workers. Like the other factory, this one employed men in the management positions and in a few of the assembly operations; women did the majority of the assembly operations and the clerical work. The work floor was divided into different areas and different rooms. Sandra, approximately 35 years old, operated a large machine located in a separate room with another woman operating an identical machine. Their separation, she explained, was because of the noise levels of the machines. She wore earplugs but had, nevertheless, experienced a moderate hearing loss. In addition, because the machine required very intricate work in threading series of needles, she had some vision problems. Further, the intricacy of the machine precluded all but a few skilled workers from operating it, and Sandra was forced to work ten-hour shifts rather than the usual eight-hour shifts. The factory had attempted to institute two twelve-hour shifts each day for the women working these machines, but Sandra said that her nerves could not stand it and she would not have had time to commute home, to do her housework, or to sleep. She said that she became "stressed out." As it was, she planned to request a different work assignment because of her failing sight and hearing.

Women who worked in these factories tended to be loyal employees. In 1982, average production workers earned between

$4 and $5 per hour, which they considered good pay. Moreover, hiring was done impersonally. Anyone who learned the work within the required training period was acceptable. Personal life was not a factor, as long as there was no talk of unions.

Iowa is a right-to-work state, which means that employees must vote to have a union if they are to bargain collectively. I did not talk to anyone in Open Country who opposed the right-to-work principle, although some believed that establishing unions would be a good thing. The prevailing opinion was that if unions were established, manufacturing plants, such as the apparel plants, would be less likely to remain in Iowa. A unionized meat packing plant in a nearby city closed in 1984, but the nonunionized lamb plant in Farmtown remained open. Union organizers distributed literature outside one of the factories where women worked, but they had no success in establishing contact. When complaining about their jobs, women often voiced the opinion that they *needed* a union, but this did not mean that they actually *wanted* to talk about a union. Without thinking I placed my position as fieldworker in jeopardy one evening early in the year when I supported a hospital worker's we-need-a-union statement. The next week the town of Center had figured out what I was really doing in Open Country: I was a troublemaker who had come to unionize the hospital workers. I met stony stares and general silence when I went to a gathering in Center the next week. A woman who had heard the original conversation rescued my reputation, smoothed over the situation, and explained to me what had happened. A decent woman did not talk about unions.[8]

Developers continue to court manufacturing industry, one of rural Iowa's major attractions being the right-to-work clause and the promise of no unions. While the factories pay more than most other employers, the pay is considerably less than that of the majority of industrial workers in the United States. The urge to approach rural problems by recruiting manufacturing industry is impeded only by the competition among rural areas for manufacturing plants. If development succeeds, increasing numbers of rural women will work in factories, but there is no guarantee that factory management will concern itself with the health of the workers or the well-being of Open Country. Where the responsibility for this concern will lie is unclear, but at present it is defined as an individual problem for a woman and her family. Yet rural family is becoming a smaller, less responsive institution than it was previously.

Conclusion

While the women's job market in Open Country seemed informal, it in fact had its own rules and structure. Just as the early Open Country women experienced their work options within the constraints of their families, the modern rules drew directly from the assumption that women should remain within their families. The idea that women belonged in the family survived the breakup of the family economies that dominated Open Country before World War II. Farm women, ousted from their traditional enterprises, could work for their husbands or for other employers, but they could not work in settings that were structurally similar to earlier positions. Except for those farm women who worked for their husbands, *work* and *family* have come to represent contrasting, often conflicting, responsibilities because the postwar nuclear family with male wage earners does not afford many women income-generating enterprises on home ground (although some women maintain their own economic operations with home dealerships). By 1982, women's family roles as wives did not automatically mean that they were business partners.

Even though many women worked outside the home or worked from their homes for money, they tended to denigrate the importance of what they did. One woman after another spoke of having a little job that brought in a little extra money, but they did not consider themselves *working women.* Ellen, who worked in the chicken packing enterprise, spoke of having "little job" that helped "a little bit" with the money. This may have meant that the pay was so little that she was embarrassed to call it her paying job. Like the farm women who *helped* rather than *worked* on the farm, these women denied the significance of what they did. With their economic feet in the home, women made forays into the work world, but they did not claim this world as their own.

Different business interests found different ways to extract surplus value from rural women. The companies which supplied the cosmetics and vitamins women sold from their homes increased their profits by saving retail distribution costs. When women sold products from their homes the costs of store rental, utilities, and maintenance were not counted as business expenses. With less *acknowledged* overhead, the companies realized extra profits by charging higher wholesale prices without having correspondingly higher consumer prices.

Small town businesses, like the dealership companies, depended on women's willingness to sell their labor cheaply. Retail businesses remained solvent only by paying women low wages. Women who had businesses maintained them on slender or negative profit margins. The fact that women teachers were hired or laid off with ease provided the rural schools with the flexibility that enabled them to adjust to declining enrollments and difficult state education standards. Pastors and mayors all agreed that women were the heart of the spirit that kept churches and small towns alive.

For the most part, women professed agreement with a non-materialistic ideal that made it easy for employers to pay them little or nothing. At a woman's club meeting I heard the statement, "The difference between doing a job for money and doing that same job for no money is the difference between night and day." *Night* was working for money and day was working for love. Night, in other words, was being in need; day was having a wealthy husband. Many Open Country women had high expectations for what a family would provide. By not passing the state Equal Rights Amendment in 1980 and in other anti-feminist statements they put their faith—and fate—in the hope that family would provide what they needed, or that family would be friendlier to their interests than the legal system would be. If family failed and a woman needed to find employment, she hoped that a pastor would ask her to work in the church office, or that a discrete inquiry would uncover a part-time job in a school or at the courthouse. The strategy for being favored in this way was to be nice, to get along with people, to be a Republican, and not to talk about unions or women's rights.

This was a more realistic short-term survival strategy than trying to make basic changes by agitating for women's rights or unions. When Open Country women rejected feminism, they were in part saying that feminism had little to offer them in their immediate struggles as they coped with the daily realities of surviving. Women in other parts of the country who were entering the field of medicine or being nominated for Vice President of the United States were taunting rather than inspiring the majority of Open Country women.

The rural poverty rates put the realities of Open Country women's lives into stark relief. In 1979, before the farm crisis began in earnest, 15.6 percent of Iowa's farm population was living below the poverty level (USDC 1983A: 485). In Open Country, among farm and nonfarm people, 10.7 percent were existing below the poverty level (USDC 1983: 472). By 1982, in the United States as a whole,

22.1 percent of the farm population was living in poverty, a higher rate than in central cities.[9] The 1982 poverty threshold for a single parent with three children was $9,817 yearly income (USDC 1984:181). The average income of an Open Country woman was less than one-half the poverty level (see Table 7.8). If a woman had a factory job and was fortunate enough to earn $4.50 per hour for a 40-hour week, she would have made $9,360 per year, still below the poverty threshold. Men's help was indeed necessary to raise women's standard of living.

Open Country has some of the richest farmland in the United States. Just 100 years ago this rich land drew northern Europeans into the area. Both the women and the men worked hard to claim the land. The land's yield has increased greatly over the years, and the rich agricultural base supports the strength of the country as a whole. But this increase has not brought general prosperity to Open Country. Open Country women who worked on the farm lost their farm enterprises. The minority of women remaining on the farm either work for their husbands or work off the farm. The farm enterprises that women once operated have been absorbed by large-scale entrepreneurs and removed from Open Country. While some women shared the fortunes of the successful men in their families, others were pushed into increasingly precarious economic positions. Working long hours at substandard wages, many women hover around the edges of poverty; others live firmly entrenched in poverty. These women are the daughters of northern European immigrants; they have attended church and maintained their belief in the work ethic and free enterprise, yet the system they have supported has not been kind to them. There is no culture of poverty in Open Country—no received behavior patterns that predispose these people to poverty. Their ancestors were hardy pioneers. These women are white, but in losing their livelihood on the land, in increased dependency on men, and in becoming cheap labor for corporations they share the economic predicaments of many black, Hispanic, and Asian women. The following chapter examines the way this affects their nonworking lives.

household farm was about to be put on the market and he thought the Walters might be interested: they could farm the land, initially with the older son's help and eventually have both sons operate the farm alone. The Walters felt the farm was a good opportunity and bought it.

Max thought of himself as a benevolent person who helped keep farmland locally owned and who helped deserving young men get into farming. Others, such as a farm business consultant who worked locally, were in a similar position to find out about plans to sell farmland. These key people were men who passed their inside information on to other men. The idea of passing along an opportunity to a young women who might want to go into farming would have seemed incredible to them; it was not within their realm of thought. When land auctions were held, women technically could have bid on land, but they never did. In fact, anyone entering farming needed significant wealth, access to credit, or substantial family support—usually all three. Each of these was much more likely to fall to a man than to a woman.

The majority of land transfers were intergenerational within families. The preferred form of inheriting farmland was patrilineal, whereby a son assumed his father's (or parents') farm. If the son did not want to farm the land, it was either sold or inherited by the son, who then rented it. Some daughters, like the Walters' daughter, asked for a share in the home farm, but they were denied the opportunity. As Mrs. Walters said, "It never would have worked to have him [the daughter's husband] and our boys trying to farm together." Some daughters remained in Open Country without receiving shares in their family farms.

Even when a daughter was the only heir, it was not certain that she would inherit the family farm. Hazel, born in 1926, was the oldest of three daughters of a farmer who had a purebred livestock business. Because he had no sons, her father eventually sold the farm. If Hazel had been given some encouragement and support, she might well have seriously considered farming. Growing up, she and her sisters did fieldwork with tractors and horses. When interviewed, she described many details of this work, of the mechanics of breeding, and of figuring feeding rations. She told of cold hands in the winter, chipping the ice from the watering tank so animals could drink, and the tonics and extra care given to sick animals. She said somewhat wistfully, "If I'd been a boy, we'd probably have carried on with the farm." As it was, Hazel and her husband ran a small business in Farmtown. Reflecting on the farm and its present owners, who had two sons going into farming, Hazel said, "They have built it up nicely. I think it probably shows the fact that there were sons in that family."

When women did gain control of land it was by default: if no brother was willing and able to take over the farm, a sister was sometimes allowed to do so. Carla, who returned with her husband to her family farm in 1966, was such an example. When it became obvious that Carla was the only sibling who wanted the farm, her father stopped attempting to improve the farm and eventually sold her the existing farm at a price above the usual level for in-family transactions. Carla described the negotiations involving her father's attempt to lure her brother who lived in another state into farming:

> My oldest brother had just gotten his master's degree in educa-tion in '64. He has four kids. My father was going to quit farming in '66. That was going to be his last year. He asked my brother if he wanted to come home and farm. . . . He had the chance to buy the farm right across the road down here for $400 an acre. I really wanted him to buy it in the worst way, but he couldn't see going into debt. My brother said, "No, I'm not going to farm. I can't hack it with four kids, with farming these two places and no [read, less] income until you retire."

> My dad would like to have had the oldest boy take over. Well, he [Dad] turned it [the land offer] down and didn't make any effort to go and talk with the guy and buy it anyway. It would have made it really nice for us because we would have had a half section [320 acres]. Now we've only got a quarter [160 acres]. . . .

> So my dad came to my husband, who was going to retire from the Air Force and said, "What do you think about coming home to farm?"

> I told my husband, "It will be entirely up to you. I won't say one way or another."

When they decided to farm, they had to cajole her father into turning over the land to them, even though he had no intention of working it and was planning to retire to Montana.

> No way are they going to leave this place and we sit here and work this land, fix all the buildings and then have to pay through the nose because it's part of the estate. . . . I said, "Either we buy it or we don't. We want to know now."

My father said okay.

We went in to the lawyers. He had promised me since whenever that when we started farming that he would sell it to me for $500 an acre. We got into the lawyer's office and the lawyer said that was pretty cheap. [The lawyer suggested $550.] I didn't look at Dad's face. I said, "Well, Dad, you promised me that you'd let us have it for $500." Then I thought, for $8,000 I'm not going to worry about it. . . . We finally got those papers signed.

Even when the land was Carla's family farm and she had made her desire to farm known to her father when he was considering buying more land two years before his retirement, he approached her husband and asked him for a decision. Carla played the wife by saying that it was entirely her husband's decision, in spite of her clear involvement in all of the negotiations. If Carla had not had a husband, she proabaly would not have wanted to return to Open Country; furthermore, her father probably would not have considered her even as a second choice for taking over the farm; finally, she probably would not have been in a financial position to buy the farm.

The other way a woman got land by default was as a widow. The 1982 U.S. agricultural census listed 23 Open Country women as farmers (USDC 1983B:2), and most, if not all, were widows. Inheritance tax laws were revised so that widows could inherit substantial farm property without paying tax, and this eased the latter years of some women, but typically a widow held the land only until it could be passed to another male family member. One such example was a woman with a 13-year-old son who was suddenly widowed. Because the son wanted the farm, his mother managed during the intervening years with the help of a hired man. Usually, a widow was an older woman with younger male relatives actually farming the land. Sonya Salamon and Anna Keim found in their study of Heartland, an Illinois farming community, that while such women ceded daily control of farming to the younger men, they gained some status within the family by virtue of their ability to confer land. In spite of women's legal ownership of land, they never developed or expanded their landholdings. Salamon and Keim (1979:115) wrote, "In Heartland, though women may own and manage farms, operation is always associated with or attributed to a male." Seena Kohl (1976:107), who wrote about Jasper, an agricultural community in Saskatchewan, concluded,

Women are precluded from effective entrance into the agricultural occupation except as wife, regardless of the household focus and the style of the mother's participation.

Although she recorded some exceptions to this, they were exceptional exceptions.

In Open Country, as in Heartland and Jasper, a woman's access to farmland was through a man—she had no access to farmland unless she married. A man did not have to be married to own land (although he typically had his mother or another woman to cook, clean, and launder for him). This asymmetry created a material base for male dominance.

Nor was it only within the family farm that men controlled women's livelihoods. Since men held most of Open Country's capital, they usually hired and paid women for their nonfamily work. The boards of directors of the cooperatives and banks, the business operators substantial enough to hire workers, and the school superintendents who hired the teachers were all men.

A working woman's pay rarely constituted a living wage. As illustrated in the previous chapter, a working woman made only a small percentage of what a man earned; her average annual income was less than one-half of the established poverty level. Therefore, a woman's access to a living wage was most often through a man—usually a husband, sometimes a father. A woman living in poverty or forced to hold three jobs in order to survive was hardly a model that many women sought to emulate in trying to take control of their own lives.

The solidarity that women had with each other in their extended families faded with the heavy out-migration and the post-World War II focus on the nuclear family. Extended family relations remained a shadow of what they once were. The women of one of the pioneer families had a family club that met monthly for visiting and eating together, but they said that a major reason for having the club was that they did not see each other much outside of this meeting. Most of the club members were older than age 50. Of the approximately 25 club members, only four had joined after 1960. Three of these four were family members by marriage; the only young woman member by birth subsequently left the area for economic reasons. The young women who were new to the family and to the club had weaker ties; they attended meetings less frequently and did not host meetings in their homes.

Nuclear family identity created heavy demands on the marital relation, but this relation was structurally strained. Because women needed men for economic reasons, marriage was not symmetric. Women had more to gain economically by marriage, and they had more to lose with the dissolution of a marriage. Men, particularly those living in town, had a much greater latitude to have extramarital sexual affairs than did women. Wives were reluctant to leave husbands even when they realized emotional alienation, which many of them did. Perhaps because farm men were busier and did not have as much leisure, they were less likely to have extramarital relationships, but they were also less likely to spend time with their wives. In addition, farm women were somewhat more likely than town women to help their husbands work; the loss of a farm wife involved a certain economic (as well as social) loss for the man. As one farm woman said, "A man really *needs* a wife on the farm." One man explained that if a husband and wife living in town had major marital problems they would probably get a divorce; if a farm couple had major marital problems they would probably remain married. The husband needed the wife, and the wife's major work experience was often connected to the farm. As a domestic violence worker stated, "Farm women often have spent years developing the farm as a family business and can't afford to leave when severe marital problems arise." (Quoted in Levitas 1983:7). Several Open Country cases supported the hypothesis that farm couples would rather endure a bad marriage, while town couples would rather divorce. With or without formal divorces, however, disrupted marriages were a reality.[2]

Bescher-Donnelly and Smith (1981:168) reported that the rural-urban gap in the divorce rate was narrowing; the divorce rate among farm as well as nonfarm rural couples was increasing. Younger farm women seemed more likely to leave a marriage. Carole, a young farm woman married in 1981, felt conflicts that she explicitly connected to farm life: She wanted more intellectual stimulation and was afraid of being trapped in a spiritually and socially stifling situation. She left her husband after two years of marriage. With a part-time teaching job and no financial support from her family, she supplemented her teaching salary by working as a waitress until she could leave Open Country. She finally moved to another job with little pay, but one that was intellectually stimulating and that allowed her to live close to some friends in another state. She had had little time and no inclination to invest herself in the farm operation.

Even though the divorce rate among farm people was rising, a divorcing woman rarely gained access to the farmland. Like Carole, most divorced women left Open Country. They suffered social scorn and economic problems, and they certainly did not become local models of independence.

The post-World War II nuclear family and the weakening of the extended family meant that a woman's access to the goods and services generated in the family were directly dependent upon marriage, but a busy husband could not provide all of what was once shared among women in an extended family. While the state assumed some of the extended family's functions, particularly with regard to the care of the elderly and ill, women realized big gaps in social services once available within the family: Open Country had no licensed childcare, and no domestic violence or sexual assault centers existed within 50 miles. Available professional counseling involved a 25-mile commute to one of the nearby cities, and even then the range of these services was not extensive. When asked about women's needs for domestic violence shelters and childcare facilities, a development planner explained that domestic violence was an urban problem and that rural women had always managed without childcare facilities because they had family. Yet domestic violence occurred in Open Country, and urban shelters across the state answered calls from rural women in their immediate areas (Levitas 1983:7). While most women who needed childcare could usually find another woman to provide those services cheaply, the quality of the care was not always comparable to that found in facilities that met state standards or in homes where grandmothers, aunts, and cousins shared the care. The nuclear family did not provide the range of services available in an extended family, but women seldom pressed effectively for more extensive public services for themselves and their children.

Women's economic dependency constituted a material base for male dominance by enforcing asymmetric marriages that often did not provide settings for meeting the needs of women. By controlling land, wealth, and social services, men were in a position to have their wishes heeded. One farmer, who had a close and long-lived marriage, explained his wife's position on their farm. His wife was a major factor in their farm operation—she drove a tractor and did the bookwork. While she never made farm decisions, she was an important factor in her husband's decisions because she listened to him and supported him. Sometimes she also added her opinion. In fact, he felt that the wife was so important to the farming operation that he never hired a farm hand without meeting his wife and making sure she was supportive of his farming work. No wife at all was better than an unsupportive wife.

Another farmer, giving his views on land ownership, said that a farmer deserved to have enough land to support his wife. He was the worker, she was the beneficiary. Farming was a labor of love.[3] This trickle-down theory of benefits to women worked in many cases and left women very comfortable: many men shared both the toils and the fruits with their families. That some men dominated unselfishly, gently, and lovingly did not negate the reality of domination, and it was not something that most women could escape while living in Open Country. Gentle domination did not address women's need for emotional, economic and social choices in their lives.

Another element in Hartmann's definition of *patriarchy* is that it is a hierarchical set of social relations among men. Patriarchy, which literally means the rule of the fathers, is a system by which more powerful men dominate less powerful men. Women are extraneous to this hierarchy in that they do not assume a position within it, but are, rather, a factor that holds it together and supports it. In Open Country, as in the rest of the United States, this hierarchy has been determined by class.

Capitalism has dominated United States agriculture since the Civil War era. Because of the ready availability of farmland on the western frontier, this domination worked through a different historical process in the rural United States than in Europe and in American cities, and it generated a different ideology. The process has moved, however, toward a polarization of capital and labor increasingly similar to that of other industries. As previously discussed, household production and commodity production were parts of a dual farm economy in the early years of Open Country settlement. Women, as producers for household use and for exchange for household needs, defended their interests and tried to further their position through local support of these interests, especially through the institution of the extended family. Within the national system, however, their position was weak.

During World War II, with the total effort for maximum production on the farm, women were drawn more fully into commodity production. The expanding market claimed increasing control of women's poultry production. Women, forced to compete as commodity producers in the post-World War II poultry products markets, lost their enterprises. Although women remained the chief housekeepers and farm helpers, their major production functions have been assumed by larger and more powerful commercial producers. Farm commodity producers, as well as household producers, are, in fact, a transitional, intermediate class that is diminishing as the process of capital accumulation proceeds. As has been shown, commodity production alone was never a viable, stable system; rather, it depended on resources generated by home production for consumption and for household income, and since World War II it has depended on increasing injections of federal subsidies. As Michael Merrill (1977:62–3) wrote about commodity production as a mode of production in the eighteenth and early nineteenth centuries,

> The only secure basis for opposition to capitalist forms of production in the nineteenth century was a non-commodity mode of production. . . . A commodity world, on the contrary, is the Ur-world of capital. . . .
>
> Commodity producers threaten their own reproduction as independent producers if they do not keep their accounts balanced. But household producers, who reproduce themselves independently of the market, are not under this compulsion.

Commodity production involved mutually independent laborers who sold the products of their labor in the market. The distribution of the products in the market determined the distribution of labor—of people (Merrill 1977:55). Family farmers are known for their independence, with each farmer owning or managing his own tract of land and presenting the product of his labor for exchange on the market. The impersonal market and the quantified, money-based exchange system determines the size of farms, the number of farmers, and the distribution of farm labor. Thus, when farmers discuss farming they usually begin by expressing good feelings about owning land, and controlling their work and lives—about natural freedom. The profanity and frustration come when the discussion turns to the market. They cannot set their prices; they cannot give themselves fair treatment precisely because their values of independence and lack of coordination work against a class response. Capital understood this.

Kevin Goss, Richard Rodefeld and Frederick Buttel (1980), in describing the process of capitalist penetration of U.S. agriculture, delineated two ongoing processes: the progressive removal of capital from the farm sector and the progressive consolidation of capital remaining in the farm sector. Agriculture, the production of food and fiber, has three stages: an input stage (providing such farm inputs as chemicals, machinery, fuel, and finance), a farm stage, and an output stage (processing and marketing). The transition from horsepower and simple farm equipment to modern machinery, chemicals, and fertilizers transferred much of what previously was farm labor to factories. On the output end, food marketing, processing, and distribution have also expanded in size and in their control of agriculture. In 1973, the total U.S. agricultural cash income was $243.6 billion, but only $22.7 billion was farm income (Goss et al. 1980:98). Unlike the farm stage, the input and output stages of agriculture have been organized according to capitalist principles, with the separation of ownership and labor and the consequent unlimited growth in size. Large grain companies, farm equipment manufacturers, and food corporations dominate nonfarm agribusiness. Under these conditions, the myth of the independent family farmer keeps the farm stage politically weak and exploitable.

John Davis (1980) described the exploitation of the propertied laborer under these conditions. The continuing existence of the family farm signifies to some that American society has not been and will not be polarized into capitalist and working classes, but Davis argued that the family farm is not incompatible with capitalist relations. By controlling nonfarm agricultural industry, capitalists control prices of farm inputs and agricultural produce, thereby exerting indirect but efficient control over the family farmer. This control forces working conditions on farmers that could not be forced on hired labor: low producer prices induce farmers to work longer hours for little extra income. In other words, a capitalist cannot produce a bushel of corn for less than he can buy it from a family farmer, who exploits his family, works overtime, and assumes the risk. Besides setting the price, the capitalist is not forced to handle whatever does not meet his quality standards (Davis 1980:143). The years between 1949 and 1968 saw a tenfold increase in the rate of exploitation of the propertied farm laborer (Goss et al. 1980:107).[4] The state furthered the process by enhancing the capitalist controlled sectors of agriculture (Goss et al. 1980:116).

Another effect of capitalist penetration of agriculture has been deepening inequalities within the farming stage itself. Among farm operations there has been an increasing concentration of land and other farm capital, an increasing concentration of hired workers, and an increasing proletarianization of small farmers (Goss et al. 1980:106,110). Federal subsidies to farmers went, in disproportionate degree, to large farmers, thereby encouraging their growth (Drabenstott and Heady 1980:21–2). Moreover, the government's extension service taught farmers to attack their economic problems by increasing production and efficiency to make themselves individually more competitive, rather than by class action (Goss et al. 1980:118).

Several studies of rural communities have indicated that, in spite of gains for a shrinking group of large-scale farmers, the overall consequences of the ascendancy of large-scale farms are negative (Buttel 1980:8).[5] Earl Heady (1980:15) found that "total farm income, rural area employment, and income stands to be reduced when farms are larger." An important result of the polarization, or the weakening middle, of the farm population was an increased outflow of capital from rural areas.

Open Country has been a part of the process of class development. The total number of farmers declined, while the percentage of large- and small-scale farms has increased. In 1982, nearly 40 percent of Open Country farmland was owned by slightly more than 10 percent of the farmers; 10 percent of the land was owned by 40 percent of the farmers.[6] The large-scale, full-time family farmers were commodity producers who were the core of a local elite class. They and the substantial Open Country businessmen and professionals controlled the land, equipment, and buildings they used to make a living. Although they hired some workers, their own labor was the central part of their business operations; they were not capitalists. Because this upper class owned a large share of Open Country's resources, they claimed the lion's share of local power.

The situations of upper-class farm and nonfarm women were similar. In 1982, the most prominent Open Country women, married to successful farmers and professionals, enjoyed a range of opportunity not previously open to rural people. They and their families took trips to Asia, Europe, and Africa; some had swimming pools and private racketball courts; some had vacation homes or condominiums at a lakeside vacation area approximately 60 miles away. The children of the upper class selected college educations without considering cost. With the exception of the sons who took over the farms, sons and daughters of the prosperous Open Country residents left Open Country permanently after high school graduation, returning only to visit their parents and to attend weddings and reunions.

This upper class is intermediate in that it is a local collection stage for capital leaving the area; it is transitional in that its members are gradually being absorbed either into the working class or into the capitalist class. The recent loss of a bank and the bankruptcies of some large farms serve as reminders of how ephemeral this class is. Yet in the mid-1980s, the upper class continues to present an imposing profile in Open Country political life. In contrast to this upper class is the working class, consisting of part-time farmers and others who must sell their labor in order to survive. Dependent on the local upper class or factory-owning capitalists for their livelihoods, they have been politically subordinate.

In this analysis, class is considered a fundamentally male hierarchy; a woman's husband's class position conferred class membership on her.[7] Those women without husbands, living or dead, formed a special subclass of social outcasts. As Hartmann wrote, the male hierarchy allowed men to dominate women. While men and women were both oppressed by the class system, women had to contend with the further oppression of a patriarchal system.

In this context, Open Country women maintaned an ongoing struggle, not only for survival but also to find a basis of support and solidarity with other women. Open Country in the 1980s posed gender-specific challenges.

Women and Open Country Organizations

Women's church club activities claimed less of their time and energy in the 1980s than they had earlier. The women of a Farmtown church consolidated their separate women's clubs and federated nationally in 1945. From this point, much of their agenda and program was generated outside rather than developed by the local women. Where a variety of locally organized groups had controlled substantial budgets, the new organization aroused less interest and had less power in church affairs. Membership declined more than one-third from 1950 to 1970. A church history listed the following as the church service of the Guild, an organization founded by young mothers in 1931 and continuing until it joined itself to the federated club in 1945: tuning the piano; buying hymnals, dishes, carpeting, curtains, screens, vesper chimes, flags, vases, oak collection plates and gifts for the minister; contributing to the church's Missionary Society, flood relief, cancer fund, County Welfare, Salvation Army, and funeral memorials; donating labor and materials for the church repairs; and contributing hundreds of dollars to the church trustees. Other women's groups in the same church made similar contributions before they were consolidated in 1945. In 1974, women's club members visited shut-ins, made quilts for the needy, distributed 41 plates of Christmas foods, and con-tributed $44.72 to church projects, a service record that did not begin to match that of even one of the women's organizations of the 1930s.

A man who had followed the politics of a Center church throughout the years explained that in the 1930s and 1940s women ran the church. They raised most of the money, and they controlled most of the decisions. In the 1950s, the pastor and trustees decided they did not want to be so dependent on the women. They increased the budget for the church as a whole, encouraged couples' clubs, and worked to raise funds that would free them of women's domina-tion. A few key women joined the ranks of the trustees. As this oc-curred, women discovered they had even less time for church club involvements. A woman in her sixties attributed this change to women's employment:

> The young women don't get involved in church circles because so many have jobs. We're finding it difficult in filling our offices in our circles because so many will say, "Well, I have a job,"—and they have their family and it's hard. It was hard when we had our chickens and our families, too. I look back on it and I don't know how I did it.

But she did it. While jobs were occupying some women's time in the 1980s, increasing employment was not solely responsible for the declining interest. Church clubs no longer had the power and prestige they had in prior years. Women put their energies into ac-tivities that would help them gain some control of their lives; by the 1980s, this was not church clubs. Although membership and activ-ity level varied, the 1980s organizations were smaller, the members were older, the meetings fewer, the activities more limited, and the monetary power much less than was the case in the earlier period.

Interdenominational Bible study clubs were more popular than church clubs among working class women. A professional man's wife made it her mission to establish these groups, which became a central element in Open Country's religious life in the 1980s. Having purchased a fundamentalist Bible study program, this woman telephoned women she knew to interest them in trying to form a group. Women who had experience with one group recruited their friends and neighbors to another study unit. The study groups met, read the lessons, and answered the prepared questions; they had no further service agenda than intensifying and sharing the Christian religious experience. Although some men and upper class women participated, the majority of the participants were working class women. Those with liberal theological views, mostly educated, upper class women, were critical of the uniformity and the literal interpretations of the study modules and did not become deeply involved in the movement.

One earnest participant was Diane, who came to Open Country in 1975 as a farmer's wife. She had a college degree which she had been unable to translate into an acceptable job in the area. Fundamentally religious and lonely as an outsider wife, she saw Bible study as a way to bridge the gap separating her, as a city person, from her rural neighbors:

> Bible study is a good way for me to meet people from this area. . . . Talk over something as intimate as your faith, you get to know what things are important and not so important to people. I've really enjoyed Bible study groups. All but one of them have been through this Friendship Bible Coffee, which you hear mixed reviews of. Some people don't appreciate it at all and some people like it. . . .
>
> They try and stay away from controversial areas. They don't like to cover baptism and communion—things where people from different churches get uptight if you question them about those things. We try and stay with things that people can talk about without having to defend why they do something a certain way.

Bible study groups met to complete one of the lesson units. Different, but overlapping, groups continued further lessons. Membership in these groups lessened the isolation of the nuclear family and provided a woman with a core of supportive, intimate female friends.

Like the formal church clubs, the secular Federated Women's Club had trouble attracting young women and maintaining its level of enthusiasm. Several women's clubs disbanded in the 1960s and

1970s, as the members became too old and too few to continue. The P.E.O. in Farmtown and the Progress Club in Center (which allowed only 12 active members) remained as clubs for upper class women. A service sorority, which attracted young women, was established, but membership was by invitation.

Even though the number of clubs was declining, no one in Open Country lacked an organization to join. Most of the modern organizations have had service themes. The hospital auxiliary and the Jaycee Ettes attracted a wide membership. The American Legion Auxiliary, established to further the activities of the American Legion, was also very popular among women. Some of the recently established organizations were founded for both men and women, although the most active organizational workers were women. Community betterment councils, a service club, a theater organization, Parent Teacher Association, an American Field Service chapter, and senior citizens' organizations had a preponderance of women members, although they consistently tried to recruit men into active involvement. Organizations that handled relatively large sums of money, such as the Centennial Committee, with a $40,000 budget, and development corporations, which raised funds to attract industry, were dominated by men.

The most thriving formal organization of women was the Farm Bureau Women. As previously explained, the Farm Bureau had its initial impetus through its connection with the extension service, which supervised the local agricultural and home economics extension agents, funded with federal and state funds. In the post-World War II years, as the Farm Bureau turned more explicitly to conservative political themes, the Farmers Union, and other centrist farm organizations protested the government subsidization of the Farm Bureau more vehemently.[8] In 1955, the Farm Bureau and extension service were officially separated, but the Open Country home economics extension program was still called the Farm Bureau–Home Economics Extension Program in that year. In spite of the separation, the extension service and Farm Bureau continued formal and informal ties; they maintain adjoining offices; and extension agents present programs for Farm Bureau meetings. Indeed, many Open Country people have not yet perceived the separation. In fact, the separation was probably more difficult for extension personnel than for the Farm Bureau, who continued to consult with extension workers, but did not perform organizational work of 4-H or extension meetings. Farm Bureau Women continued as a committee within the Farm Bureau. As before, a woman was a member if and only if her husband joined the Farm Bureau. Although the Farm Bureau claimed wide membership among farm and nonfarm people in Open Country, its leadership came from among the full-time, large-scale farmers.

In 1982, the Farm Bureau remained the only active farm organization in the county, and the most active segment of the Farm Bureau was the Farm Bureau Women. All members received the monthly *Farm Bureau Spokesman*, a readable compendium of Farm Bureau news and opinions on current issues. Although some of the Farm Bureau policies were controversial, this was the major source of information regarding farm politics, and most people did not delve into the political complexities. Farm Bureau Women had clubs in most of the townships and a central county committee composed of county officers and representatives of local clubs. The county organization had an annual meeting of all women members, sponsored a talent contest each year, and sold hamburgers and pie at the county fair; but most members had their strongest links in the local clubs. At local monthly meetings women were encouraged to write to legislators supporting Farm Bureau issues and were given lessons (often by extension personnel) on topics such as farm safety, estate planning, home decoration, coping with family problems, and political participation. One meeting which I attended involved a 40-mile trip to a florist who sold Christmas decorations and taught a lesson in Christmas crafts. At another meeting, the agricultural extension agent gave a lesson on hedging in livestock futures and how women could help with marketing. Like nearly all organizations in Open Country, Farm Bureau Women began meetings with prayer and the Pledge of Allegiance and ended with food and visiting.

Women also meet on a less formal basis for recreation and relaxation. A group of single, widowed, and divorced women met in a bar nearly every evening after work. Working class women had bowling leagues that brought small groups together for weekly fun and conversation. Others had card groups that met regularly. As in the chartered organizations, women categorized themselves by class in these less formal contexts.

Martha's group was one example of these more informal collections of women. The wife of a prosperous, full-time farmer, Martha had a close, supportive circle of four women in similar circumstances. These four women gathered together once a week for more than 25 years. Originally, they got together during the day while their children played, and they continued to take a morning or afternoon each week. They had their husbands join them for dinner parties, picnics, and holiday celebrations. All four came to Open Country around 1950 as college-educated wives of college-educated farmers. As Martha explained,

> It's kind of like a psychiatrist in a way because these women are all former urban people and we've all had similar problems in trying to learn about farming and trying to adjust to the changes and the fact that we don't have immediate families around here. . . . We've been like sisters to each other. It started because of our children, so they'd have someone to play with. It's just been very good. . . . I would have been kind of lonely if it hadn't been for them. You need someone you can share things with.

Two of the women belonged to the same church and two lived close to each other, but the group as a whole found each other in spite of the miles separating their farms. As Martha explained, they did not like to talk about it much, but their college education was a major factor that brought them together. All of them were politically and religiously liberal, with a particular passion for disarmament and anti-nuclear issues.

Thus, new voluntary associations of women replaced the older church and family associations. Women found other women in similar situations and became, in Martha's words, "like sisters to each other." They needed these new sisters because their biological sisters and other female kin lived elsewhere, no longer shared the same interests, or no longer had access to the same experiences. These new groupings were the basis of political interest groups.

Politics

Although all local partisan elective offices went unfailingly to Republicans, political power at the local level was less clearcut than this would suggest. When an office was about to be vacated, a primary race was held among several Republican candidates. Democrats often changed parties temporarily in order to vote in these elections. In addition, school board, town council, and mayoral offices were nonpartisan and Democrats were sometimes elected to these offices. Women, both Democrats and Republicans, were elected to offices. The presidents of the Farmtown school board and the Center school board were women in 1982, and women were on the town councils and on the hospital board.

Marjorie, who came to Center to run a store with her husband in 1951, served on the hospital board as one of its first two women members. She and another woman were appointed when the existing male board decided to expand its membership to involve women in hospital governance. At the next election, Marjorie ran and was elected as an incumbent. She saw her political involvement as a good part of Open Country life:

> This [being on the hospital board] is probably one of the most exciting things I've ever done. It's hard for me to believe. I'm from Chicago; you get lost in Chicago. You'd never get a chance to do anything like this unless you are a member of the ruling body of the city.

In Chicago she was not in the ruling elite; in Open Country she was connected to the upper class. In Chicago she felt no comparable sense of participation or power.

Of course, decisions were made by the town councils and boards, but in Open Country, where people knew and interacted with the same people on the street, in the grocery store, at work, and at the high school basketball game, formal political bodies were a thin veneer over the ongoing political action. Things got done in Open Country when someone had an idea and was able to rally enough support to see the idea through to fruition. When someone in power tried to enact a private agenda, public opinion could force a reversal. Two women who worked many years in government jobs were fired in 1982 by angry supervisors. In both cases the women rallied enough support to reverse the decisions, and the supervisors were forced to leave their jobs, although their dismissals were brought on by a history of arrogant behavior rather than by single events. In other words, Open Country politics worked on the principle of consensus, with power resting more in the ability to marshal support than with the officials who expressed the decisions. A controversy involving the Farmtown school board illustrates this principle.

Farmtown teachers discovered that they had the lowest pay base of any teachers in Iowa. This, together with an authoritarian school superintendent who was not willing to listen to teachers' complaints (and who, incidentally, was one of those forced from his position), moved them to the unpopular step of forming a union to negotiate salary increases. When this negotiation failed, the union and the school board submitted the question to binding arbitration, which was decided in favor of the teachers. The school board then had to decide whether to accept the decision or to appeal. The total in question was only $7,500, approximately the cost of the appeal; therefore, the issue became a matter of principle. Acceeding to the union's wishes might imply weakness; on the other hand, they agreed that the teachers were inadequately paid. Farmtown did not pass a special school enrichment tax levy that many small Iowa school districts used to support their schools when faced with declining enrollments. The Farmtown board was therefore faced with a very limited budget and the possibility of having the school closed by state officials. Board members discussed the issue with influential members of the community to try to determine popular opinion, but no clear consensus was evident.

The school board held an open meeting in the school gymnasium, and many men, and a few women, spoke on both sides of the question in what proved to be a long and emotional session. While no good solution was in sight, several said the enrichment levy might be feasible now. At one point, when asked if the members of the school board had any thoughts on the issue, the school board president responded that she did not think it was appropriate for the school board members to comment! When the public finished, a board member moved to accept the arbitrator's decision. A long pause fell before a weak second was heard. The measure passed with no discussion and no dissent.

This incident underscored the fact that although the school board members were the elected decision makers, they acted only with the public's approval. The board's confusion came when conflicting messages were received. When they themselves refrained from articulating what was involved in the issue, they were attempting to avoid losing the support of any powerful person. No board member wanted to be a dissenter; each could say that he or she simply went along with the majority. No board member was ever required to take a strong stand, even after the fact. Like many elected officials, they were followers rather than leaders.

Although determining to whom the board members spoke before the meeting is difficult, those who spoke most persuasively at the public meeting were upper class males, who clearly constituted the most significant public. They had the skill and confidence to mix humor and muscle in their words. Very few upper class women spoke at the meeting. The men who spoke slowly and deliberately commanded attention and defined the issue's parameters. While these men probably formulated their positions through discussions with their wives, they, and not their wives, governed public opinion. After the meeting, a college-educated, large-scale farmer who had spoken well in favor of the teachers' position explained privately that full-time farmers could speak out on issues and express views that no one else could because they did not have to worry about losing their jobs or damaging their businesses.

Upper class women had a strong sense of political efficacy, although they seldom exercised their political power in obvious ways, such as speaking at public meetings. Their most effective political forums were quiet ones. In the 1980s, a northwest Iowa peace and justice organization was formed through women's organizing efforts. Although the group's officers were men, the women provided much of the dedication, the energy, and the bulk of the membership. The major project in 1982 was collecting signatures for the Bilateral Nuclear Freeze petition and these women worked passionately on it, ordering films to be shown in the schools and churches and absorbing the hostility of strong militarists. One of the most successful women carried a petition with her at all times and asked everyone she met to sign it. Enthusiastic Open Country Freeze supporters secured official endorsement by the Federated Woman's Club on the local and state levels. They also obtained signatures from the majority of the Farm Bureau Women's county officers. They managed to avoid casting the question in partisan political terms, thereby garning the support of Republicans as well as Democrats and obtaining an impressive collection of signatures.

The Bilateral Nuclear Freeze campaign pushed on the edges of what was socially permissable for women. In general, their efforts were devoted to enhancing community life within the limits of the class-based, patriarchal structure. As before, when women had rights allowing them to do any kind of work if it was done within the context of a family economy, upper class women had recognized rights to work unobtrusively for unselfish goals.

Ironically, women could do things unselfishly for others that they could not do for themselves. Chris, a politically astute young farm woman, joined with some other women to promote the primary candidacy of a friend's husband who was seeking a seat in the Iowa Legislature. A core of women worked very hard on the campaign, which they saw as a turning point in local politics. While the women spent the week before the election mailing campaign flyers their candidate went golfing. This was frustrating for Chris, who said, "I just wish he wanted it as badly as we want it." What prevented one of the women from running rather than supporting a less-than-enthusiastic male candidate? She would never have been elected. No woman, not even in the upper class, was allowed to be that aggressive without becoming ridiculous. So, Chris and her friends worked together, sharpened their political skill, and learned something about male dominance through their campaign effort.

Even the limits of the patriarchal, class-based structure allowed for creativity and a sense of accomplishment for those willing to work within them. Bertha was a woman who was able to put through her projects, albeit with a great investment of time and energy. Bertha moved to Center as a home extension agent in 1935 and retired to marry a local businessman in 1940. She epitomized the volunteer, unselfish spirit of Open Country women. Her many services included: serving as president of the school board in the 1950s; holding many offices in her church; organizing and serving as president of the town betterment council; serving as president of a housing board that built two Federal Home Administration housing complexes for the elderly; establishing a senior citizens meal program; establishing a farmers' market; and initiating the committee that got a community center built. When The Bilateral Nuclear Freeze petition campaign started, Bertha courageously—but discretely—promoted the measure and collected signatures.

Bertha was definitely a member of the more prosperous and better-educated upper class (although she was not wealthy enough to build buildings or make large donations to community projects). As a home extension agent, she had experience mobilizing people and spurring them to action. Although severely criticized as she worked on many of her projects, she was always able to rally supporters, due in large measure to her personal skills in offering friendship and support to those buffeted by the ill winds of rural society. She was extremely astute in lobbying for the right program in the right time and place.

Upper class women like Bertha and Chris were noted for their community service, as they did the hard work of almost all of the community organizations. Their work was limited in scope by the fact that, in the patriarchal culture, women were not permitted to promote structural changes that empowered them as women. Their ability to act on their own behalf was mostly untried, but the 1980 Equal Rights Amendment (ERA) campaign was an opening. They found that although working to save the world was permissable, working to better the position of women was not.

In 1980 the Iowa Equal Rights Amendment was being placed on the ballot for ratification by the electorate. The Iowa Women's Political Caucus contacted Martha and Joan, the wife of a banker, to cochair a county committee in support of the Amendment. At that time, Martha did not clearly identify as a feminist and she wanted to study the issue first. She and Joan began by planning a group of six public programs with invited speakers to teach themselves and the public about the issues involved. From the women who attended these programs and showed a strong interest, they organized an ERA coalition that was comprised of the wives of prominent business and professional men. This group then developed a list of all the county's organizations and contacted each one to see if the coalition could present an ERA program for them. Some of the women had never spoken in public before, so they observed others before they themselves did their own speaking. Through this work, the women welded themselves together as a supportive group. Matha described her experience:

> I'd never really done political work before. It was the first time for me. . . . Joan had more experience than I did, I'm sure. We were a good team, because I didn't mind doing the upfront things like speaking and she didn't mind doing the background work. She would do a lot of sending of letters. We divided the work.
>
> The speaking didn't bother me as long as I knew the information. We got that all together in the first study series. . . . After studying that I read a lot of other things. I felt pretty comfortable with the material. . . .
>
> We tried hard with the ERA to learn what our group was like and to speak to their needs. . . . I think that was pretty successful. There were a few times when we had two or three antis who took the whole time. That was a few, I think, out of 65 or 70 [programs].
>
> I felt really good. I said we did our best, the best strategy, the best people I could think to do it. . . . You give it your best shot.

The group's bond was further cemented by their tears when the ERA was defeated, and it became obvious that even their close neighbors had not supported the measure. The group continued to meet and support each other as feminists and to reach out to other women. In 1982 when Roxanne Conlin ran for Governor of Iowa the group formed a core of support for her.

The Iowa ERA referendum, coming at a critical time before the temporary end of the national ERA battle in 1982, was a disappointment, particularly after polls indicated that it would pass. Iowa was one of the first states to ratify the national Amendment, and as such was heavily targeted by anti-ERA forces—women who had the advantage of presenting themselves as unselfish and wanting nothing but what was good for others. In Open Country, however, an element of class antagonism was apparent.

Rejection of the Amendment was broad-based in Open Country, but the hostility to upper class women showed most clearly through a group at the opposite end of the Open Country class structure. There was a group of women who chose not to have male partners; as a result they were living in the social and economic margins of Open Country. Consisting of divorced and never-married women, these outsiders had their primary emotional ties with each other. Without husbands to provide them with a place in society and to provide a living wage, these women worked hard, often pooling their resources. As secretaries, health care personnel, factory workers, and other blue collar workers, these women had no choice but to take care of themselves economically and socially. They smoked and swore and used their limited resources on such things as motorcycles and cars rather than on the home improvements and clothing others in Open Country used to signal status. They gathered in a local bar in the evenings after work; they celebrated birthdays and holidays together and took vacations together. Some of them shared living quarters.

These outsiders saw the underside of Open Country society. While upper class women did not enter local bars, upper class men frequently did. In the bars, these men told misogynist jokes and sexually propositioned the outsider women, who occasionally accepted. Through this contact and through their general observations, these women became cynical, but penetrating, commentators on Open Country society. They articulated the class structure lucidly with concrete examples.[9] They understood local relations of power. They realized that they violated the patriarchal principle that women were to be defined in terms of their relationships with men and were keenly aware of their marginality: they understood the root of their social ostracism. Their drinking and carrying on was an overlay rather than a cause of their separation.

Some of the outsiders performed community services, for example, hauling newspapers for a paper drive, operating lights for a theater production, and helping to organize the summer car races held at the fairgrounds. Although they sneered at the family life of the married, they were hurt by the social snubs they experienced. One painful example came when one of the women, Sue, understood that she was invited to a party hosted by several upper-class couples, only to discover when she arrived (after boasting of the invitation to her friends), that she was asked to attend as the bartender, not as a guest. Another woman who helped with a newspaper collection drive was left out of the informal gathering of workers after the day's activities. One who worked on a committee with an upper class woman sat with her head in her hands saying, "If only she would say *something* nice to me."

This feeling of alienation came to bear directly on the ERA issue. Before World War II, unmarried women were not allowed to live alone, and the outsiders relished the modern freedom they had to be outrageous in many contexts; they had a lot to gain with feminism. They did not make enough money to support families, but they did have some material comfort and security from their incomes. Although they felt and expressed the oppression of women more directly than most women and although they were generally in favor of the ERA, they did not support it and few of them voted for it. Besides their low sense of political efficacy, they were hostile. They had a freer relationship with the husbands of many in the ERA coalition than they did with the coalition members. They wanted to associate with the coalition women, but barring full acceptance they were not about to submit to their political leadership. One of the women attended an open study session, but she did not return for another, and she did not join the coalition. Another explained that people in general went where they felt comfortable and accepted. She did not feel comfortable or accepted among the ERA coalition women, and both groups of women were poorer for this separation.

As Richard Sennett and Jonathan Cobb (1972:170–71) explained the hidden injuries of class,

> Class society takes away from all the people within it the feeling of secure dignity in the eyes of others and of themselves. It does so in

two ways: first, by the images it projects of why people belong to high
or low classes—class presented as the ultimate outcome of personal
ability; second, by the definition the society makes of the actions to
be taken by people of any class to validate their dignity—legitimiza-
tions of self which do not, cannot work and so reinforce the original
anxiety.

. . . In other words, the psychological motivation instilled by a class
society is to heal a doubt about the self rather than create more
power over things and other persons in the outer world.

The hidden injuries of class perpetuated the injuries of sexism.

Conclusion

Men's domination of women supported the class structure.
Men, not women, owned the land and other wealth of Open Country;
men, not women, controlled the jobs that paid living wages. But the
class structure also served male domination. Men who had little
wealth could still dominate some women; they could still claim
higher pay and more privileges than women. Thus, they had a stake
in maintaining the structure. While women could work for various
"Good Causes" within the limits of patriarchy, they could not suc-
cessfully press for structural change. In Open Country, class,
however illusory and ephemeral from the larger social perspective,
divided women with common interests from each other.

All of the churning of power interests in Open Country has occurred as capital has been draining from the area, and maintaining
the ideology of the family farm as the cornerstone of rural America
is becoming increasingly difficult. As other rural analysts have
predicted, new things are on the horizon. What these new things will
be, whom they will benefit, and whom they will oppress depends on
the ability of rural women—and men—to claim their rights to act on
their own behalf. The deepening difficulties in the farm economy
make it clear that the present system must change, and rural
women are struggling to find their place in the change.

Open Country women have struggled and continue to struggle
for control of their lives. They have formed links with each other
and with these links they tested the limits and came to new
understandings of themselves as women. In the Bible study groups,
in the ERA coalition, and in the bar, women sought contact with

other women—women who shared their basic convictions, women they could trust, women who would listen and reflect on their views of life, women who cared about them. The way an earlier generation of Open Country women did these things has been largely unsuited or unavailable to women in the 1980s. In the past, as in the 1980s, women together have validated each others' experiences and clarified their options for change.

Marjorie, in reflecting on the defeat of the ERA referendum, talked about the power of women together:

> I have never in my life known of a group of women that wanted to accomplish something who really did not accomplish it. Women have tenacity. . . .

> I think our coalition gave a lot of people a lot of things to think about that they never thought about before. I think the next time around those objectives will be accomplished. How many times have you talked to women that didn't even know what this movement was all about? They're beginning to finally realize it.

Women have been learning about themselves, about rural life, about their connections with other women, and about their separations. They will continue to learn. They will be formulating their response.

CHAPTER 9

A Concluding Perspective

Open Country is a small world unto itself. In my year of fieldwork, I found it natural to assume that Open Country was the center of the universe and that the rest of the world was noise on the periphery. The earth and the elements were there—the wind blew harder, the stars shone brighter, blizzards were more frightening, and the smells of nature were more pungent there than in any city. Open Country seemed to be a place where nature lent its power to privileged humans and the rest of the world should have stood in awe as it lived off the bounty. The history of Open Country with its fertile, cheap land, its European immigration, and its role in building the large corporations that control the capitalist economy helped to construct a uniquely North American rural experience and a uniquely North American ideology that has obscured connections with the rest of the world.

But Open Country is part of a world economy, and it is dependent on its linkages with this economy. Beef from Central America, the strength of the dollar on the world market, the amount of rainfall in the Soviet Union, and the availability of cheap labor around the world affect Open Country. Moreover, Open Country cannot control either these conditions or their effects. The linkages are controlled by economic elites who are not accountable to Open Country or to any other well-defined public interest. The privilege of living in North America does not grant anyone immunity from exploitation; it does not shelter anyone from the realities of a capitalist economy.

It is appropriate to ask the same kinds of questions about North American agricultural development that are pertinent to agricultural development around the world. Who benefits? Who suffers? Does it effect a broad-based economic development or are the benefits funnelled out of the area? Although Open Country is unique, Open Country women share elements of their experience with women in other times and other places. Identifying common experiences provides a perspective on Open Country that allows a realistic assessment of the possible directions for the future.

Women in Farming

Women have a long history of involvement in farming. In the Neolithic, when plant food was first cultivated rather than gathered, women were cultivators, and they have remained as the predominant cultivators in societies practicing hoe agriculture today (Martin and Voorhies 1975). Among the horticultural Native American groups who lived in Iowa before European settlement women were the ones who traditionally did the planting and harvesting.

White women also farmed. European peasant farming was based on household labor, and women were involved in this system through the nineteenth cenury (Tilly and Scott 1978). The intensification of European agricultural production in the eighteenth and nineteenth centuries increased women's farm labor on the European continent. Denmark, for example, developed its specialties in poultry and dairy products in the late nineteenth century, and women, not men, milked the cows and managed the poultry. Furthermore, women did the stoop labor in the sugar beets when they were introduced as a cash crop that radically changed the farming of eastern Denmark in the 1870s. Although the work that women did varied according to class, farm women, smallholder women, and landless women were all part of the farm workforce (Fink 1982). Farming was the largest employer of women in France and was a substantial source of women's employment in Great Britain in the nineteenth century (Branca 1975:133). Thus, when northern Europeans invaded Iowa, women's participation in the farm economy was not anomalous.

In the dual economy of early Open Country farm men and women were interdependent. Men handled the market sphere of the farm economy: They secured and kept the farm, they paid the taxes, and they reinvested income in the farms—either for expansion or simply to hold onto the land. Women handled the household sphere: They raised poultry, gardened, and helped their husbands with livestock chores and fieldwork; they produced chicken, eggs, butter, potatoes, and other foods eaten in the homes; their egg money or egg trade bought flour, spices, cloth, and school pencils. As household producers, they were doing an immediate, material, and essential part in reproducing the farm labor force. Women's rights to benefit from their work were upheld through the social sanctions of their extended families and public opinion within the moral community. The bonds among women were central in maintaining the social consensus which, in the absence of legal rights, protected women's interests.

With post-World War II modernization women's poultry and garden production was transferred to large commercial workplaces. As work on the farm became less labor intensive and the farm population declined drastically, women's traditional work in farm production and in reproduction became superfluous. The impact of modernization was, however, uneven. While some farms and a few town businesses prospered, the majority lost their economic bases. A woman working in her own family's business is now the exception rather than the rule. The remaining family operations are in peril.

There is a growing cleavage between those who have prospered with modernization and those who have not. Rural America, which only 100 years ago provided the basis of the ideology of opportunity and economic mobility, has, through the free market arena, come to see a "closure in the mobility changes of individuals" (Coughenour and Christenson 1980:4). The recent economic developments have shown that this closure of mobility is more real for those on the lower end seeking upward mobility than for those with small businesses or farms. These people have been losing their livelihoods and joining the nonpropertied at an increasing rate, creating what is called the *farm crisis*. The mobility door is only locked in one direction.

Certain aspects of this modernization process in the United States have parallels in developing countries. Agricultural development in Third World countries has led to concentration of land ownership and imbalances in the distribution of resources (Perelman 1977). Ester Boserup (1970) was the first to focus on agricultural development from women's perspectives. Boserup found that when African men adopted cash cropping women were faced with intensified subsistence work. When cash crops claimed the best land, women raised food on the marginal lands: women worked harder in the subsistence economy. The growth of export industries provided jobs for men in the cities, leaving women and children in the farming villages. Boserup (1970:79) wrote, "The burden African women take on in manless villages is their contribution to Africa's export economy."

Rather than being forced into intensified farming, as were the African women, Open Country women were forced out of the greater part of their subsistence activity. They absorbed a heavy load in producing food for World War II, but this increased production lasted only for the duration of the war. Because of the rapid industrial development in the rural United States, brought on in large part by the increased wartime injections of capital, Open Country women's subsistence work was absorbed by large-scale industries in the years immediately after the war.

American women's exclusion from egg and poultry production resulted from a conscious policy decision on the part of agricultural program planners. Women did not have the same access to the agricultural extension service that men had. Rather than encouraging and sheltering women's poultry production, the postwar extension service ceased to include women in the poultry demonstration flock project unless their husbands were also participants. Although extension was divided into a home economics component for women and an agricultural component for men since its inception in 1914, the division was more sharply delineated between 1945 and 1970. While the current policy allows no discrimination in access to services, the majority of women had relinquished their poultry operations by 1970. Carolyn Sachs (1983:90) described a U.S. woman farmer taking an extension class where the women learned picture framing and the men learned farming. The women suggested that classes on small motors, building repairs, and veterinary medicine would improve the extension program's service to women involved with farming. Information particularly directed to women's problems in credit and finance would also be helpful if the extension service envisioned women as farmers and wanted to plan for their needs. While not engaged in overt gender discrimination in recent years, extension has continued to design its farm and home programs on a gender-based model.

Basically, in the United States a *farmer* is a man; a woman who farms is usually called a *woman farmer*. This does not mean that women have not done farming, but that only men are recognized and supported as farmers. Census takers recorded male heads of households as farmers; women did not appear in the statistical records of the farm workforce if they were married to farmers. As a result, men have had preferential access to the social resources (land, information, and capital) associated with farming, and women have typically gained access to farming only by default, as wives helping their husbands or as marginal farmers. In the past, women had customary rights to their own production enterprises, but these rights have largely dissolved; and they have not been replaced with full legal and economic rights in the present. There are almost no instances of women assuming farm operations or production enterprises within farm operations in the face of husbands', brothers', or capitalists' counterclaims on the work setting.

American gender biases, when carried to development programs, have exacerbated women's difficulties in farming. Western developers participating in agricultural planning in developing countries carried biases about men and women in farming with them. They have talked primarily to men and have not included women in agricultural development planning (Nash 1977; Staudt 1978). As a result, development programs have worked to push women out of farming and heighten their dependency on men. The plan for the developing economies was that women would turn over their farm production to men, just as the majority have done in the United States. In the meantime, development projects have taken land from women and their families and left them as destitute squatters in cities.[1]

Rural Women and Nonfarm Work

What do women do when they lose their subsistence production? Boserup believed that women must be educated in order to establish careers. Modernization was a good thing if women adapted themselves through education and change of attitudes and goals, so that they, too, could gain access to the benefits of increased production and industrial transformation. Development programs were faulty not by design, but only in not including both men and women. Lourdes Benería and Gita Sen (1981) examined this assumption closely. They contrasted two models of development: modernization and accumulation. The modernization model used by Boserup assumes that modernization is beneficial and that complete modernization, that is, modernization for women, will alleviate the problems. Against this model, Benería and Sen posed the accumulation model, in which the uneven distribution of benefits is a structural product; more of the same results in more uneven distribution. Consistent with the accumulation model, Benería and Sen (1981:290) saw the benefits of development as being necessarily selective:

> [T]he problem for women is not only the lack of participation in this process as equal partners with men; it is a system that generates and intensifies inequalities, making use of existing gender hierarchies to place women in subordinate positions at each different level of interaction between class and gender.

Thus, while some men and fewer women find jobs and economic enhancement in the new structure, others lose their jobs and their means of production and find no comfortable position in the modern economy. Increasingly, unemployment plagues well-educated women. Constitutional guarantees of equal rights for women in many countries (but not in the United States) and the various equal pay and nondiscrimination laws in the United States have failed to produce equity for women because the basic development model is flawed (Leacock 1981:475).

Rather than finding *careers* that use their education in the developing economies, many Third World women have been led into factory work in more than 100 free trade (or export processing) zones around the world. As described for Ciudad Juarez, the Mexican city just across the border from El Paso, Texas, the wages of women working in factories in this free trade zone, while high by local standards, do not approach the level of U.S. factory workers (Fernández-Kelly 1983). The Mexican women have been vulnerable because of their lack of other economic options. Poor work conditions are also found in Asia: Annette Fuentes and Barbara Ehrenreich (1983) described conditions of extreme squalor for Asian women working in free trade zones.

The Heritage Foundation, a conservative think tank, proposed establishing similar zones in the United States (Shapiro 1982:36). Called urban-enterprise zones, they would be modelled on 11 such zones established by the Thatcher government in Great Britain. President Ronald Reagan advocated the creation of urban-enterprise zones, including the waiver of minimum wage requirements for workers younger than age 21, in his 1982 State of the Union address (New York Times 1982). To date, no legislation on urban-enterprise zones has been passed, although key elements are still being debated.

In the capitalist system, underdevelopment, as well as development, is structured into the modernization process. Capitalist economies, with their continuing needs for low-cost raw materials and cheap labor, have developed and perpetuated dependency relations (Nash 1983). Laurel Bossen (1984) examined the effects of the capitalist penetration by studying four Guatemalan communities in different stages of integration into the world economy. She found that in the peasant village, the least integrated into the world system, the women and men were interdependent. While there was some subordination of women, they had a measure of autonomy and formed strong associations among themselves. Women in communities located in a sugar plantation and in a middle class urban area had weaker positions because of their dependence on male income and, indirectly, on the capitalist economy. The women of an urban barrio were politically active and had a degree of freedom from male control in their households, but they lacked power in the larger political and economic structures in which they operated daily. Bossen (1984:318) suggested that male privilege was less a product of indigenous Guatemalan culture than a product of the imposed hierarchy. Such a system was functional from the viewpoint of the capitalist elite in that it rewarded the participating men with their own domain of control outside of the workplace; it made women into a special segment of the labor force available to be hired at lower wages; it provided for the reproduction of the labor force at less expense to the elite; and it divided the interests of the working class.

Like other sites of capitalist penetration, Open Country combined the introduction of manufacturing industry with the restructuring of farming in its development. Community Development Corporations were organized in Farmtown and Center to attract factories, which have tended to be viewed as a panacea for the pain of rural underdevelopment. When the *Des Moines Register* ran a series of articles on Pocahontas, Iowa, and its failing economy, the writer described the city's Industrial Committee and its search for a manufacturing industry to save the town:

Here, as in small towns across the state, industrial development has become the rallying cry. Everyone is trying to diversify by nabbing new industries that will create jobs and a little hope in their communities (Westphal 1985).

Small town development committees were seldom in a position to request good working conditions for those getting jobs.

Frederick Buttel (1980) explored the phenomenon of industrial development in the rural United States. Beginning in earnest in the 1970s, rural manufacturing industrialization provided some jobs, thus ameliorating the devastating effects of the outflow of capital and the concentration of wealth within the farm population. By providing jobs for farm men and women unable to live on farm income alone and for others leaving farming, rural industrialists prevented a major social upheaval. But one of the issues Buttel raised was the "disarticulation" of rural industry, referring to its linkages with the local economy. The extent to which the rural community provides the raw materials and consumes the industrial product affects the degree to which the rural area will benefit from the industry's presence in terms of broad-based local economic development. When the only point of articulation is the local supply of cheap labor, the industry becomes an "export enclave." The strategy of "chasing smokestacks" is not viable for broad-based rural development because not enough smokestacks are available, the tax incentives given to industry strain local resources, and the local community sees few benefits and many social problems from the industry (Buttel 1980:19).

Iowa is above all an agricultural state, and its natural industrial development prospects are in food. Buttel saw some hope in articulation of rural industry in a more decentralized food processing and marketing system. The energy crisis raised the possibility of more regional self-sufficiency in food production in the northeastern United States. But in Iowa this has not occurred. Meat packing plants, a major industry employing unionized workers, have closed throughout the state. Although several nonunion plants (including the small lamb packing plant in Farmtown) have opened, the overall trend is toward fewer jobs in the meat packing industry. Iowa still produces very few of its commercially sold fruits, vegetables, and grain products.

The modern increase in women's unemployment is not immediately apparent because their work on farms was not counted as employment. Therefore, when women accepted jobs in factories, offices, and stores, most were statistically counted as economically productive for the first time. Moreover, there is now a great deal of unrecorded unemployment and underemployment among women, since married women search for jobs informally.

When women do find jobs, they are often part-time, temporary jobs paying subminimal wages, and rarely afford career paths to better work with higher pay. In terms of the theory of labor market segments, this work falls into the secondary market. Richard Edwards (1979:167–68), in describing the secondary labor market, wrote,

> What marks these jobs as secondary is the casual nature of the employment. . . . Such jobs offer low pay and virtually no job security. They are, in other words, typically dead-end jobs, with few prospects for advancement and little reward for seniority in the form of either higher pay or a better job. With little incentive to stay, workers may move frequently, and turnover in these jobs tends to be high.

Women who compete for the few, low-paying women's jobs in Open Country often view even the stressful, nonunionized factory work as an improvement. Thus, as June Nash (1983) wrote, the ills of modernization are not confined to Third World countries.

The impacts of multinational practices on the labor process that Nash described are similar to those which occurred in Open Country. The lower level of employment, decline of social welfare (through the loss of the traditional support system), and the decline in worker control of the workplace (which happened as women lost their poultry businesses) have occurred. Marginal regions of the United States are as prone to economic disintegration as are Third World countries.

Rural Development in Iowa

Iowa, with its rich soil and level land, is second only to California in farm production. Since the populated world will always need food, viewing agriculture as the basis for its future economy is rational and logical. Saving the family farm has become a rallying cry for a diverse group of farm organizations and coalitions. Organizations including the conservative American Farm Bureau Federation, the liberal National Farmers Union, National Farmers

Organization, and Iowa Farm Unity Coalition, join in the effort. An array of smaller organizaitons such as the Grange and the U.S. Farmers Association have more limited constituencies. In addition, there are commodity organizations such as those for corn, soybean, beef, pork, and lamb producers, many of which have overlapping membership. These organizations are joined by a number of professional farm experts from the state universities, research centers, and agribusiness corporations who have interests in farm production and structure changes.

All support the preservation of the family farm. Although the leadership of all of these particular groups lies with men, women's organizations such as WIFE (Women Involved in Farm Economics) and American Agri-Women (whose Iowa affiliate is Iowa Organization of Women for Agriculture, or IOWA) also exist. Furthermore, the major farm organizations have women's committees or women's auxiliaries—Farm Bureau Women is a committee of the Farm Bureau, Porkettes is an auxiliary of the pork producers' organization, and CowBelles is an auxiliary of the beef producers' organization. Members of these organizations, as typified in the WIFE acronym, see themselves as "farm wives." The president of American Agri-Women, addressed the IOWA organization by saying,

> You meet the guy you want to marry, and if he's a farmer, you become a farmer's wife. . . . But we've become partners on the farm. The farm wife walking three paces behind can now stand beside her husband and do a very professional job (quoted in Erb 1984).

Women's groups joined the men's organizations in viewing farm women as wives of farmers who could stand beside their husbands, help and support them. None except the short-lived Rural American Women had a women's agenda that defined women as having their own interests. When I participated in a program on the work of farm women with a panel of Farm Bureau Women, I asked them what they saw as their issues as farm women in the 1980s. All described their husbands' or sons' desire to continue farming and their worthiness as farmers; they said that this was not the appropriate time to speak of women's concerns. As Cornelia Butler Flora (1981:386) noted,

> Farm women's organizations positively sanction the public activity of women (a non-traditional female role) while defending their families'

class interests (a traditional female role). . . . Clearly the better-off farm women are more organized and have the capital and management skills to devote to making their organizational clout felt on the state.

But the bow to stereotypical gender hierarchy is not limited to the conservative or wealthier farm families. The limitation of a farm woman's political interests to those of her husband extends across a broad spectrum of agrarian political views.

Although the programs of the different farm organizations vary considerably, particularly in the extent to which each group relies on the free market as opposed to state control, there is widespread agreement on the goal of saving the family farm. Definitions of the family farm vary, but those most commonly used specify that the bulk of the land, labor, and capital are provided by the farm manager and his or her family (Goss et al. 1980:113). As Frederick Buttel pointed out, a problem with this definition is that it is imprecise and impossible to operationalize in terms of available statistics. However, he estimated that of the 3.3 percent of U.S. farms which accounted for 44.2 percent of gross agricultural sales in 1978, 90 percent had hired laborers, the average number being eight. These were larger-than-family farms. On the other end of the spectrum, 65.9 percent of all farms grossed less than $20,000 (which produced a net income of approximately $2,000); these were *subfamily farms*, which provided a total of only 8.8 percent of gross sales (Buttel 1983:93). Thus, by 1978 the family farm was no longer dominant either in numbers or in sales in the United States. In 1982, what George Anthan (1984) called "true family farms," (the units with sales of between $40,000 and $100,000 per year), represented only 16 percent of the total farm operations and 19 percent of the total sales in the United States. Even these farms were not providing a family living: they averaged $4,650 in net farm income and the family members made an average of $10,600 off the farm. Thus the fight to save the family farm, in which the family employs its own labor and provides its own work setting, has so far been a losing one.

The struggle is made more difficult by the ambiguity of the family farm concept. What frequently passes as a family farm is a larger-than-family-sized operation that capitalizes on the family farm appeal. Thus, when H.H. Adams of Piedmont, Alabama, testified before the U.S. Senate on behalf of highly integrated egg operations of up to one million hens, operations which had their own hatcheries and feed mills, he stressed that he represented family farmers and that their land, homes, children's futures, and lives were in jeopardy (U.S. Stnate 1983:23). John Block, President Ronald Reagan's former U.S. Secretary of Agriculture, refers to himself as a family farmer, although neither he nor his wife contribute significantly to the farm labor. Defined broadly, a *family farm* can include just about any farm, and one is left to wonder why a farm run by a single person or unmarried partners should be less worthy than one run by a family.

The word *family* adds a great deal of ideological force to the family farm cause (Fink 1984). The conservative right celebrates a patriarchal family with a husband at the head, and the family farm is, in this rendering, a place where this independent family unit can live apart from the turmoil of competing norms. The neopopulist left sees the family farm as the last bastion of decentralized power protecting the country from total domination by capitalist corporations (Hightower 1975). The family as a haven in a heartless world (Lasch 1977) is, in this sense, a source of strength to fight the good fight for personal freedom.

Open Country's history reveals that *family* has had different meanings, and that the extended family of the early years of this century offered women an economic niche and a community of women that the modern nuclear family does not. Women did not have equal rights, but their dependence on men was balanced by men's dependence on them. Their customary rights to control over their workplace were stronger on the farm than they were in the nonfarm business world. A single woman found a place on the family farm when families were large and inclusive. The family farm of the 1980s can mean husband and wife, but increasingly it is coming to mean father and son (or sons) or brothers farming together. Women enter in as wives, but they are seldom equal partners, even if they perform a significant degree of farm work. One farm woman who cosigned all the loans for her family farm was barred by her father-in-law from participating in discussions about the farm operation. He told her that she was not allowed a voice, first, because she was a woman, and second, because she was not a member of the family. Although he later apologized for his remarks, he said that never before had his orders been challenged and that it was indeed a sad day to have a young woman speak to him in that way. Granted, women previously had little to say with regard to men's work, but they had their own work and men took at least as little interest in the details of this work as women did in their work.

Farming shifted from mixed subsistence and commodity production to specialized commodity production, but women have not moved in a parallel direction into comanagement of commodity production enterprises. As Carolyn Sachs (1983:69) maintained, the farm family suffers from domestic violence, incest, and spouse abuse, just as do other families in the United States. While these problems were possibly present in the earlier families, the one-sided dependency of modern rural women makes the problems more inescapable, even as the awareness of the problems grows.

The *family farm* is a misnomer in that families do not own farms. Typically the owner is a man; sometimes it is a legal partnership of a husband and wife or a father and his sons. Although family farms are often contrasted with corporate farms, many corporate farms are also called family farms when the corporation is owned predominantly by members of one family. Wives are often included in the family corporation only after years of proving themselves by contributing labor or capital or both to the farm operation. As Max Hedley (1981:74) found,

> In Canada and the United States, the term *'family farm'* or *household*, tends to embody, at least implicitly, the connotation of family collective ownership, a tendency reinforced by the fact that it is normally a commensual unit in which the funds for consumption are derived from the earnings of the farm as a whole. By implicitly working with a notion of collective ownership of the means of production we fail to reflect on the inequalities that are structured into units of production by the particular nature of the underlying relations of production. We need to recognize that while there is private ownership of the means of production by an individual who applies his own labour to the productive process, there is also a considerable amount of labour by nonowners of the means of production.

Women working on family farms have supplied a large amount of this nonowner labor. They have been remunerated in different ways—by provision of basic needs, by love, by part ownership of the farm, or by a share of a considerable cash income. At present, neither law nor custom grant women any specific form of remuneration.

Most rural women have not fared well with the uneven benefits conferred by rural development in the United States. The structural changes in agriculture relieved the majority of their place in farming, and modern agribusiness has not been hospitable toward them. They have been marginalized from the operation of the large farms.

While they do more work on the smaller, more labor-intensive farms, no evidence is found of a lesser measure of male dominance (Vail 1982). Moreover, they have not been able to enter the more varied and better paying occupations in nonfarm agribusiness firms (Hacker 1978:20). Local employment prospects for women in the rural nonfarm economy have been—and continue to be—bleak.

Moreover, a family farm program is not necessarily inconsistent with the unequal treatment of families. U.S. policies on farm taxes and price supports have done the most to help large farm operators: they contributed to the land inflation of the 1970s and the inability of the average person to enter farming. Alain de Janvry (1980:163) wrote,

> These [family farm] claims, while sincerely motivated by the defense of farmers' welfare and traditional agrarian values, serve the purpose of prolonging the myth of the family farm and of providing the ideological backdrop to legitimize an attempted return at highly inequitable and inflationary farm income support policies based on the production costs of an average (and, hence, family) farm. The result is the possibility for the larger farmers with production costs below average to capture substantial excess profits at the expense of consumers and taxpayers.

De Janvry believed that the family farm concept was dead and deserved a respectable burial rather than an artificial life support system. Others, such as Mark Drabenstott and Earl Heady (1980:86) argued for the development of a specific small farm policy rather than a family farm policy which, although it would entail a higher federal farm budget, would stem the economic decline in rural America.

Another remedy would be to look at the basic philosophy of the family farm rather than any historic form, thereby viewing the family farm in terms of its original rationale of democratization rather than as an end in itself. To the people of Open Country, *family farm* means living on the land and exerting a measure of control over the workplace; it means a person is not alienated from the work. As such, it remains an emotional issue for both farmers and nonfarmers. The family farm ideology owes its strongest appeal to its promise of "broad access to the productive resources of the society, of narrowing city-countryside disparities of income and wealth, and of ensuring that agricultural development contribute[s] to economic development as a whole, although not on unequal or exploitive terms" (Buttel 1983:89). This does not tie policy to a particular structure, but evaluates alternatives in terms of democratic ends, and is the basis of a policy which, unlike other price support and "save the family farm" measures, allows for a basic rethinking of agriculture and rural problems from a woman's perspective.

Conclusion

The question of who will own the land strikes home for all the people of Open Country. Who will control the basis of wealth, who will live on the land, and who will have a legitimate right to control the future are all interconnected. Considering women's experiences and the nature of their claims is only one part of redefining the debate in terms of the needs of the people rather than the profits of the few.

Notes

Chapter 1

1. In order to protect the identities of my research subjects I have used pseudonyms for most of the proper names throughout the book. Elsa, Open Country, Farmtown, and Center are among the names I have changed. I have also altered specific details in two instances in order to more completely ensure the anonymity of those involved.

2. To enhance readability, all interviewees are hereafter referred to as women.

Chapter 2

1. Peter C. Hainer (1985), who did anthropological fieldwork in a black community in the northeastern United States, has explored some of the misunderstandings that can arise from the application of census classifications that do not reflect the social reality of the persons being counted.

2. These figures were tabulated from U.S. census schedules, censuses of 1900 and 1910. While these data have some value, there are a surprising number of errors in the recording of family relationships. The kinship statuses of many of Ruth's relatives were incorrectly listed. Another entry listed a woman, age 76, having three children younger than age four. Another entry showed a household consisting of a 77-year-old male head, his 12-year-old wife, a 5-month-old son, and a 13-year-old unmarried son-in-law.

3. In addition, some of the hired hands who were kin were not listed according to their kinship relations.

4. Figures from U.S. Bureau of Agricultural Economics, crop report-ing district farm commodity prices, Iowa, 1910-1925.

5. This is not written as a criticism of the extension service; it is an observation. Obviously, the extension service was not the only or first source of the "cult of domesticity" (see Cott 1977:1-3). Extension home economists of Open Country have been intelligent women who have work-ed for the welfare of their communities.

Chapter 3

1. Among the problems of estimating the value of food produced for home consumption is the question of whether to value the produce at the price for which a farmer would buy the food or the price at which a farmer would sell the food. For example, potatoes purchased at a grocery store, at a roadside stand, or by a wholesale buyer would bring different prices. Margaret Liston, an Iowa State University home economist of the 1930s, says that a frequent fault of these studies was their failure to clarify the way home production was valued (personal communication). Stenswick (1939), in the study quoted here, uses a combination of retail prices that yielded a low retail value for the goods but that were still presumably higher than the wholesale value. Monroe (1940) does not clarify the basis of her figures.

2. This information is from U.S. census schedules, Iowa, 1900 and 1910. See Chapter 2 for a discussion of household membership.

3. Assessing the way women have been recorded as farm workers in census publications is frustrating. Censuses do list some women as farm workers, but they are both understated and overstated. The 1940 official labor force statistics for Open Country lists 24 women as farmers, 10 women as farm laborers, and 6 women as unpaid family farm workers (USDC 1943:919,925). Clearly, many more than six women were working on family farms at this time. On the other hand, the 24 women listed as farmers was overstated, if a farmer is taken to be the manager of a farm operation: The majority of these "farmers" were widows who had given all but formal title of the farms to the younger males in their families. I doubt that there was one independent woman farmer in Open Country in 1940.

As Bossen (1984:32) notes, since the incidence of rural women's farm labor is so inadequately reported, many researchers have chosen to disregard the figures for women' farm work. My use of official statistics is restricted to nonfarm employment of Open Country women.

Chapter 6

1. Records at the Poultry Department, Iowa State University, Ames.

2. Records at the Poultry Department, Iowa State University, Ames.

3. While cream money is not discussed in detail, it was often a parallel source of income for farm women. In the early years of this century, farm women churned butter, which they marketed with eggs for their household money. As cooperative creameries appeared in the 1920s, marketing the cream and buying butter became more common. Most farms had major beef enterprises, but dairying was more labor intensive and, consequently, was not as common on Iowa farms. The usual practice entailed keeping a few cows that supplied the household with milk and provided a nominal additional income for the farm woman. In the instances in which there was a major dairy enterprise with more than ten cows, the dairy income became part of the farm commodity economy, and as such, the farm man controlled this money. The Iowa dairy industry, like the egg industry, has since been concentrated in a small number of production sites.

4. Women who were egg breakers comprised the majority of the labor force of these plants. As cooks, women had experience breaking eggs, and the companies used this experience in their businesses. Just as with women's tradition of egg production on the farm, wartime industry tapped a traditional role and put it to use for its own purposes.

5. Eggs had been exempt from the Agricultural Marketing Act of 1937, but they were included as of 1983. With this legislation, the egg industry had the option of establishing marketing orders. With a marketing order a producer would submit to industry controls on the size of production in return for more stable markets.

6. This information was supplied by William Owings, Extension Poultry Specialist, Iowa State University, Ames.

7. Ironically this operation was called FarmEgg. It sold eggs under the label Nature Maid, which traded on the symbolism of women and unpolluted freshness.

Chapter 7

1. For census purposes, *farm* is defined as an establishment normally selling at least $1,000 of agricultural products annually. Approximately 90 percent of this gross income was paid out in production expenses; therefore, this definition clearly includes farms which would not support any kind of household. Considering a slightly more restrictive definition of farm, those marketing a minimum of $10,000 of agricultural products annually, the average farm size was 294 acres rather than 271 acres in 1982 (USDC 1983:4). But even 294 acres was a marginal operation; 155 farms were larger than 500 acres. In some cases, small farms were operated in

close association. For example, often a father and one or two sons combined their land, labor, and capital and actually operated as a single larger unit while nominally maintaining multiple farms. Thus, the census data, even though they record the increased concentration of landholdings, do not reflect the degree of concentration.

2. The average Open Country household had 4.4 persons in 1920 (USDC 1924:46); in 1970, it had 3.0 persons, which is the same as Polk County, the most urban county in Iowa (USDC 1972:167).

3. In 1930, 10.3 percent of the county's population was younger than age five (USDC 1932:810); in 1970, 7.4 percent was younger than age five (USDC 1972:162). While the crude birthrate has become greater in urban than in rural Iowa, the fertility rate is still somewhat greater in rural Iowa. In 1980, there were 3,244 children born per 1,000 white Iowa farm women between ages 35 and 44; 2,671 children were born per 1,000 white urban women in the same age range (USDC 1983A:62.). The lower crude birthrate in rural Iowa reflects the relatively fewer number of women in childbearing years in rural areas, a result of the out-migration of young adults.

4. The estimated cost of seed and chemicals for planting an acre of corn was $91.90 if the land had been planted in soybeans the preceding year, and $107.95 if it had been planted in corn the preceding year (ICLRS 1983:89).

5. These farmers were mostly male. Each farm was accorded one and only one farm operator in the census classification. While the 1982 census reported female farm operators (23 of them in Open Country), this gives a misleading picture of the actual farm labor and management, as the majority of female "farmers" were widows who had not yet officially turned over the farms to sons or other male relatives. I did not locate a single example in Open Country of a woman who was operating a farm independently.

6. These figures were disaggregated by race in the published statistics. Since no blacks or Asians and very few Hispanics lived in Open Country in 1979, I have used the figures for whites rather than attempting to aggregate the figures for all races.

7. Nursing homes are now required to pay minumum wages if they receive federal payments for the care of patients.

8. Some unions existed for Open Country workers. One of the meat packing plants which drew workers from Open Country was unionized. The teachers in Farmtown formed a union, a move which was not welcomed. The Rural Electrification Cooperative workers were nominally unionized.

9. Local poverty computations are done only for census years. The last year for which the poverty statistic was published for Open Country was 1979.

Chapter 8

1. Personal communication from Louie Hansen, Extension Resource Development Specialist, Iowa State University, December 13, 1982.

2. But marriage was a difficult area to study using the anthropological methods of participant observation and interviews with women.

3. This was Elsa's husband, whose work was described in the beginning of Chapter 2.

4. The rate of exploitation is defined as (capitalist share/labor share).

5. This is the *Goldschmidt hypothesis*, which is drawn from the study of two rural California towns in the 1940s (Goldschmidt 1947, 1978). Walter Goldschmidt supervised a comparative study of Arvin, a town dominated by large-scale absentee landlords and Dinuba, a town dominated by smaller-scale, farmer-owned farms. He found more retail trade, a better school system, and more religious organizations in Dinuba than in Arvin. Dinuba had paved streets, sidewalks, garbage collection, sewers and public parks, all absent in Arvin. The Goldschmidt hypothesis relates these quality of life indicators to farm structure.

6. These figures are computed from the 1982 federal agricultural census of Open country (USDC 1983:1), which gives the number of farms of each size group in 1982, and the state agricultural census, which gives the percentage of land in each farm size group in 1981 in northwest Iowa (ICLRS 1983:5). While census figures do not allow for a clear comparison with earlier times, they do show a much more pronounced majority of intermediate-sized farms in 1940: 57.2 percent of all farms were between 50 and 179 acres; only one farm was larger than 1,000 acres (USDC 1943:148).

7. This analysis of class as being defined in terms of the men's ranking is the same as Kohl (1976:18) established in the rural community of Jasper.

8. The American Farm Bureau Federation, of which the Open Country organization is a part, has generally opposed support prices for farm commodities in favor of a free market in agricultural commodities. It has opposed farm workers' unions, and it has declined to support strict conservation measures for farmland, supporting instead weaker measures based on voluntary participation. Outside of farm politics, it has been vigorously anti-socialist and has supported a military build-up; it has opposed civil rights legislation, the sovereignty of Native Americans, the Equal Rights Amendment, the Occupational Safety and Health Act, food stamps, and the metric system.

9. Unfortunately, but understandably, these women did not like tape

recorders. They knew what I was doing in Open Country, and they were mildly resentful of my probing. After spending time with them, I wrote what they said as accurately as my memory allowed.

Chapter 9

1. For an example of a land takeover in the Philippines, see Kamel, 1985.

References Cited

Anand, Anita
    1983   Rethinking Women and Development. *In* Women in Development: A Resource Guide for Organization and Action. Pp. 5–11. Geneva: ISIS International Women's Information and Communication Service.

Anderson, Karen
    1981   Wartime Women: Sex Roles, Family Relations, and the Status of Women During World War II. Contributions in Women Studies, Number 12. Westport, CT: Greenwood Press.

Ankarloo, Bengt
    1979   Agriculture and Women's Work: Directions of Change in the West, 1700–1900. Journal of Family History 4:111–120.

Anthan, George
    1984   Des Moines Register. December 10.

Atkeson, Mary Meek
    1929   Women in Farm Life and Rural Economy. Annals of the American Academy of Political and Social Science 143:188–94.

Bailey, L. H. et al.
    1911   Report of the Commission on Country Life. Chapel Hill: University of North Carolina Press.

Baker, O.E., and Conrad Taeuber
    1940   The Rural People. *In* Farmers in a Changing World. Yearbook of Agriculture 1940. U.S. Department of Agriculture. Pp. 827–848. Washington, DC: U.S. Government Printing Office.

Benería, Lourdes, and Gita Sen
    1981   Accumulation, Reproduction, and Women's Role in Economic Development: Boserup Revisited. Signs: Journal of Women in Culture and Society 7:279–298.

251

Berger, Samuel R.
  1971   Dollar Harvest: The Story of the Farm Bureau. Lexington, MA: Heath Lexington Books.

Bescher-Donnelly, Linda and Leslie Whitener Smith
  1981   The Changing Roles and Status of Rural Women. *In* The Family in Rural Society. Raymond T. Coward and William M. Smith, Jr., eds. Westview Special Studies in Contemporary Social Issues. Pp. 167–185. Boulder: Westview Press.

Bodensteiner, L. J.
  1949   Farm Flocks that Fit. Iowa Farm Science 3(11):10–12.

Boserup, Ester
  1970   Woman's role in Economic Development. New York: St. Martin's Press.

Bossen, Laurel Herbenar
  1984   The Redivision of Labor: Women and Economic Choice in Four Guatemalan Communities. Albany: State University of New York Press.

Branca, Patricia
  1975   A New Perspective on Women's Work: A Comparative Typology. Journal of Social History 9:129–153.

Buttel, Frederick H.
  1980   Farm Structure and Rural Development. Paper presented for Farm Structure and Rural Policy Symposium, Iowa State University, Ames.

  1982   Agriculture in Advanced Industrial Societies. Current Perspectives in Social Theory 3:27–55.

  1983   Beyond the Family Farm. *In* Technology and Social Change in Rural Areas: A Festschrift for Eugene A. Wilkening. Gene F. Summers, ed. Pp. 87–107. Boulder: Westview Press.

Campbell, D'Ann
  1984   Women at War with America: Private Lives in a Patriotic Era. Cambridge: Harvard University Press.

Cather, Willa
  1918   My Antonia. Boston: Houghton Mifflin.

Cherokee Times
  1943   June 22.

"Chickens?—That's a Woman's Job."
  1948   Wallaces' Farmer 73:805.

Cochran, Wendell
1982   Des Moines Register. January 17.

Cochrane, Doris Herrick
1943   Equal Pay for Comparable Work. Independent Woman 22:197,
        216.

Cochrane, Willard W.
1979   The Development of American Agriculture: A Historical Analysis.
        Minneapolis: University of Minnesota Press.

Collier, Jane, Michelle Z. Rosaldo, and Sylvia Yanagisako
1982   Is There a Family? New Anthropological Views. *In* Rethinking the
        Family: Some Feminist Question. Barrie Thorne and Marilyn
        Yalom, eds. Pp. 25–39. New York: Longman.

Cott, Nancy F.
1977   The Bonds of Womanhood: "Woman's Sphere" in New England,
        1780–1835. New Haven: Yale University Press.

Coughenour, C. Milton, and James A. Christenson
1980   Farm Structure, Social Class, and Farmer's Policy Perspectives.
        Paper presented at Farm Structure and Rural Policy Symposium,
        Iowa State University, Ames.

Country Air
1936   Wallaces' Farmer 61:297.

Country Cooking? I Eat It!
1948   Wallaces' Farmer: 281.

Danbom, David B.
1979   The Resisted Revolution: Urban America and the Industrialization
        of Agriculture, 1900–1930. Ames: Iowa State Press.

Davidson, Jay Brownlee, Herbert Hamlin and Paul Taff
1933   A Study of the Extension Service in Agriculture and Home
        Economics in Iowa. Ames: Iowa State Press.

Davis, John Emmeus
1980   Capitalist Agricultural Development and the Exploitation of the
        Propertied Laborer. *In* The Rural Sociology of the Advanced
        Societies: Critical Perspectives. Frederick H. Buttel and Howard
        Newby, eds. Pp. 133–153. Montclair, NJ: Allanheld, Osmun.

Davis, (Mrs.) Lavinia K.
1867   Female Life in the Open Air. Report of the Commissioner of
        Agriculture for the Year 1866. Pp. 430–440. Washington, DC:
        U.S. Government Printing Office.

de Janvry, Alain
  1980   Social Differentiation in Agriculture and the Ideology of Neopopulism. *In* The Rural Sociology of the Advanced Societies; Critical Perspectives. Frederick H. Buttel and Howard Newby, eds. Pp. 155–168. Montclair, NJ: Allanheld, Osmun.

Des Moines Register
  1943A May 6.

  1943B May 12.

  1943C May 26.

  1955A July 6.

  1955B August 4.

  1955C October 20.

  1966   December 18.

Dodds, John Perry
  1940   Production and Marketing of Eggs in Lake Township, Cerro Gordo County, Iowa, M.S. Thesis. Ames: Iowa State College.

Drabenstott, Mark R., and Earl O. Heady
  1980   Small Family Farms in American Agriculture: Projected Income for North Central Iowa Small Farms. CARD Report 96. Ames: Center for Agricultural Research and Development, Iowa State University.

Edwards, Richard
  1979   Contested Terrain: Transformation of the Workplace in the Twentieth Century. New York: Basic Books.

Erb, Gene
  1984   Des Moines Register. September 9.   •

Evans, Sara
  1979   Personal Politics: The Roots of Women's Liberation in the Civil Rights Movement and the New Left. New York: Vintage Books.

Executive Council of the State of Iowa
  1916   Census of Iowa for the Year 1915. Des Moines.

Faragher, John Mack
  1981   History From the Inside-Out: Writing the History of Women in Rural America. American Quarterly 33:537–557.

The Farm Flock
  1942   Wallaces' Farmer 26:442.

  1948   Wallaces' Farmer 73:360.

Farm Records are Important
1948   Wallaces' Farmer 73:185.

Farmtown Centennial Historical Committee
1983   Farmtown Centennial. 1883–1983.

Fernández-Kelly, María Patricia
1983   For We are Sold, I and My People: Women and Industry in Mexico's Frontier. Albany: State University of New York Press.

Fink, Deborah
1982   Women, Eggs, and Wages in Denmark: Industrial Marginalization. Ethnology 21:137–149.

1984   Rural Women and Family in Iowa. International Journal of Women's Studies 7:57–69.

Fink, Deborah, and Dorothy Schwieder
1984   Iowa Farm Women in the 1930s—A Reassessment. Paper presented at Conference, American Farm Women in Historical Perspective, Las Cruces, NM.

Fite, Gilbert C.
1974   The Farmers' Frontier 1865–1900. Albuquerque: University of New Mexico Press.

Flora, Cornelia Butler
1981   Farm Women, Farming Systems and Agricultural Structure: Suggestions for Scholarship. The Rural Sociologist 1:383–386.

Food Wins Battles
1943   Wallaces' Farmer 68:473.

Friedan, Betty
1963   The Feminine Mystique. New York: Dell.

Friedmann, Harriet
1978   World Market, State and Family Farm: Social Bases of Household Production in the Era of Wage Labour. Comparative Studies in Society and History 20:545–86.

Fuentes, Annete, and Barbara Ehrenreich
1983   Women in the Global Factory. Institute for New Communications Pamphlet Number 2. Boston: South End Press.

Gabelmann, Bertha
1912-66, 1971
        Diaries, Clarksville, Iowa. Photocopy. Iowa State Historical Department, Iowa City.

Gallaher, Ruth
 1918   Legal and Political Status of Women in Iowa. Iowa City: Iowa
         State Historical Society.

Gates, Paul W.
 1964   The Homestead Law in Iowa. Agricultural History 38:67–78.

Gilman, Charlotte Perkins
 1909   The Rural Home Inquiry: Why Are There No Women on the Presi-
         dent's Commission? Good Housekeeping 48:120–122.

Goldschmidt, Walter
 1947   As You Sow. New York: Harcourt, Brace.

 1978   As You Sow: Three Studies in the Social Consequences of
         Agribusiness. Montclair, NJ: Allanheld, Osmun.

Gordy, Amelia S. and Gladys S. Gallup
 1952   Progress in Home Demonstration Work: A Statistical Analysis of
         Trends, 1910–1950. Extension Service Circular 479, USDA.
         Washington DC: U.S. Government Printing Office.

Goss, Kevin F., Richard D. Rodefeld, and Frederick H. Buttel
 1980   The Political Economy of Class Structure in U.S. Agriculture: A
         Theoretical Outline. In The Rural Sociology of Advanced
         Societies. Frederick H. Buttel and Howard Newby, eds. Pp.
         83–132. Montclair, NJ: Allanheld, Osmun.

Gough, Phyllis Elvira
 1943   Tasks Done by 100 Iowa State College Freshmen Women Living
         on Farms During 1942 in Iowa and Surrounding States. M.S.
         Thesis. Iowa State College, Ames.

Grundy Center Register
 1943   July 29.

Hacker, Sally
 1978   Farming Out the Home: Women and Agribusiness. Science for
         the People 10:15–28.

Hainer, Peter C.
 1985   Census Definitions and the Politics of Census Information. Prac-
         ticing Anthropology 7(3):7–8.

Hall, Florence
 1943   They're Getting in the Crops. Independent Woman 22:194–196.

Hampton, Wallace B.
 1946   Iowa Agriculture—The First Hundred Years. In Iowa Year Book of
         Agriculture 1945. Pp. 19–44. Des Moines: State of Iowa.

Hargreaves, Mary W. M.
   1976   Women in the Agricultural Settlement of the Northern Plains. Agricultural History 50:179–189.

Hartmann, Heidi
   1981   The Unhappy Marriage of Marxism and Feminism: Towards a More Progressive Union. *In* Women and Revolution: a Discussion of the Unhappy Marriage of Marxism and Feminism. Lydia Sargent, ed. Pp. 1–41. Boston: South End Press.

Hartmann, Susan
   1982   Home Front and Beyond: American Women in the 1940s. Boston: Twayne.

Harnack, Curtis
   1981   We Have All Gone Away. Ames: Iowa State University Press (originally published in 1973).

Heady, Earl O.
   1980   Economic Policies and Variables Relating to the Structure of Agriculture, with Potentials and Problems for the Future. Paper presented at Farm Structure and Rural Policy Symposium, Iowa State University, Ames.

Hearst, James
   1978   We All Worked Together: A Memory of Drought and Depression. Palimpsest 59 (May/June):66–76.

Hedley, Max
   1981   Relations of Production of the 'Family Farm': Canadian Prairies. Journal of Peasant Studies 9:71–85.

Henderson, E. W., and W. M. Vernon
   1934   Feeding and Management of Hens. Extension Circular No. 200, May. Iowa State College, Ames, Extension Service.

Hightower, Jim
   1975   Eat Your Heart Out: Food Profiteering in America. New York: Crown Publishers.

Hill, Reuben, and Elise Boulding
   1949   Families Under Stress: Adjustment to the Crises of War Separation and Reunion. New York: Harper.

How Farm Women Help
   1943   Wallaces' Farmer 68:84.

ICLRS (Iowa Crop and Livestock Reporting Service)
   1983   Iowa Agricultural Statistics. ISDA, Des Moines and USDA, Washington, DC.

1984   Iowa Agricultural Statistics. ISDA, Des Moines, and USDA, Washington, DC.

ISDA (Iowa State Department of Agriculture)
1940   Iowa Year Book of Agriculture 1940. Des Moines: State of Iowa.

1946   Iowa Year Book of Agriculture 1945. Des Moines: State of Iowa.

ISES (Iowa State Extension Service)
1929   A Project of Marketing and Nutrition Relating to Eggs. Ames: Iowa State College.

1931   Agriculture and Home Economics, Annual Report. Ames: Iowa State College.

1930- 39
       Poultry Record Report (Yearly). Ames: Iowa State College.

1944   What's Ahead for the Livestock Farmer. Pamphlet 92. Ames: Iowa State College.

1950, 1960
       of Work: Cooperative Extension Work in Agriculture and Home Economics. Ames: Iowa State College.

1954, 1955
       Report. Iowa Poultry Demonstration Flocks (Yearly). Ames: Iowa State College.

Iowa State Planning Board
1952   Statistics and Data for Iowa: Vital Statistics and Health. Ms. Des Moines.

Jensen, Joan M.
1980   Cloth, Butter and Boarders: Women's Household Production for the Market. Review of Radical Political Economics 12(2):14–24.

1981   With These Hands: Women Working on the Land. Old Westburg, NY: Feminist Press.

1985   The Role of Farm Women in American History: Areas for Additional Research. Agriculture and Human Values 2(1):13–17.

Jones, Calvin and Rachel A. Rosenfeld
1981   American Farm Women: Findings from a National Survey. National Opinion Research Center Report No. 130. Chicago.

Kagerice, M.
1950   Let's Do Dishes. Home Economics Circular HE-17. Ames: Iowa State College.

Kamel, Rachael
1985 Filipinas Mobilize Against Marcos, TNC. Listen Real Loud: News of Women's Liberation Worldwide 6(2):A1,A4,A5.

Kohl, Seena B.
1975 Working Together: Women and Family in Southwestern Saskatchewan. Toronto: Holt, Rinehart and Winston of Canada.

Lasch, Christopher
1977 Haven in a Heartless World: The Family Besieged. New York: Basic Books.

Leacock, Eleanor
1981 History, Development, and the Division of Labor by Sex: Implications for Organization. Signs: Journal of Women in Culture and Society 7:474–491.

Levitas, Daniel
1983 Farm Crisis. Rural America 8(4):6–7.

Martin, M. Kay and Barbara Voorhies
1975 Female of the Species. New York: Columbia University Press.

Mason, Earl
1946 History of Iowa Poultry and Egg Industry. In Iowa Year Book of Agriculture 1945. Pp. 109–115. Des Moines: State of Iowa.

McNall, Scott G., and Sally Allen McNall
1983 Plains Families: Exploring Sociology Through Social History. New York: St. Martin's Press.

Merrill, Michael
1977 Cash is Good to Eat: Self-Sufficiency and Exchange in the Rural Economy of the United States. Radical History Review 4(1):42–71.

Moberg, David
1985 Disappearing Dreams. In These Times. February 13–19:8–10.

Moen, Elizabeth, Elise Boulding, Jane Lillydahl and Risa Palm
1981 Women and the Social Costs of Economic Development: Two Colorado Case Studies. Boulder: Westview Press.

Monroe, Day
1940 Patterns of Living of Farm Families. In Farmers in a Changing World. The Yearbook of Agriculture 1940. Pp. 848–869. Washington, DC: U.S. Government Printing Office.

More Chicks This Year
1943 Wallaces' Farmer 68:118.

Muhm, Don
1982A Des Moines Register. January 10.

1982B Des Moines Register. August 15.

1984 Des Moines Register. December 21.

Murphy, Zoe
1948 We Have a Freezer. Wallaces' Farmer 73:28.

Myres, Sandra L.
1982 Westering Women and the Frontier Experience, 1800–1925. Albuquerque: University of New Mexico Press.

Nash, June
1977 Women in Development: Dependency and Exploitation. Development and Change 8:161–182.

1983 The Impact of the International Division of Labor. *In* Women, Men, and the International Division of Labor. June Nash and María Patricia Fernández-Kelly, eds. Pp. 3–38. Albany: State University of New York Press.

New York Times
1982 January 27, Pp. 16–17.

Noll, Margaret
1945 "When I Husk Corn." Wallaces' Farmer 70:860.

Open Country Bulletin
1894 February 15.

1897 April 22.

1924 December 4.

1933A May 10.

1933B November 15.

1937A January 13.

1937B April 3.

1942A March 11.

1942B April 15.

1942C April 22.

1942D June 17.

1943 August 18.

Open Country Extension
1934, 1939, 1943, 1946
    Annual Narrative Reports. County Extension Activities. Ms.

Papanek, Hanna
1979   Family Status Production: The "Work" and "Non-Work" of
        Women. Signs: Journal of Women in Culture and Society
        4:775–781.

Peck, J.L.E., O.H. Montzheimer, and William J. Miller
1914   Past and Present of O'Brien and Osceola Counties, Iowa. In-
        dianapolis: B.F. Bowen and Company.

Perelman, Michael
1977   Farming for Profit in a Hungry World: Capital and the Crisis in
        Agriculture. Montclair, NJ: Allanheld, Osmun.

Pfeffer, Max
1983   Social Origins of Three Systems of Farm Production in the United
        States. Rural Sociology 48:540–562.

Poole, Dennis L.
1981   Family Farms and the Effects of Farm Expansion on the Quality
        of Marital and Family Life. Human Organization 40:344–349.

R.L. Polk and Company
1918   Iowa State Gazeteer and Business Directory, Des Moines.

Rapp, Rayna
1982   Family and Class in Contemporary America: Notes Toward an
        Understanding of Ideology. In Rethinking the Family: Some
        Feminist Questions. Barrie Thorne and Marilyn Yalom, eds. Pp.
        168–187. New York: Longman (originally published in 1978).

Riley, Glenda
1981   Frontierswomen: The Iowa Experience. Ames: Iowa State Univer-
        sity Press.

Rogers, George B.
1979   Poultry and Eggs. In Another Revolution in U.S. Farming? USDA.
        Pp. 148–199. Washington, DC: U.S. Government Printing Office.

Rosenfeld, Rachel A.
1984   U.S. Farm Women 1980: Work, Farm and Family. Paper given at
        Conference, American Farm Women in Historical Perspective.
        New Mexico State University, Las Cruces, New Mexico, February
        2–4, 1984.

Sachs, Carolyn E.
1983   The Invisible Farmers: Women in Agricultural Production.
        Totowa, NJ: Rowman and Allanheld.

Salamon, Sonya, and Anna Mackey Keim
  1979   Land Ownership and Women's Power in a Midwestern Farming Community. Journal of Marriage and Family 41:109–19.

Sawyer, Gordon
  1971   The Agribusiness Poultry Industry: A History of its Development. New York: Exposition Press.

Schrader, Lee F., Henry E. Larzelere, George B. Rogers, and Olan D. Forker
  1978   The Egg Subsector of U.S. Agriculture: A Review of Organization and Performance. North Central Research Publication 258. West Lafayette, Ind.: Purdue University Agricultural Experiment Station.

Schwieder, Dorothy
  1980   Labor and Economic Roles of Iowa Farm Wives, 1840–80. In Farmers, Bureaucrats, and Middlemen: Historical Perspectives on American Agriculture. Trudy Huskamp Peterson, ed. Pp. 152–168. Washington, DC: Howard University Press.

  1983   Rural Iowa in the 1920s: Conflict and Continuity. Annals of Iowa 47:104–115.

Sennett, Richard and Jonathan Cobb
  1973   The Hidden Injuries of Class. New York: Vintage Books.

Servants on the Farm
  1937   Wallaces' Farmer 62:754.

Sheldon Mail
  1982   January 13.

Shannon, Fred A.
  1945   The Farmer's Last Frontier: Agriculture, 1860–1897. Volume V, The Economic History of the United States. New York: Farrar and Rinehart.

Shapiro, Harvey D.
  1982   Now, Hong Kong on the Hudson? Saving the Slums with 'Enterprise Zones.' New York 15 (April 26):35–37.

Should Egg Money Be Mary's Share?
  1942   Wallaces' Farmer 67:140.

Skold, Karen Beck
  1980   American Women in the Shipyards During World War II. In Women, War, and Revolution. Carol R. Burkin and Clara M. Lovett, eds. Pp. 55–75. New York: Holmes and Meier.

Smith-Rosenberg, Carroll
1982 The Female World of Love and Ritual: Relations between Women in Nineteenth Century America. *In* Women's America: Refocusing the Past. Linda Kerber and Jane DeHart Mathews, eds. Pp. 156–178. New York: Oxford University Press (originally published in 1975).

Staudt, Kathleen
1978 Agricultural Productivity Gaps: A Case Study of Male Preference in Government Policy Implementation. Development and Change 9:439–57.

Stenswick, Mildred L.
1939 Farm Security Studies I. Certain Home Management Practices of 73 Families in Union County, Iowa. M.S. Thesis, Iowa State College, Ames.

Stewart, George F.
1946 Eggs and Meat from Iowa Poultry. *In* A Century of Farming in Iowa 1846–1946. Pp. 154–166. Ames: Iowa State College Press.

Stewart, (Mrs.) Elinore Pruitt
1914 Letters of a Woman Homesteader. Boston: Houghton Mifflin (reprinted by University of Nebraska Press).

Straub, Eleanor F.
1973 United States Government Policy Toward Civilian Women During World War II. Prologue 5:240–254.

Suckow, Ruth
1926A The Daughter. *In* Iowa Interiors. Pp. 37–49. New York: Knopf.

1926B Renters. *In* Iowa Interiors. Pp. 132–138. New York: Alfred A. Knopf.

1930 The Kramer Girls. New York: Knopf.

1934 The Folks. New York: The Literary Guild.

Swelling Family Incomes
1933 Wallaces' Farmer 58:220.

Swierenga, Robert P.
1968 Pioneers and Profits: Land Speculation on the Iowa Frontier. Ames: Iowa State University Press.

Termohlen, William Dewey
1928 A Study of Egg Marketing in Iowa. M.S. Thesis. Ames: Iowa State College.

They'll Get More Eggs Now
   1943   Wallaces' Farmer 68:219.

Thompson, Arthur T.
   1942   Also Let's Keep 'Em A-Laying. Wallaces' Farmer 67:61.

Tilly, Louise A., and Joan W. Scott
   1978   Women, Work, and Family. New York: Holt, Rinehart, Winston.

Toledo Chronicle
   1943   July 15.

U.S. House of Representatives
   1974   Egg Price Situation. Hearing before the Subcommittee on Domestic Marketing and Consumer Relations, Committee on Agriculture. 93rd Congress, 2nd Session, April 30, 1974.

U.S. Senate
   1983   Egg Handling Regulations. Hearing before the Subcommittee on Agricultural Production, Marketing and Stabilizaiton of Prices of the Committee on Agriculture, on S. 1368, 94th Congress, 1st Session, July 14, 1983.

USDA (United States Department of Agriculture)
   1863   Hardships of Farmers' Wives. In Report of the Commissioner of Agriculture for the Year 1862. Pp. 462–470. Washington, DC: U.S. Government Printing Office.

   1915A Social and Labor Needs of Farm Women. Report 103. Washington, DC: U.S. Government Printing Office.

   1915B Economic Needs of Farm Women. Report 106. Washington, DC: U.S. Government Printing Office.

   1940   Iowa Agricultural Statistics. Statistical Bulletin Number 2. Des Moines: Office of the Agricultural Statistician.

   1942A Farm Women on the Home Front. Extension Service Circular 390. Washington, DC: U.S. Government Printing Office.

   1942B National Summary of Inquiry into Changes in the World of Farm Women and Girls caused by War Labor Shortages. Extension Service Circular 395. Washington, DC: U.S. Government Printing Office.

   1945A Ceremonials. Extension Service Circular 443. Washington, DC: U.S. Government Printing Office.

   1945B You Can Work It Out Yourself. Extension Service Circular 430. Washington, DC: U.S. Government Printing Office.

1950   Extension Work in Urban Areas. Extension Service Circular 462. Washington, DC: U.S. Government Printing Office.

1960   State Estimates of Farm Income, 1949–59. Agricultural Marketing Service. FIS–179 (Supplement). Washington, DC: U.S. Government Printing Office.

1965   Prices Received by Farmers for Chickens, Turkeys, and Eggs. Statistical Bulletin No. 357. Crop Reporting Board. Washington DC: U.S. Government Printing Office.

1973   Farm Income State Estimates 1959–72. Economic Research Service. FIS–222 (Supplement). Washington, DC: U.S. Government Printing Office.

USDC (United States Department of Commerce) Bureau of the Census
1924   Fourteenth Census of the United States. State Compendium. Washington, DC: U.S. Government Printing Office.

1932   Fifteenth Census of the United States: 1930. Population. Volume 3. Part 1: Alabama-Missouri. Washington, DC: U.S. Government Printing Office.

1942A   Sixteenth Census of the United States: 1940. Agriculture. Special Poultry Report. Washington, DC: U.S. Government Printing Office.

1942B   Sixteenth Census of the United States: 1940. Agriculture. Volume I. Washington, DC: U.S. Government Printing Office.

1943A   Sixteenth Census of the United States: 1940. Housing. Volume I. Data for Small Areas. Part 1: United States Summary and Alabama-Nebraska. Washington, DC: U.S. Government Printing Office.

1943B   Sixteenth Census of the United States: 1940. Population. Volume III. The Labor Force. Part 3: Iowa-Montana. Washington, DC: U.S. Government Printing Office.

1952A   1950 Census of Population. Volume II, Characteristics of the Population. Part 15, Iowa. Washington, DC: U.S. Government Printing Office.

1952B   U.S. Census of Agriculture: 1950. Counties and State Economic Areas. Iowa. Volume 1, Part 9. Washington, DC: U.S. Government Printing Office.

1953   County and City Data Book 1952. Washington, DC: U.S. Government Printing Office.

1963   Census of the Population: 1960. Volume I, Characteristics of the Population. Part 17, Iowa. Washington, DC: U.S. Government Printing Office.

1972   County and City Data Book 1970. Washington, DC: U.S. Government Printing Office.

1981   1978 Census of Agriculture. Volume I, State and County Data. Part 15, Iowa. Washington, DC: U.S. Government Printing Office.

1983A   1980 Census of Population. Volume 1, Characteristics of the Population. Chapter C. General Social and Economic Characteristics. Part 17, Iowa. Washington, DC: U.S. Government Printing Office.

1983B   1982 Census of Agriculture. Preliminary Report. AC82-A-19-141(P). Washington, DC: U.S. Government Printing Office.

1983C   Lifetime Earnings Estimates for Men and Women in the United States: 1979. Current Population Reports, Series P-60, No. 139. Washington, DC: U.S. Government Printing Office.

1984   Characteristics of the Population Below the Poverty Level: 1982. Current Population Reports. Series P-60. No. 144. Washington, DC: U.S. Government Printing Office.

Vail, David Jeremiah
1982   Women and Small Farm Revival: The Division of Labor and Decision-Making on Maine's Organic Farms. Review of Radical Political Economics 13:19–32.

Van der Zee, Jacob
1912   The Hollanders of Iowa. Iowa City: State Historical Society.

Vanek, Joann
1980   Work, Leisure, and Family Roles in Farm Households in the United States, 1920–1955. Journal of Family History 5:422–431.

Vidich, Arthur J., and Joseph Bensman
1968   Small Town in Mass Society: Class, Power and Religion in a Rural Community. Princeton: Princeton University Press.

Wallaces' Farmer
1935   Volume 60:299.

1943   Volume 68:112, 177.

1945   Volume 70:232.

1948   Volume 73:211, 250, 281, 297.

War Jobs at Home
1945   Wallaces' Farmer 70:232.

Westphal, David
1985   Riches to Rags: Iowa's Economic Upheaval, Part 3. Des Moines Register, June 18.

What Education Do Farmers Need?
1948   Wallaces' Farmer 73:134.

What'll You Buy?
1945   Wallaces' Farmer 70:785, 821.

What Price for Eggs?
1945   Wallaces' Farmer 70 (April 7):1, 30.

When Frank Gets Back
1945   Wallaces' Farmer 70:611.

Wherry, Elizabeth
1943A Country Air. Wallaces' Farmer 68:19.

1943B Country Air. Wallaces' Farmer 68:86.

1945A Country Air. Wallaces' Farmer 70:145.

1945B Country Air. Wallaces' Farmer 70:233.

1945C Country Air. Wallaces' Farmer 70:811.

1948   Country Air. Wallaces' Farmer 73:83.

Wilson, Meredith
1942   Progress of the Neighborhood Leader Plan. Extension Service Circular 393. United States Department of Agriculture. Washington, DC: U.S. Government Printing Office.

Wisconsin State Extension Service
1956   Trends in the Poultry Industry. . . . Effects on the Midwest. Bulletin 523. Agricultural Experiment Station. Madison: University of Wisconsin.

Wylie, Philip
1955   Generation of Vipers. New York: Holt, Rinehart and Winston.

York, Mrs. Virgil
    1945   "Don't Wake Me Up." Letter to Homemaking Editor. Wallaces'
            Farmer 70:856.

Young, Kate
    1980   A Methodological Approach to Analysing the Effects of Capitalist
            Agriculture on Women's Roles and their Position within the Com-
            munity. *In* Women in Rural Development: Critical Issues. Pp.
            6–12. Geneva: International Labour Office.

Index